MW00356964

JEAN JAURÈS

GEOFFREY KURTZ

JEAN JAURÈS

THE INNER LIFE OF SOCIAL DEMOCRACY

The Pennsylvania State University Press
University Park, Pennsylvania

Library of Congress Cataloging-in-Publication Data

Kurtz, Geoffrey, 1974– author.
Jean Jaurès : the inner life of social democracy /
Geoffrey Kurtz.
pages cm
Summary: "A study in social democratic political
theory that examines the writings of Jean Jaurès
(1859–1914), the parliamentary and philosophical
leader of French socialism"—Provided by publisher.
Includes bibliographical references and index.
ISBN 978-0-271-06402-4 (cloth : alk. paper)
1. Jaurès, Jean, 1859–1914—Political and social views.
2. Socialism—History.
I. Title.

HX264.7.J38K87   2014
320.53'1092—dc23
2014009217

FOR *Alyson*

CONTENTS

ACKNOWLEDGMENTS

My work on this book was supported by a Borough of Manhattan Community College (BMCC) Faculty Development Grant (2008) and by two Professional Staff Congress–City University of New York (PSC-CUNY) Research Awards (2008 and 2009). I presented parts of my research at a 2011 Faculty Salon held by BMCC's Department of Social Sciences and Human Services and at the New York Political Science Association's 2012 meeting, and I benefited from discussions at both events. I would like to acknowledge *Logos: A Journal of Modern Society and Culture* for publishing "Jean Jaurès: A Portrait" (2006) and *New Political Science* for publishing "A Socialist State of Grace: The Radical Reformism of Jean Jaurès" (2006) and "An Apprenticeship for Life in Common: Jean Jaurès on Social Democracy and the Modern Republic" (2013).

Reading and writing about Jaurès has been part of my life for more than a decade now, and during that time many people have contributed to this project. I am grateful to all the teachers, colleagues, neighbors, comrades, friends, and family members who have guided and supported me in this period. I would like to acknowledge by name the following people who played a part in the making of this book. My thanks go to each of them.

Early in my graduate studies, Stephen Eric Bronner extracted from me a promise to turn a short paper on Jaurès into "something publishable." Although I now consider that obligation discharged, my intellectual debt to Steve remains, and I am happy to acknowledge it.

The staff at Pennsylvania State University Press, most notably, my editors— Sanford Thatcher at the beginning of the process and Kendra Boileau at the middle and end—shepherded this book to print with patience and forbearance. Copy editor Jeffrey H. Lockridge pushed me to sharpen my argument, improving the text tremendously. Michael Forman and Leslie Derfler reviewed an early version of the manuscript for the Press, and two anonymous reviewers commented on a later version.

Dorothea Coiffe and other librarians at BMCC's A. Philip Randolph Memorial Library provided indispensable help. The staff and librarians at the New

York Public Library's Stephen A. Schwarzman Building—especially Jay Barksdale, liaison for the Allen Room and the Wertheim Study—made it possible for me to read and write in beautiful places.

Over the past few years, I have been shaped by an intellectual and political community in and beyond New York. Many of that community's members have influenced or supported this book through conversations or correspondence (sometimes without knowing so, and sometimes despite—or through—their disagreements with the ideas I present here). Among them, I would particularly like to thank Kate Bedford, Melissa Brown, Mark Engler, K. E. Saavik Ford, Roger Foster, Brian Graf, Andrew Greenberg, Kristy King, Jacob Kramer, Daraka Larimore-Hall, Penny Lewis, James Mastrangelo, Charles Post, Joseph M. Schwartz, Jessica Shearer, Nichole Shippen, and Michael J. Thompson. Others—Matthew Ally, Michael Rabinowitz, and Brian Stipelman—also offered helpful comments on sections of the manuscript. I thank Matthew in particular for his questions about Jaurès's first doctoral thesis, which steered me away from a number of serious errors.

I have benefited continually from the gracious generosity of my family: Wayne and Kathleen Kurtz, Jeremy and Stefanie Kurtz-Harris, Deborah and Mark Andstrom, and (smallest but not least) Miriam, Lewis, and Ginger. If ever I doubted that we are born and remain dependent on those who love us, writing this book has taught me all over again that this is so.

My wife, Alyson Campbell, has done more than any other person to make this book possible, from commenting on drafts of the manuscript to answering questions about French, to patiently performing the practical work of partnership, to showing me what it is to be a citizen, to having more confidence than I often had that the project would eventually be finished. I dedicate this book to her.

ABBREVIATIONS

For works by Jean Jaurès cited frequently, I use the following abbreviations. Translations from these texts are my own. I have retained Jaurès's fully capitalized words within quotations as well as his italics except where doing so would require putting an entire quotation in italics.

AN   *L'organisation socialiste de la France: L'armée nouvelle*. Paris: L'Humanité, 1915.

HS   *Histoire socialiste, 1789–1900*. 13 vols. Edited by Jean Jaurès. Paris: Jules Rouff, 1901–8.

OJJ   *Oeuvres de Jean Jaurès*. 9 vols. Edited by Max Bonnafous. Paris: Rieder, 1931–39.

PTA   *Philosopher à trente ans*. Vol. 3 of *Oeuvres de Jean Jaurès*. Edited by Annick Taburet-Wajngart. Paris: Fayard, 2000.

TAD   *Les temps de l'affaire Dreyfus, novembre 1897–septembre 1898*. Vol. 6 of *Oeuvres de Jean Jaurès*. Edited by Éric Cahm and Madeleine Rebérioux. Paris: Fayard, 2000.

INTRODUCTION
The Problem of Hope

A political tradition has its characteristic principles, policies, and strategies. Beneath or behind these, it also has its characteristic patterns of coherence and instability, its sources of courage and anxiety, its hopes and worries. We recognize a political tradition by its outer features, but it thrives or fades according to its inner rhythms. Debates in recent years about the "renewal of social democracy" have focused on the feasibility and justification of policy programs.[1] This book, in contrast, is an essay on the inner life of the social democratic tradition. Looking at the political thought of one of the giants of social democracy's founding generation, it aims to recover certain questions asked by that generation, questions that might profitably be asked again by those who would like to see a democratic Left in the twenty-first century that is able to preserve and extend the best of what the twentieth-century Left achieved.

The story of social democracy's outer life is well known.[2] During the middle half of the twentieth century, parties and movements of the democratic Left constructed a new, social democratic model of political life. This model—as momentous an innovation as the nineteenth-century development of political parties based on mass suffrage or the eighteenth-century invention of the constitutional republic—comprised a comprehensive welfare state, extensive collective bargaining, and economic rules that favored equality and stability, all in the context of representative democracy and a market economy. Cultivating broad coalitions rooted in the labor movement and operating both inside and outside government, social democrats were able to reduce material poverty, foster associational life, create beautiful public spaces, and protect civil liberties and democratic institutions. No other version of left-wing politics has been so successful at realizing the Left's dream of a modern society made fit for human habitation.

When I describe social democracy as a political tradition, I mean that it is not only this set of actions and results. More fundamentally, it is a distinct way of thinking about and approaching politics that has been sustained over time. Those who have championed the social democratic model have not always called themselves "social democrats"; some have instead called themselves "socialists" or "democratic socialists" or, in America, "labor liberals" or "left-liberals." Nevertheless, they have been linked with one another by a consistent sense of purpose, by a project capable of being revived even when the tradition's particular efforts failed or its particular achievements were undone.[3] The social democratic tradition is thus defined not only by its strategy and its policy program but also by its broader commitment to freedom, equality, and solidarity. Just as fundamental as those principles is social democracy's commitment to a genuinely political engagement with the modern world. Social democracy has been among the modern traditions that defend the classical Greek and Roman image of public talk in public spaces and the classical claim that human beings living together in ordered societies have the capacity to change or preserve their social orders through such talk, and, in doing so, to realize common goods.[4] Thus social democrats have prized political life, with all its uncertainty and messiness; they have sought coalition and compromise rather than absolute victory; they have valued the continued possibility of dissent over the perfect realization of principles. They have declined to seek a society in which conflict has been abolished, in which politics has been transcended, and thus they have been able to embrace the fact of human plurality.[5]

This history and these orienting commitments are what make social democracy an appealing tradition to me and to many others. That said, I want to point out something about social democracy that may be less obvious, especially in our time. During the last years of the nineteenth century and the first years of the twentieth, before there were social democratic governments with the power to enact a policy model, social democrats built a movement. At first no more than an unconventional style within the international socialist movement, this new politics gradually differentiated itself from the rest of the socialist family and emerged as a distinct movement with a forthrightly reformist and democratic character.[6] In that movement's early years, as its leaders and members thought about what they were doing and why they supposed it worth doing, they found that the ideas of nineteenth-century socialism (or, for that matter, those of nineteenth-century liberal republicanism) did not allow for an adequate account of their circumstances or their activities, and that they would need a new understanding of political life. That would have been challenge enough, but they also found—and this is what we are less likely to remember— that they had to reflect on the inner life of their movement.

This was no simple thing to do. For the first generation of social democrats, committing themselves to the practice of democratic politics meant abandoning the extravagant expectations that had oriented the nineteenth-century Left. Utopia, revolution, unbounded progress—what happens when these ideas lose whatever plausibility they may once have had? If the daily work of the socialist movement was not to be seen as a series of steps on the road to a wholly new and fully just society, what reason could the movement's members have for making the sacrifices demanded by political life? If a final victory was not written into the trajectory of history, what could make participation in the movement worthwhile? What would bind the movement together? The early social democrats seem to have been surprised by the urgency of these questions, and some members of that first social democratic generation tried harder to think through the problems of their movement's inner life than their descendants would in the period when social democracy moved from success to success. Building a movement, the first social democrats were haunted by the problem of hope.

Seeking to rebuild that movement, social democrats today are haunted by the same problem and need not face it as if for the first time. Since the last quarter of the twentieth century, adherents of neoliberal market fundamentalism have attacked the social democratic model with devastating results. Over the same period, the character of election campaigns has changed; the demographic bases of left parties have shifted; globalization has altered the terms of national policy making. Social democrats in recent years have found their confidence enfeebled, their sense of a common project less sure than it once was. Old questions about social democracy's inner life have a new relevance.

That the polemics and introspections of social democrats a century ago might be of interest today may seem an odd notion. Why read old arguments against revolutionary politics when there are no longer any viable revolutionary movements to argue against? Nevertheless, this is just what I want to propose. Because those first social democrats could not take for granted the appropriateness of a commitment to democratic reform, they—or at any rate some of them—not only examined the outer shape of their politics but also attended to the problems that accompanied their new commitments. We might say that they listened not only to the melody but also to the undertones of social democratic politics. Social democrats' multiple commitments—to principles like freedom and solidarity but also to the worth of political life itself—raise difficult questions, today as in earlier periods, about the sources of political motivation and the kind of political hope that can orient a project of democratic reform. I am convinced that the original social democrats can help today's social democrats not only to develop an account of what they—or, rather, we—are doing and of why our political commitments might be worthwhile, but also to confront the consequences of those commitments. I should add that, although I write here with those purposes, I am also aware that social democracy's problems are neither all new nor all unique to the Left. In many respects, they are iterations of the oldest problems of Western politics and political thought, and so I would suggest that the travails of social democracy ought to be of interest to anyone who wants to defend the possibility of political life in the modern world.

This book, then, should be understood as a study in social democratic political theory that reconstructs the questions asked by the first generation of social democrats in order to pose those questions in a way that might be useful to the democratic Left today.[7] Its medium is the political thought of Jean Jaurès, a French writer and politician whose career in public life lasted from his first election to public office in 1885 to his assassination in 1914.[8] Jaurès was one of many people in several countries who contributed to the birth of the reformist socialism that would grow into the tradition of social democracy. Except in France, where he is fondly remembered, Jaurès is not the best known of the early social democrats; Eduard Bernstein, his German counterpart, has received more attention.[9] Studying Jaurès makes sense for my purposes, however. Like other reformists of his generation, Jaurès thought through the consequences of the social democratic commitment when those consequences were new and surprising. It seems to me that he undertook that intellectual work with exceptional vigor and creativity. He also did so with exceptional prominence: in a way Bernstein never did, Jaurès became an international spokesman for the new reformism; indeed, "Jaurèsism" was one of the first names for social democracy.[10]

In some ways, Jaurès was a representative member of the first generation of social democrats, albeit a particularly vocal and prolific one. He also contributed something unique to the new politics. Jaurès was unusual among his contemporaries in that he was not only a journalist and a parliamentarian, but also a historian and a philosopher, distinguished by the uncommon breadth of his curiosity and intellectual aptitudes. Although he never wrote a systematic statement of his ideas—in itself a suggestive fact—he thought broadly about both the outward and the inward consequences of social democratic commitments. Best of all, he wrote blazing prose and gave intricate and soaring speeches. These traits have sometimes been seen as faults. I want to suggest, however, that Jaurès's writerly prowess should be seen not as a quirk of temperament, but as an indication of the kind of political thinking appropriate to social democracy.

Irving Howe, who knew something about both rhetoric and social democracy, wrote: "It has been customary in radical circles to praise Jaurès as a brilliant personality, a scintillating orator, a fine leader, but to condescend a little toward his intellectual powers, often because he was far from Marxist orthodoxy. But time is a cruel teacher. Many of the clogged Marxist tracts of theoreticians allegedly more profound than Jaurès are now all but unreadable, while his writings, for all their oratorical quality, retain a clear vision of the indissoluble link between democracy and socialism."[11]

I would go only slightly farther than Howe: Jaurès's works convey something about the link between democracy and socialism *because* of their oratorical quality and because of the poetic mood of his oratory. Theory can be allied with rhetoric, ideas with imagery, and when citizens talk with one another, this alliance is not only possible but also indispensable. When we aim to illuminate a shared moral world, we need words that touch the intangible: we need symbols. When we aim to move listeners to political commitment, or to give an account of such commitments, we need models of speech other than those we associate with scientific discovery and technological invention.[12] Because Jaurès's works were elements of his own thoughtful engagement in the democratic politics of his time, they pursue those aims, they meet those needs, and they rely on that alliance. That is no small part of why they remain useful today.

Accordingly, this book reflects on the social democratic tradition by presenting and interpreting the political thought of Jean Jaurès both because he is representative of social democracy's founders and because he has something unusual and valuable to say. Although it resembles a work of intellectual history, it attempts to project the lines of Jaurès's thought beyond his own situation; its purpose is as much rumination as exposition. I am concerned with what Jaurès said because I want to figure out what his political thought might mean now. To that end, I write with an eye toward *how* Jaurès thought; I try to show the process by which he responded to concrete political problems as much as I try to show what his responses were.

Thus, although I try to explain enough about Jaurès's life to put his thought in its proper context, I offer no full-fledged biography of Jaurès, nor even an intellectual biography, no history of the socialist movement in the France or Europe of his time, nor an account of Jaurès's historical legacy or influence on later generations. I also offer no apology for social democracy itself. Instead, I write here as a "connected critic" of social democracy; I start from the assumption that social democratic politics is worth practicing and worth thinking about.[13]

With that in mind, I look at Jaurès's political thought in order to explore certain questions, thinking with and alongside Jaurès in order to discover what he has to say to us today, at a time when the social democratic tradition seems unsure of its way forward. I ask, what follows from the decision to engage in social democratic politics? What account can those who make this decision give of what they are doing? What tends to trouble them, and how can they think clearly and usefully about those troubles?

In exploring these questions, I argue that Jaurès's account of the public character of his politics makes a connected whole out of the principles and method that later became the hallmarks of the social democratic tradition. Jaurès was able to give this account of social democracy's outer life in part because he drew on the vocabulary and imagery of classical political thought. When he uses the word "republic" to describe his political commitments, he is expressing an understanding of reformist socialism that is not peculiarly French. Social democracy, though a distinctively modern tradition, is also a tradition that can be best accounted for by drawing on certain premodern resources. And no one can show us the republican—or, to use the equivalent Greek-rooted word, the political—quality of social democracy better than Jaurès.[14]

What I have found most interesting in Jaurès's writings and speeches, however, are those points at which his thought becomes murkier. Jaurès is not shy about revealing the inner life of social democracy, but his account of that inner life is not entirely consistent, and when he spoke to his contemporaries, he at times contradicted himself. Jaurès wants to understand what can motivate a political tradition that does not expect to fully realize its ideals; he wants to give an account of social democratic hope. This, it seems to me, was the deepest concern of his intellectual life. That his account of this hope never became entirely clear may have been less a failure on his part than a feature of the problem he faced.

The subsequent chapters are a reading of several of Jaurès's major writings and speeches.[15] These span the years from his young adulthood to the end of his life and are situated in the context of French and European socialist politics and the events of Jaurès's own life, with occasional, briefer references to other writings or speeches by Jaurès or his contemporaries.[16] Because how Jaurès says things is important to what I want to show about his political thought—and also because so few of his writings have been translated into English[17]—I often quote substantial sections of his texts in my own translations. Although I have tried to convey both the sense and the sensibility of Jaurès's words, as an amateur translator, I have certainly fallen short of that aspiration. But if the inadequacies of my efforts spur someone more competent to undertake a fuller and better translation of Jaurès's writings into English, that alone will justify the existence of this book.

Each chapter examines either one major text or a small number of related texts, set in their respective contexts. There is one chapter each on Jaurès's doctoral theses (chapter 1), his *Histoire socialiste* (chapter 2), his major speeches during the reformism debates toward and just after the end of the nineteenth century, especially his 1900 speech on "the evolution of socialist method" (chapter 3), his *Études socialistes* of that period (chapter 4), and his *L'armée nouvelle* (chapter 5). In the conclusion, I try to make room for both clarity and murkiness, piecing together the implications of Jaurès's thought for politics in our time.

1

THE BATTLE IS NEVER WON

Jean Jaurès is remembered as a speechmaker and a polemicist, as a tribune of the labor movement and the helmsman of a political party. I propose, however, that the best way to understand his political thought, the relationship of his thought to his own times, and the meaning of his thought for us today is to begin by considering his two doctoral theses, especially—as strange as this may sound—his first thesis, "De la realité du monde sensible" (On the reality of the sensible world). Jaurès's early scholarship on metaphysics might seem far removed from politics, but in it he developed ideas about conflict and conciliation, the limited and the absolute, space and spirit that would set the pattern for his account of social democracy and its inner life. By the time he completed his theses in 1892, Jaurès had confronted the contrasts between country and city, classical and modern, philosophy and politics, republic and socialism. It is not surprising that he seems to have been preoccupied with reconciling what common sense would say cannot be reconciled. The quest for harmony that began in Jaurès's early years would come to define his mature political thought.

Although Jaurès would live in Paris for most of his life, he was born 350 miles to the south, in the small commercial town of Castres, which sits on the river Agout in the department of the Tarn, a region of hills and river gorges. By the time of his birth in 1859, some mining, metallurgy, glassmaking, and textile manufacturing had come to the Tarn, but it was for the most part a place of grain fields, vineyards, and orchards.[1] The Jaurès family—Jules, an unsuccessful businessman, Marie-Adélaïde, a devout Roman Catholic from a family of textile merchants, and their sons, Jean and Louis (a daughter, Louise, died in infancy)—spent part of each year in a townhouse but lived the rest of the time on their farm, La Fédial Haute, about 3 miles outside Castres. Jean and Louis began their education at a small school run by a Castres clergyman and continued it a few years later at the Collège de Castres. The boys walked about an hour each day from La Fédial to reach their schools; when not in class, they spent much of their time out of doors.[2]

Jaurès excelled in his Greek and Latin studies, which most likely included readings in Homer, Thucydides, the classical Greek playwrights, Plato, Aristotle, Plutarch, and Cicero.[3] In 1875, he was recruited to attend one of the best Parisian lycées, Sainte-Barbe, where he would prepare for the entrance exams to the École normale supérieure, the elite institution of higher learning for future academics, teachers, and civil servants. In the fall of 1876, Jaurès left the Tarn for Paris.[4]

Absorbed in the Greek and Latin classics during his two years at Sainte-Barbe, Jaurès spent most of his time in classes or studying in a small room at the student *pension* where he lived.[5] In one of his student writings, Jaurès argued that the classics "have, after their long sleep, a youthful freshness and vivacity." They are important not so much for their doctrines as for their sensibility: they "refresh and revive" modern minds. In particular, Jaurès commended Plutarch's *Lives* to a modern world too ready to surrender to the debilitating idea that history is a continuous sequence of causes and effects. Plutarch's writings, he declared, refute the proposition that "everything is enchained, and necessity directs even the heroes," and they show modern people that one can "ally valor with prudence, liberality with respect for law, freedom with rule, and that good things do not lose their worth by avoiding extremes."[6]

Jaurès entered the École normale supérieure in 1878 and soon decided to focus his studies on philosophy.[7] Although some French philosophers of that time had become interested in the work of Immanuel Kant, the core texts of the École's philosophy curriculum remained the works of Xenophon, Plato, Aristotle, Cicero, Seneca, and Epictetus, with only secondary attention paid to Kant and other modern thinkers.[8] The École sequestered its students in poorly lit and stuffy buildings, allowing them only two afternoons a week to explore the city. Although Jaurès apparently found time to read works by the French utopian socialists Claude Saint-Simon, Charles Fourier, and Pierre-Joseph Proudhon, his course work took most of his attention. The *normaliens* did discuss politics, and most were supporters of France's new republican regime—among them, one of Jaurès's friends, the future sociologist Émile Durkheim, was known to attend republican rallies[9]—but Jaurès would remark years later on the lack of connection between his studies at the École and the political life of the city around him. "In minds nurtured in that fashion," Jaurès wrote, "the most subtle and profound knowledge is found side by side with the most extraordinary ignorance. It is like a vast secluded room where the light penetrates only dimly." Studying the ancients' ideas about justice and friendship and the utopians' visions of cooperative societies, he "did not know that there were socialist groups in France and a whole agitation of propaganda and fervor of sectarian rivalry."[10] The idea that classical republican thought might be relevant to political life in the French Republic was at least one of the reasons that the École retained a classical curriculum. However, as Jaurès would later write, although "the idea of freedom in Cicero and Tacitus was honored" there, "popular protest was scornfully treated as intemperate brawling."[11]

What did it mean to speak of a republic in France in the 1880s? For the ancient Romans, "res publica" (literally, "public thing") had meant a political order in which the Senate and the popular assemblies each had some power, much like the blend of oligarchy and democracy that the Greeks before them had called a "politeia" (meaning something like "the political way of doing politics"). A "res publica" meant not only a system for making and enforcing law, but also an aspiration toward a certain moral order, toward a devotion to the common good. A classical republic was a regime of mixing and balancing, and of shared life in public spaces.

What use these ideas might have under modern conditions has never been self-evident. Classical republicanism assumed independent cities with a stability of culture and economy, not to mention a scale of social life that has long since become unavailable. By the end of the nineteenth century, the French word "république" had its own complex relationship to modern upheaval. When the First French Republic was declared in 1792, "république" meant, above all, a regime in which the sovereignty of the monarch had been overthrown and had been replaced by the sovereignty of "la nation," the people as a whole. The close association between "république" and "révolution" continued through the series of uprisings and regimes—empires, monarchies, and the Second Republic of 1848 to 1852—that followed. "République" came to mean not only the people ruling, but also the people rebelling; it meant violent and disruptive acts by the people en masse, as well as the state of affairs those acts were intended to create.

The Third Republic was something different. When Emperor Napoléon III was captured by the Prussians in the summer of 1870, France's previously weak National Assembly became the country's only available government. The Assembly called for elections, after which a new National Assembly was to decide what sort of regime would govern France. In the meantime, the National Assembly would serve as a provisional parliament in what amounted to a provisional republic. But when the monarchist majority in the new National Assembly found itself unable to unite around a single royal house, the provisional republic remained in place. Patiently, the republican minority managed the country's affairs, outlasted the internecine fights among the monarchist factions, and negotiated a peace with Prussia. In 1875, a new election gave the republicans enough seats in the National Assembly to establish, by a one-vote margin, a new set of governing institutions: a Chamber of Deputies and a Senate, a cabinet, a prime minister, and a president of the Republic. The provisional government had become a permanent government, not through a dramatic uprising but through an unheroic combination of political gambits, competent governance, and good luck.[12]

"République" now meant a regime that was anything but revolutionary. In fact, the militants of the Paris Commune, who briefly created a radical urban democracy in the spring of 1871, had been among the first foes of the nascent republic. Adolph Thiers, one of the Third Republic's early leaders, spoke frankly: "The Republic will be conservative, or it will not be."[13]

This was the "Republic" that Jaurès and his friends at the École normale supérieure knew and supported, the Republic that the student Jaurès endorsed when he became, according to the reminiscences of a friend, "a republican in the style of Ferry and the Opportunists of 1880."[14] Jules Ferry, along with Léon Gambetta, led a faction of republicans who wanted to consolidate the institutions of the new republic while putting off unwinnable or controversial social reforms until more opportune times. Their opponents thus named them the "Opportunists." Ferry and the Opportunists were men of the Enlightenment tradition; they saw free thought and public debate as weapons against outmoded dogmas and as tools for building a modern republic. At the same time, they were in at least one sense republicans in the classical style: they thought of civic education—that is, the moral formation of a citizenry capable of self-government—as an essential element in the constitution of a republic. Thus, once the structure of the parliament, cabinet, and presidency had been settled, the Opportunists turned their attention to local government, to public education, and to citizens' freedom of association.[15]

In 1881, just before he completed his studies, Jaurès began his involvement in political life. He joined a committee of Paris republicans, mainly Opportunists, that met to nominate a candidate for the Chamber of Deputies.[16] Jaurès would not be long in the city, however. After finishing third in that year's *aggregation*—the competitive exam for École graduates seeking teaching positions—he requested a position as *professeur* at a lycée near Albi, where he would be only 25 miles from his parents. He left Paris that summer to take up his teaching duties.[17]

Jaurès's lectures at Albi take up themes that he would later develop. Because mind and matter act on each other "in constant rapport," Jaurès taught his students, "we cannot understand the essence of matter without the essence of mind, and the reverse as well."[18] Made of mind and matter, human beings are obligated to uphold the dignity of the individual person, as Immanuel Kant had demonstrated: "In the individual we see one man, one example of human life in its ceaseless flux, one form and incarnation of the human person from which we must displace suffering and degradation" (*PTA*, 102).

Along with Kant, Jaurès worried that human beings rarely obey the moral law for its own sake: "It commands, and we do not listen to it." Because of the rapport of mind and matter, Jaurès proposed, if we are to obey the moral law, we need not only the rational conviction regarding morality that Kant had described, but also a "feeling of duty," a deep sensation of moral obligation that is to the human personality "as the core of the trunk is to the tree" (*PTA*, 90).

Asking how someone might acquire this moral feeling, Jaurès found himself turning toward public life. In 1882, only months after he arrived at Albi, Jaurès wrote his École classmate Charles Salomon that he might run for the Chamber of Deputies in 1885 if a seat was open: "When I shall have fathomed the depths of the universe, I will have to come back to the surface. . . . I tell you, my dear friend, that instead of taking me away from politics, my studies push me into it." Jaurès began to attend meetings of the local republican club. After his father died in the spring of 1882, Jaurès no longer felt bound to remain in Albi. He found a position teaching philosophy at the University of Toulouse and moved there, bringing his mother with him, in the fall of 1883. He began to write articles for the local republican journal, *La Dépêche de Toulouse*, and won notice as a public speaker eager to defend the Republic against its critics. In 1885, he asked the Toulouse republicans to include him on their list of candidates for the Chamber. They agreed. Jaurès's political career had begun.[19]

Republicans and socialists won 383 seats in the Chamber of Deputies in the 1885 elections, against 201 for the monarchists and Bonapartists of the Right. This meant a continued left majority in the Chamber, to be sure, but a narrowed majority: the Right had almost doubled the number of its seats since 1881, and its partisans remained unreconciled to the Republic. Although the basic institutions of the Republic had been in place for nearly a decade now, the regime's stability was still in question. One reason why the Left's candidates did not win as many seats as they had in 1881 was that the republicans were now divided into two loosely organized parties. Once republicans had to govern, they faced decisions about how to use their power, and such decisions are hardly ever simple. Ferry's Opportunists were now met with bitter criticism from republicans who called themselves "Radicals" (or, in some cases, "Radical-Socialists"). The Radicals, led by Georges Clemenceau, deputy from and former mayor of the commune of Montmartre, differed from the Opportunists in both style and program. Enamored of the French Revolution, the Radicals saw themselves as latter-day Jacobins fighting for the purity of the Republic, and they disdained those who did not share their sense of urgency. They objected to the Opportunists' policy of imperial expansion, and they insisted on immediate social reforms such as a progressive income tax, the introduction of pensions, the nationalization of the railroads, and limits on the length of the working day and on child labor. "Everything all at once," sneered the Opportunists.[20]

There were only about half a dozen deputies in the Chamber of 1885 who could properly be called "socialists." French socialism was eclectic, and the socialists were even more fractious than their republican colleagues. Different from one another in mood and in strategy, these groups were nevertheless recognizable as members of the same political family. For socialists of that generation, "socialism" (or "communism" or "social democracy"—at this point, the terms were more or less interchangeable) meant a commitment to replacing the existing society with an utterly different social order based on mutuality, community, and cooperation. In the short term, most socialists sought to strengthen the labor movement, win social welfare legislation, expand voting rights, and eliminate oligarchic institutions like upper legislative chambers and standing armies. They wanted what the revolutionaries of 1848 had called "la république démocratique et sociale."[21] But most nineteenth-century socialists also made a qualitative distinction between their proximate and their ultimate goals. Marx and Engels's *Communist Manifesto*—a document with a modest but increasing number of enthusiasts—promised that in time "the public power will lose its political character."[22] Or, in the words of Eugène Pottier's "L'Internationale," the movement's anthem:

> The world shall rise on new foundations;
> We are naught, let us be all.
> This is the final struggle.[23]

These were aspirations that pushed beyond the bounds of politics. Democratic in practice, the nineteenth-century socialists drew previously voiceless members of the working class into political action. For many socialists, however, their democratic practices seemed no more than means to the end of a society in which political action and political movements would no longer be needed.

The first French socialist party had been organized in 1879, as the exiled revolutionaries of the Paris Commune returned; by 1885, there were at least five socialist groups. Although Marxism was an increasingly prominent tendency among socialists in some parts of Europe—most notably in Germany—Marx's ideas were but one current among several within French socialism. The series of revolutions in France from 1789 to 1830 to 1848, the memory of the

Paris Commune, and the utopians of the early nineteenth century—especially Proudhon, with his vision of a federation of local democracies—all informed and inspired French socialists.[24]

That is not to say that Marxism was unimportant in France. The Parti ouvrier français (POF), led by Jules Guesde, was the largest and most organizationally coherent of the French socialist groups. Anomalous within the free-wheeling French Left, the POF fiercely defended its rigid catechism of Marxist doctrines. Its style was marked by disdain for compromise, skepticism toward the institutions of the Republic, and unshakable confidence in the prospect of revolution. For Guesde and the POF, Marxism meant class struggle between the bourgeoisie and the proletariat and the promise of a dramatic break between capitalism and the socialist system that would succeed it.

Quite different from the Parti ouvrier français in outlook was the small group of "independent socialists" influenced by the writings of Benoît Malon, a veteran of Marx's International Workingmen's Association and of the Paris Commune (where he was a Proudhonian dissenter against the Jacobin majority). Malon wanted to turn the moral impulse of French utopian socialism toward what he called the "reformist" and "experimental" process of change that was now possible within the Third Republic.[25] Aside from Malon's circle of followers, the Marxists' main rival among the socialist factions was a group led by Paul Brousse, labeled by Guesde the "Possibilists" for their interest in advancing the class struggle bit by bit and by any means possible. Indeed, it may have been Brousse who invented the term "Marxist" as an unfriendly label for his opponents in the POF.

To both Malon and Brousse, the Guesdists of the Parti ouvrier français seemed slavish followers of an authoritarian—and, worse, a foreign—thinker. As one associate of Malon wrote, Marxism was "essentially un-French," mired in German "local prejudices," and utterly lacking the "flexibility" and "passion" of French political thought.[26] Moreover, the Guesdists' insistence that socialism was the inevitable result of historical processes left socialists without an intellectual guide to the complicated work of achieving reforms that might be immediately possible. Other smaller groups of French socialists—followers of Auguste Blanqui, who dreamed of a revolutionary conspiracy led by a small band of devotees, or of Jean Allemane, who wanted a revolutionary movement composed solely of real workers with "calloused hands"—added their own criticisms of the POF's Marxism, but the common refrain was that Marxism, in addition to being a German import, seemed to lead its followers into a closed world of military-style party discipline and deterministic think-ing, in which the lessons of France's revolutionary past and the benefits of life in a republic were forgotten.[27]

The newly elected Jaurès had little interest in any of these socialist groups. He found them self-marginalizing and simplistic, and he thought that none of them understood the importance of consolidating recent republican achieve-ments before pressing for further reforms. Even Brousse's Possibilists seemed narrow in their perspective and sectarian in their style, despite their interest in gradual change, and the Radicals' impatient condescension toward the Oppor-tunists dismayed him. Unwilling to join any of these groups, he declared him-self an unaffiliated "republican at large" with an interest in the reconciliation of, or at least mutual respect among, all republican groups. The youngest member of the Chamber, he was slow to draw attention to himself. He sat quietly with the Opportunists and voted with them more often than not.[28] The question for Jaurès was, how to build and keep a republican majority? The best approach, it seemed to him, was to begin with the largest republican group and make it more inclusive. Aligning with the Opportunists required patience. It meant working for a distinctly nonrevolutionary republic and making majority building a higher priority than any policy question. To Jaurès, this was acceptable.

Jaurès had only an informal connection with the Opportunists; sitting with them in the Chamber did not make him a member of an organization. He would not remain unorganized for long, however. In 1886—which was also the year of his marriage to Louise Bois, the daughter of a wholesale merchant from Albi—Jaurès helped to found a labor caucus within the Chamber. Since his department included coal-mining towns like Carmaux, he had some acquaintance with the miners' union, one of France's first significant indus-trial unions. Composed of socialists, Radicals, and a few independent deputies like Jaurès, the labor caucus was formed in the wake of a bloody miners' strike in Decazeville, some 100 miles northeast of Toulouse. Caucus members trav-eled to Decazeville, conducted an investigation there, and returned to the Chamber to call for policies that would benefit workers.[29]

The caucus's open and organized support for strikers was a scandal accord-ing to the dominant interpretation of the French republican tradition. With few dissenters, Radicals and Opportunists alike shared the horror that the Jaco-bins of the First Republic had felt toward any organization that set itself apart from the general will of the nation. A trade union, in this view, was no better than an aristocratic house or a monastic order. Although an Opportunist-led government had legalized unions in 1884, partly as a response to an unprecedented wave of strikes, for most French republicans, this law represented an unhappy accommodation with a new and disturbingly significant force in French society, a foreign object too firmly lodged within the body politic to be safely excised. The labor caucus represented a dissident variety of republicanism in France, in some ways closer to the classical model of making latent conflicts public, of openly balancing different classes and interests.[30]

After joining the labor caucus, Jaurès drew closer to the miners' union. In 1886, not long after the Decazeville strike, he was invited to the congress of the miners' federation at Saint-Étienne to speak about union rights and the prospect of pension legislation. In 1887, he led a parliamentary fight to require that miners' delegates be included in mine safety inspections, and he worked, although with little success, to introduce pensions, accident and sickness insurance, and other social welfare measures that would benefit his working-class constituents.[31]

In the Chamber and in the *Dépêche*, Jaurès defended the place of unions in the Republic. René Waldeck-Rousseau, the interior minister who had ushered in the labor law of 1884, had argued that "the association of individuals in accordance with their professional affinities is not so much a weapon of combat as an instrument of material, moral, and intellectual progress."[32] Jaurès, however, insisted that unions were instruments of moral progress in part *because* they engaged in political combat. The strike might be a "terrible weapon," he wrote in 1887, but it was necessary if civic life were to be possible under modern conditions, since "there [was] no other way to reconcile humans than to render them truly equal," and equality was not achieved without the development of organizations that could guarantee some measure of power to those previously powerless. At the same time, unions showed the republic what it was like for citizens to be not only neighbors but fellows as well. "The greatest good that the Revolution has given to men is surely liberty," Jaurès wrote, but "liberty without solidarity is only a word, and solidarity itself is nothing if it remains a mere sentiment, if it does not take institutional form." When unions engaged in peaceful strikes and orderly collective bargaining on progressively larger scales, they enlarged their circles of solidarity. With this organizational expansion would come a new consciousness for union members, more political and less strictly economic, more appreciative of negotiation and less enamored of revolution—but, for all that, the daily activities of unions would be no less an attack on social inequality and on the privileges of the upper class. An expansion of "association" among workers, Jaurès concluded, would provide workers with "both wisdom and power."[33]

As the elections of 1889 approached, Jaurès began to express a new confidence in his own political purposes. Campaigning in his hometown of Castres that August, he said: "I hold in my heart a dream of fraternity and justice. I want to work for it until it has been realized."[34]

Jaurès lost his bid for reelection, however.[35] Returning to Toulouse with Louise and their newborn daughter, Madeleine, he took up teaching once more and wrote frequently for the *Dépêche*. At times, Jaurès now used the word "socialism" as a name for his political position.[36] Socialism seemed a "luminous ideal that shines before the working class, guiding them," he wrote in an October 1889 essay. None of the existing socialist groups, however, had figured out how to follow the socialist pillar of fire without getting lost in the wilderness. Even the Possibilists stumbled at the same point that other socialists did: their sole political task, as they saw it, was to engage in class struggle. The Possibilists understood the need for that struggle to yield gradual reforms, but, to an extent they had not yet thought through, their acceptance of republican methods was at odds with their commitment to class struggle. The republic operated by majority rule, but the industrial working class was still a minority. "If the socialist party is right to demand a broad representation for the workers, it cannot long maintain the principle of class struggle," Jaurès wrote. "Either it must start a violent revolution or, contrary to its principles, it must seek an alliance of classes in common defense of liberty, in common pursuit of justice."[37]

The contradiction between the politics of class and the politics of the common good was not unresolvable, Jaurès wrote. The intellectual solution lay in the republican tradition, he proposed, and the organizational solution lay in the republican majority among French citizens. "There is in France an immense socialist party that calls itself simply 'the republican party,'" Jaurès wrote in October 1890. "The French republican party, basing itself on the French Revolution, is a socialist party, whether it says so or not, because the Revolution contains all of socialism." The French political tradition already contained socialism because the ideas of that tradition, if pursued conscientiously and thoroughly, required a confrontation with the new problems of a capitalist society. So far that confrontation had been the business of small and marginal socialist groups, Jaurès wrote, but he thought this need not always be the case: "Our goal must be not to found socialist sects outside the republican majority, but to bring the party of the Revolution to boldly and explicitly recognize what it is: a socialist party."[38] Existing socialist groups erred when they aimed to build a movement committed exclusively to class struggle. This might have made sense when socialism was a new movement of protest against the conditions of workers in the emerging capitalist economy. Now, Jaurès proposed, a better way to win the "broad representation for the workers" of which he had written the year before would be to build a party, or a coalition of parties, that could assemble an electoral majority in favor of social reform. Significantly, this majority would be a *republican* majority. Its members would speak the common language of republican politics: rejection of monarchy and aristocracy; commitment to liberty, equality, and fraternity; a concern with both institutions and civic virtue; an affection for the complexity of life in public spaces.

Jaurès had close at hand a model of what this republican socialist majority might look like. He had been elected to the Toulouse city council in a July 1890 special election and served as a member of the governing coalition of socialists and Radical republicans. There were tensions between republicans and socialists—and between socialists, to be sure—but the liveliness and durability of coalitions like that in Toulouse heralded a new kind of politics, as different from older kinds of socialism as socialism was from the liberal republicanism of previous generations.[39]

Jaurès's "dream of fraternity" was taking shape. By the end of 1890, he had a rough idea of the political path he wanted to follow: republican-socialist coalitions, a legislative and electoral strategy coupled with support for striking workers, the expansion of collective bargaining, and the introduction of social welfare measures. He was developing a social theory as well. Under the influence of Lucien Herr, who had become librarian at the École normale supérieure in 1888 and with whom he had struck up a friendship while conducting research for his Chamber speeches, Jaurès began to read the writings of Karl Marx. Aside from the *Communist Manifesto,* a full translation of which had been published only in 1885, few of Marx's works had been translated into French—Jaurès would read most of them in the original German—and Herr was among the few French socialists who knew them well. Jaurès filled the margins of his copy of Marx's *Capital* with notes. He was impressed by Marx's exposition of the intimate relationships between value and capital, capital and labor: here was a precise and sophisticated account of the mechanics of injustice in industrial societies.[40]

As much as Jaurès thought he had to learn from *Capital*'s analysis of society, he was not moved by the *Manifesto*'s apocalyptic prophecies. Neither Marx's certainty about the inevitable fall of capitalism nor his vision of a future in which humanity has outgrown political life altogether won Jaurès over to Marx's theory of history. But the members of a political movement need to be confident that their efforts are not futile. If he was not to join Marx in awaiting a revolution, how would Jaurès explain why his republican socialism was worth pursuing? Jaurès wanted a way of thinking about politics that could account for strikes and electoral coalitions, a program of radical reform and a politics of mixing and balancing, the facts of the Third Republic and the dream of fraternity. Most fundamentally, he wanted to confront the problem of hope—but not in Marx's way. All this, Jaurès seems to have decided, would require intellectual work at some remove from politics itself.

In the 1890s, candidates for the *doctorat ès lettres* were required to complete two theses, a primary thesis in French and a secondary thesis in Latin. Jaurès had begun work on a thesis in philosophy as early as 1883 or 1884, soon after he arrived in Toulouse. Setting the project aside when he became a candidate for the Chamber of Deputies, he did not return to it until 1890. There followed two years of intense intellectual activity, alongside his service on the Toulouse city council, his journalism for the *Dépêche,* and his continued advocacy for the miners' and glassmakers' unions of the Tarn. By 1892, Jaurès had completed his two doctoral theses.[41]

Jaurès begins his French thesis, "De la realité du monde sensible," with a deceptively simple question: "The sensible world—what we see, what we touch, where we live: is it real?" (*PTA*, 113). Jaurès has absorbed part of Kant's critical philosophy; he affirms that the senses collect "fragmentary impressions" of the world while the mind acts as an "architect" to structure them (*PTA*, 113, 115). Our experiences of the sensible world take the form they do because human consciousness organizes human perceptions through categories such as time, space, and causality. For Kant, the role of consciousness in organizing perceptions means that human knowledge of the world is radically limited. We cannot know how closely things as they appear to us match things as they are in themselves: the phenomena we experience through our senses and the noumena conceived within our minds are separate from one another. Here Jaurès breaks with Kant. Whereas, for Kant, rational consciousness marks human beings as peculiar and betrays their alienation from things-in-themselves, in

Jaurès's eyes, the work of human consciousness marks human beings as full citizens of the cosmos.

What Kant and French neo-Kantians failed to understand, Jaurès argues, is the importance of *what* we see when we look at the world around us.[42] In the sensible world, we encounter not merely a series of objects and events; a world like that would be an incomprehensible "ghost in motion." Instead, we perceive a drive toward form and toward orderly relationships. Jaurès does not mean that our perception of order in the world proves that the world is orderly. He has absorbed too much Kant to make such an argument; like Kant, he thinks that we see order because our consciousness arranges our sense perceptions into ordered systems. But human consciousness is itself part of the world, Jaurès argues, and so if we have a predisposition to perceive order it must be because human consciousness shares with the world as a whole certain structures and impulses. We perceive order because human consciousness, like the rest of the world, tends toward order. That pull toward order, he writes, is the world's most fundamental trait.

> That is why there is organization in the world; or, rather, that is why each part of the world is organized: thus we have the vast ensembles of intertwined movements that we call the systems of stars, we have the systems of forces united by secret affinities that make up chemical compounds, we have living organisms, we even have higher consciousnesses that try to draw the entire universe into their own smaller unities. These organized systems do not exist in relation to a purpose outside themselves. Each only serves itself, or at any rate it is never the essence of any of these systems to serve anything but itself. . . . Each becomes real only through an interior aspiration, through an obscure and conscious effort of its own toward beauty and independence of form. (*PTA*, 120)

All the pieces of the world—galaxies, living things, cells, molecules—are by nature both individuated and relational. Every "organized system" aspires toward autonomy, toward self-rule; at the same time, these autonomous systems are each members of larger and more encompassing systems with their own orderly patterns and internal rules. Jaurès's account of the universe sounds so much like what Aristotle claimed about human beings—that we are most ourselves when we are members of communities in which members take turns ruling and being ruled, and in which the community aspires to a shared good life—that at times Jaurès seems to be writing not so much a metaphysical argument with political implications as an account of political life projected onto a cosmic screen.

Jaurès depicts this endless making of organized systems as both a physical phenomenon and a moral drive.

> It is not that these organized systems are isolated from one another and that the world finds its being only by losing its unity, for, first, no phenomenon is part of these systems without also being part of the causal and mechanical series that link it to the totality of phenomena, and, moreover, all these organizations, to various degrees and in various ways, aspire to the same end: unity, beauty, freedom, joy. They are thus all linked together outwardly and inwardly, by the exterior and indefinite bonds of the causal series, and by the inner community of the superior and divine purpose that they share. (*PTA*, 120)

Precisely because we recognize in it something ideal, we can be confident about the reality of the world as we experience it, the reality of what Kant called "the phenomenal realm" and of what Jaurès variously calls "the sensible," "the visible," "the solid," or "the palpable." We might say that, in recognizing ourselves as parts of a whole, we recognize the sensible world as real and as aspiring to order. Jaurès insists equally on the inverse claim: recognizing the sensible world as real, we recognize ourselves as parts of a whole, as participants in the universal order and dynamics of Being (*l'être*).[43]

Thus Jaurès cannot accept the "famous comparison" between Kant's critical philosophy and Copernicus's theory that the sun, rather than the earth, is the point around which the planets of our system revolve. Quite the opposite: because it treats human consciousness as an anomaly, Kant's philosophy is better compared to the medieval, earth-centered view of the cosmos. A true Copernican revolution in philosophy, Jaurès writes, would displace human consciousness from the center, treating it as simply one component of the world, not particularly different from any other; it would "place the self within the living system of infinite consciousness" (*PTA*, 356). Jaurès, in this respect, turns Kant inside out.

"Consciousness," as Jaurès uses the term, is not a distinctively human quality of rational self-awareness, but something more like purposeful existence. Jaurès rejects "the opposition, or even the radical distinction, between Being and consciousness" (*PTA*, 235). Every fragment or aspect of the world contains aspirations that are, in this sense, conscious—although those aspirations might be more obscure here and more overt there. The rational consciousness with which Kantian philosophy is concerned is not to be thought of as something separate from the body and therefore separate from the physical world. Indeed, Jaurès writes nearly as often about the brain (*le cerveau*) as about consciousness (*la conscience*) or mind (*l'esprit*). After all, Jaurès argues, consciousness is located in the brain, an organ of the body. Thus, building on his lectures at Albi, Jaurès proposes that what philosophers study is not consciousness in and of itself, as Kant had argued, but rather "consciousness in its rapport with the reality of the world."[44] This rapport, this "continuity of the Being of the world and the being of the brain," means that human perceptions give us access to the world as it really is (*PTA*, 370, 351). Our experiences of the sensible world are experiences of reality, of Being itself, and we ought to take with full seriousness the physical and sensual world as we find it.

But something other than the nature and limits of knowledge is at stake here. Jaurès has introduced the idea that Being is characterized not only by unity, but also by diversity and individuation—and by unity not only through "the causal series," but also through aspiration toward a "divine end." Jaurès's universe is neither random nor uniform, neither static nor deterministic. It— and thus the human communities possible within it—can change, in an uneven but orderly fashion, in ways not so much dictated by causal laws as motivated by moral aims.

When Jaurès writes about Being's ideal unity, he echoes the Platonic and Neoplatonic notion of Ideas or Forms more real than their tangible approximations.[45] But Jaurès wants to account for Being's diversity and complexity without repeating Platonic philosophy's denigration of the sensible world; he wants to be able to say both that Being is a perfect whole and that it is composed of imperfect parts, but he does not want to treat those parts as illusions or distractions, as shadows on the wall of a cave. To account for these apparently incongruous ideas, Jaurès borrows the categories developed in Aristotle's *Metaphysics*.[46] There Aristotle distinguished between actuality (*entelecheia*, conventionally translated into French as "acte") and potency or potentiality (*dynamis*, conventionally translated into French as "puissance"). Jaurès proposes that Being be understood as having two faces: Being in actuality (*l'être en acte*) and Being in potentiality (*l'être en puissance*). Insofar as the world is intelligible, and therefore real, Jaurès writes, it must be because "the world participates in the continuity of time and space, as in the absolute continuity of indeterminate, homogenous, and continuous Being." Being's actuality, in other words, depends on or is grounded in Being's potentiality.

> Determinedness is thus not enough to constitute the reality of the world: there must also be the absolute continuity of Being considered as undetermined potentiality. To be real, the world must participate not only in the actuality of Being, but in the potentiality of Being. . . . The permanence of a form is possible only because the potentiality of Being is always mixed in all its activities. . . . It must be that every element of Being lives its own life and at the same time aspires to harmony of form and unity of type. Thus, within each element, aside from its own activity there must be a ground of Being and, if I can put it this way, there must be stored-up aspirations toward form. (*PTA*, 123–24)

Neither "permanence of form" nor "activity"—neither the world's stability nor the evident possibility of new and surprising things in the world—can be accounted for by deterministic theories, whether of cosmology or of human history. Every phenomenon trembles with unrealized possibilities; particular facts, Jaurès writes, are comprehensible only in relation to "an ideal end," which must be "the immense harmony of all." Jaurès's occasional use of the word "unity" may be confusing since he also writes about "harmony" (*PTA*, 125). This is not a contradiction, however. The essential point is that the unity toward which Being aspires, in Jaurès's account, is not unity of identity or erasure of distinctions. Rather, it is unity of purpose, common participation in an ordered whole. Being, in Jaurès's understanding, wants to arrange itself like a musical composition whose distinct notes all harmonize with one another.

That ideal end of "immense harmony" is what Jaurès calls "Being in potentiality." Because Being in potentiality makes possible—and thus in a sense is the origin of—all particular facts, it is logically prior to them. At the same time, Being in potentiality is in another sense the goal or the end of all particular things. Being in actuality, then, is the aspect of Being that remains particular, incomplete, unharmonized. Though infinite in its potentiality, Being is finite in its actuality. Being in actuality aspires to (and is grounded in) Being in potentiality, but a gap always remains: Being's actuality never fully achieves or exhausts Being's potentiality. Given the ideal end Jaurès claims for Being—a kind of joyful sociability among its fragments—this seems to be necessarily so. Only if Being aimed at a perfect unity of identity could the actual and the potential merge. Unity can be perpetual, but harmony among moving voices gives rise to new harmonies and new dissonant overtones.

Although he takes the actuality-potentiality distinction from Aristotle, Jaurès uses it in his own way. Aristotle wrote about the actuality and potentiality of particular beings; he wanted to understand the processes of development that beings undergo as they move through actuality toward potentiality—from acorn to oak, for instance, or from a set of people in one place to a political community. For Aristotle, actuality *becomes* (or can become) potentiality. For Jaurès, however, actuality and potentiality are aspects of Being as such. The relationship between the two is not one of change over time, but of permanent co-presence. "Infinite Being is not on the way to realization; it is already the fullness of Being. Infinity does not become; it is," Jaurès writes. "The infinity of Being is present really, actually, in all fragments of reality" (*PTA*, 152). A pair of concepts that Aristotle used to account for growth and development becomes, for Jaurès, a way to give an account of the perpetual tension that constitutes Being. When Jaurès writes that the world's parts all aspire to the common end of unity, beauty, freedom, and joy, he is not making a prediction about the degree to which those ends will be realized in the future; he is proposing that we can sense the presence of those ends now, in the world as we see, hear, smell, taste, and feel it. Thus the facts of conflict, ugliness, oppression, and sadness are not the last word on reality. Writing about the concept of movement, Jaurès proposes that trajectory is more significant than extent: "Every movement—whatever it is, whatever its form, its speed, its direction—is infinite since it gives form to a part of Being; Being is homogenous and singular, and so every one of its parts shares in its infiniteness. Every movement is thus infinite from the point of view of Being and of Being's potentiality; it is so also from the point of view of Being's form and Being's actuality. . . . Each form of movement expresses in its own way the universal system" (*PTA*, 173–74). Thus, if we want to look for infinity—that is, for the potentiality of Being—we need not look elsewhere than the finite and particular organized systems and instances of movement that we meet in the sensible world. Every form, every organization, every movement intimates the unity, beauty, freedom, and joy that are the purpose of Being. The potentiality of Being is not to be waited for, but to be recognized here and now, in real spaces and at the present time. If we enter into the limited movements and not quite harmonious relationships of the world that surrounds us, we will not be distancing ourselves from the "ideal end" or "divine end" of Being. To pursue the ideal is not to depart from the sensible world, but to comprehend it. To take seriously the sensible world is not to neglect the ideal, but to find it.

Turning from the vocabulary of classical Greek philosophy to the vocabulary of biblical religion, Jaurès at times uses "Dieu" as a synonym for "l'être." Twice, he quotes Paul's "in God we live, and move, and have our being" (*PTA*, 154, 347).[47] and he writes: "God, or Being, is at the same time, and in an indestructible unity, both actuality and potentiality" (*PTA*, 129). Jaurès's God is not a self-contemplating "idol of perfection" like the god of Plato and Aristotle, but is active and "present in our struggles and in our sadness, in all struggles and all sadness."

> Because God is infinite, he has an infinite need to give himself, to pour himself out in all beings and to rediscover himself by that effort. . . . Because God is the supreme reality and the supreme perfection, he does not want to exist in a state of unperturbed and imperturbable perfection. He puts himself in question; he finds a way to give himself up to the uncertain work of the world; he becomes poor and suffering with the universe in order to complete his essential perfection through the holiness of voluntary suffering. The world is in a sense the eternal and universal Christ. (*PTA*, 154)

Always on the Cross, always rising from the tomb: that, for Jaurès, is the dynamic that constitutes Being. It is important to note here that Jaurès sees "Christ" as an appropriate symbol for the *world*, not for a particular *event* in the world. Every facet of the world's yearning for harmonious order, not only one specific instance of that yearning, shows humanity what it is to live for the sake of something outside the self. Jaurès wants to say here that there will be no one moment at which potentiality overcomes actuality once and for all, no one day when a qualitative transformation takes place. Whatever new birth or resurrection—or revolution—the world experiences will be instead a perpetual, and thus perpetually incomplete, reordering of the world into a harmonious whole.

This is not to say that Jaurès was returning to the Roman Catholic Church of his youth.[48] It is doubtful, to say the least, that his theology could have passed as orthodox. But the fondness for biblical language and sympathy for religious feeling that he shows here is more than a rhetorical decoration.[49]

Certainly the words "God" and "Christ" are likely to have a different effect for readers, especially readers schooled in the Christian tradition, than the words "Being," "actuality," and "potentiality." To say that God is present not just in *all* struggles but in *our* struggles is to invite a response that is not detached or objective, and not merely cognitive. The danger, as Jaurès sees it, is that philosophical argument involves contemplation but not commitment. "This is an era of refined powerlessness and pretentious debility," Jaurès writes. These features of the modern condition can be overcome, however, because "human consciousness needs God, and will know how to reach him," just as "human society needs fraternal justice, and will know how to achieve it," despite the "sophists and skeptics" who obscure these truths (*PTA*, 135). Philosophical language offers precision and transparency, but Jaurès suggests that theological language has its virtue, too: "The very essence of religious life is to leave behind the mean and egoistic self" (*PTA*, 347). Jaurès wants words that have effects beyond the conveyance of concepts, words that have the capacity to pull his readers or listeners out of moral isolation, or at least to instigate within them a protest against that isolation. Jaurès claims in his French thesis to be dealing in philosophical knowledge, but he lets slip now and then that he is at least as concerned with what he can express, or elicit, as with what he can prove. "De la realité du monde sensible" is—perhaps among other things, but perhaps nothing other than—an exposition of how the world looks to someone who has adopted a certain orientation toward it: active, critical, appreciative, engaged.

Every theology needs a theodicy; hope needs to be plausible. Since, by definition, Being in actuality cannot fully realize Being in potentiality, Jaurès reminds his readers, the "infinite joy" of Being in potentiality is present within and around the "infinite sadness" of Being in actuality. Joy is the ever present aspiration of all existence, but "the perfect, because of its very perfection, and to earn its perfection, unfolds the world in effort, in contradiction, in struggle, that is to say, in suffering." Being stretches toward joy and toward harmony only through an endless struggle, Jaurès writes. There can be progress of a kind, progress that "raises, transforms, and enlarges the conditions of the struggle," but the struggle is never superseded. Thus the world "oscillates between conflict and harmony." Moments of harmony are never more than provisional because "there remains at the base of the world an eternal contradiction" between Being in actuality and Being in potentiality, "a hidden root of suffering." But Jaurès is quick—too quick?—to add that suffering is never absolute because "the divine activity that pours out the world remains like an inexhaustible spring of joy." Indeed, the life of the world consists of a continual effort to achieve harmonious organization and shared joy, an effort that is always incomplete and always possible: "The battle is never wholly won; it is never wholly lost" (*PTA*, 175–77).

The important thing, Jaurès wants to say, is not a transformation that will happen in the future. What matters is the contour of the present. Tellingly, Jaurès writes little in "De la realité du monde sensible" about time and a great deal about space. For Jaurès, the reality of space is a particularly important idea because the expansiveness and three-dimensionality of space guarantees the possibility of movement, and thus of freedom (*PTA*, 129–35). He distinguishes between the idea of "place" (*lieu*) as it was studied by Aristotle and other ancient thinkers—the position of objects in relation to one another—and the idea of "space" (*espace*), properly understood. For space to be conceivable, Jaurès writes, two intellectual "revolutions" were necessary. First, Christian theology—in particular the thought of Augustine, who was "amazed that images of extensiveness can pour out and move through the nonextensive soul"—taught that "the development of interior life, the habit of contemplation" does not distract us from the sensible world, but rather grounds our comprehension of it. Then, at the beginning of the modern era, Copernican thought posited a universe of infinite space, showing us that we are located within a limitless expanse of Being. After these two revolutions, Jaurès writes, it became possible to understand space as the site where the absolute is present in the world. For Jaurès, thinking spatially involves recognizing both the inclusion of particular spaces within the infinite expanse of Being and the presence of infinite Being within particular spaces. Thus Jaurès can say that the absolute—or the infinite, or the potentiality of Being, or divine perfection—is not an unembodied spirit or an event that will reach fullness at a future time; instead, the absolute becomes available to our senses through its spatial character. Because space is real, Jaurès argues, it is in real spaces, in the present, that we are able to sense the world's aspiration toward an ideal harmony (*PTA*, 291–93).[50]

> Precisely because absolute consciousness creates the reality of the world, all the individuals and all the forces of the world keep the reality they already have and the duties that are already familiar to them. By blending into the world, God pours out not only life and joy but also modesty and common sense. Precisely because he is present in all, God does not

invalidate, does not destroy, the simple and quiet relationships among objects and beings. The lofty sky and stars find their full reality and their justification in the absolute and divine consciousness, but so also does the modest home where, between the family table and the hearth, the man with his humble tools wins for himself and his own their daily bread. (*PTA*, 374)

Instead of asking his readers to expect that the world will someday arrive at a state of perfect harmony and full joy, Jaurès asks them to consider the simple, the quiet, the contained, the humble, the quotidian. It is in these, if anywhere, that we can find the proper object of our deepest commitments and the proper sphere of our most fundamental moral and political responsibilities. If we want to see the entry of the ideal into reality, Jaurès suggests, we should look not to things distant but to things immediate, not to a time in the future but to the space in which we are already present.

To most socialists of the early 1890s, eagerly awaiting the total realization of their ideal, the moral stance revealed in "De la realité du monde sensible" would have seemed wrong, or at least unfamiliar. Nevertheless, Jaurès saw socialism as the political counterpart to his metaphysical argument. If "the deeper meaning of life" is "that the universe itself is but a boundless and muddled yearning toward order, beauty, freedom, and kindness," as he wrote around the time he began working in earnest on his French thesis, then one might claim that "the universe is, in its own way, socialist."[51] The question is what kind of socialist politics might bring that deeper meaning to the surface.

In his Latin thesis, "De primis socialismi germanici lineamentis" (The first outlines of German socialism), Jaurès transposes the "pure and contemplative philosophy" of his French thesis into a political key and begins to work out the differences between the socialism he rejects and the socialism he wants. He does this by writing about a philosophical tradition that is not only the carrier of a "doctrine," he tells his readers, but also "a party within the state," which "fights to smash the foundations of the existing society" (*PTA*, 383). For Jaurès, German socialism showed (sometimes despite itself) how the ideal of justice and harmony about which he had written in his French thesis might take shape within the world—that is, within the conflict, disharmony, and finite spaces of political life.

German socialism was naturally a subject of great interest for any socialist at this time. The German Social Democratic Party (Sozialdemokratische Partei Deutschlands, or SPD) was the largest socialist party in Europe. Even in 1890, when it was just emerging from more than a decade of repression under Chancellor Otto von Bismarck's Anti-Socialist Laws, the SPD was able to win almost one and a half million votes for its Reichstag candidates. Alone among the socialist movements of the European countries, German socialists offered a model that could be, and was, imitated elsewhere. Unlike their French and English counterparts, the Germans had a single nationwide party with a mass membership, an established party press, cultural organizations, a relatively well developed party bureaucracy, and defined roles for local branches, central leaders, and party congresses.[52]

Along with the German style of organization, new socialist parties were also adopting German ideas. German socialists had for a long time been divided between followers of Ferdinand Lassalle, who emphasized peaceful change and the role of the national state in establishing socialism, and those of Karl Marx, for whom socialism meant relentless class struggle and, as certain as sunrise, a smashing revolutionary victory in the relatively near future. But during the dark days of the Anti-Socialist Laws, Marxism's promise of an inevitable revolution won over many former Lassalleans, and, by 1890, Marx's ideas were ascendant; in 1891, as Jaurès completed his Latin thesis, the SPD's Erfurt congress would officially adopt Marxism as the party's doctrine.[53]

Jaurès sees the peculiarly German spirit of German socialism as both a fault and a virtue. Because the SPD's strategy and style respond to its own circumstances, Jaurès suggests, socialists in other countries would be unwise to imitate it uncritically. But they would also be unwise to ignore it because German socialism is the culmination of an intellectual tradition that offered to the rest of the world a distinctive and useful way of thinking. The political visions of Marx and Lassalle are rooted in the thinking of Georg Wilhelm Friedrich Hegel, Johann Gottlieb Fichte, Immanuel Kant, and Martin Luther, who together compose a tradition that "claims that there is in history and in political economy a certain dialectic that changes the forms of things and of human relations" (*PTA*, 383).[54] What Jaurès means by "dialectic" is simply this: "The Germans deliberately bring together and reconcile things that seem to be embattled opposites" (*PTA*, 398). According to the German tradition, whatever moral or political progress is to be achieved will proceed through the reconciliation of certain pairs of principles that are seen as being, but do not have to be, in conflict with each other.

This way of thinking is quite unlike the French, Jaurès writes. The Germans reconcile, whereas "the French passionately embrace one side of the contradiction, so they can more thoroughly despise and crush the other. The French oppose reason to faith, individual freedom to collective power. The Germans interpret the Christian religion rationally, and they assert that the freedom of each can only be established and secured through the legitimate power of the state" (*PTA*, 398–99). This habit of nondialectical thinking drives the French to conceive of freedom only as "the abstract faculty of choosing between contrary options, as the hypothetical independence of each citizen taken individually" (*PTA*, 383). The French "tend to treat each will abstractly, as if an individual could be separated and isolated from broader patterns of events, as if each were sufficient to himself, power for power, so that we then claim that all men are equally free. From this comes the economic maxim 'Each for himself.'"[55] This idea of freedom, Jaurès writes, is ghostly, otherworldly, immaterial, cut off from life. It is not a picture of substantive justice (*PTA*, 389). The French, as much as any nation, needed to learn something from the German tradition.

Jaurès proposes that everything really distinctive in German socialism, including its dialectic method of thought, comes from Luther. No political radical, Luther wanted "not to change society but to reform the realm of conscience and faith," and he distanced himself from the peasant rebellions he helped to inspire. Despite Luther's own intentions, however, his insistence on "the liberty to interpret and to comment" on Scripture, his doctrine of the priesthood of all Christians, and his conviction that "the sacraments only have merit when Christians have perfect equality and communion" helped to open a new era in which political life would be shaped by recurring waves of protest and reform. Luther never "wholly embraced the social question" even when he did find something to say about economic matters, as in his pamphlet on usury (*PTA*, 385–87, 397). But what interests Jaurès most is the idea at the heart of Luther's theology: the doctrine of salvation by grace. Here Jaurès finds a paradigm for understanding matters far removed from Luther's principal concerns.

In Luther's theology, human beings are weak, fallen, distorted by humanity's original sin. Under our own power, through our own merit, we are unable to fulfill God's commandments. Our judgment is flawed, and we cannot reliably carry out our own intentions. We cannot simply *decide* to do what we should. We can only do good "with the grace and help of God." Thus the source of freedom—of our capacity to make our actions follow our own wills—is not found within the individual self. The doctrine of free will, for Luther, is dangerous not only because it is incorrect, but because it "isolates man from God." Jaurès worries that there is something punishingly lonely in the idea that freedom is rooted in some quality of the individual person, and he thinks that Luther has captured something about free will, something of interest to socialists. If the individual person were already fully free, as advocates of a simplistic notion of free will would claim, then there would be no need for any change in the human condition. But we do not find ourselves, on our own, to be free, and so we know that the freedom of the human being to judge and to decide requires the establishment of a new context outside the individual. For Luther, whose concern is spiritual freedom, that context is God's grace, revealed in God's Word. For Jaurès, the political analogy to Luther's doctrine is the idea that the political freedom of the individual is possible only on a foundation of social justice. Freedom for the individual citizen, Jaurès wants to say, is possible when justice has been established in and by the society that stands outside the individual, and when the individual is not isolated from that society. Thus Jaurès argues that Luther's theology prepared thinkers in the German tradition to understand that "man is free only when truth illumines him and justice shapes him" (*PTA*, 387–88).

In Luther's soteriology, God's grace appears as the mediation between human weakness and divine perfection—an opposed pair not unrelated to the Being in actuality and Being in potentiality of Jaurès's French thesis. What Jaurès finds most interesting in Luther's doctrine of grace, in other words, is its dialectical quality. Glossing Luther, Jaurès writes:

> We must distinguish between the revealed God and the hidden God, that is to say between the Word of God and God himself. God by his Word calls all men to salvation; but God, by his will, pushes some toward salvation, some toward death. And this is not injustice, because it is not ours to judge God or to truly account for the rules of his justice. There are three levels of truth, like three kinds of light: the light of nature, the light of grace, and the light of divine glory. In the light of nature, we are offended to see how often liars and impious men succeed in this worldly life. But in the light of grace, we see that life on earth is only a part of

human life, and that beyond this a reward has been reserved for the just, a punishment for the impious. Why has God predestined some to what is good and others to what is bad? In the light of grace, we still cannot comprehend clearly, and we can only stammer unthinkingly that justice has been violated. But when we are allowed to enter into the heart of the radiant glory of the invisible God, then the divine will appear fully just and good to us. (*PTA*, 388)

For Luther, the world of suffering, of injustice, of sin and alienation that is immediately present before us is not utterly disconnected from the complete joy, perfect justice, and absolute unity of divine glory that is hidden from us. But the brokenness of the world is not the only truth about the world: human beings can experience grace. For Luther, grace—the content of the revealed Word of God—is something we experience here, within the world, although we can only comprehend that grace if we understand it as the mediation of that which remains beyond our sight and grasp. Grace is an intimation of the divine. It shapes and illuminates life in this world, even while the world remains broken and sinful. This is not so different from saying that Being's potentiality grounds Being's actuality. What Luther contributes here is the emphatically dialectical notion of a mediation between two poles, whatever names we might give them. Luther's doctrine of grace suggests to Jaurès that, in politics as in religion, the ideal for which we long can be continually present with us despite its perpetual absence from us.

This dialectic—or, better, this paradox—of the presence of the absent is what fascinates Jaurès about Luther's moments of biblical literalism. Luther insists that the Garden of Eden was a real place in the Middle East containing an actual Tree of Life because he wants to hold on to the idea that "it is not in unknown or fictional places but in the world itself" that the "struggle for good or evil" happens. Thus the centrality for Luther of the doctrine of incarnation: "What is Christ if not God himself present within the nature of things and of the visible world?" Luther believes that "human life renewed in Christ is impelled toward immortality, permeated with immortality, as if with a divine infection," writes Jaurès (*PTA*, 391). This means that

just as Luther does not want to abstract and isolate the human will from divinity, so he refuses to separate and isolate justice from the nature of things and from the nature of the visible world. Justice will not be accomplished outside nature or outside the things of the visible world, but in the world itself, corrected and amended. Justice will not shine forth in the cold regions of death, but in life itself; it will blend into the light of the visible sun. Justice is wrapped up in and interwoven with the things of the world. . . . Heaven will be made anew, earth will be formed anew—not a theological heaven, not a phantasmagoric image of the earth, but a real heaven, a true earth. We need not say: Justice is in the other world and outside this world. Justice will shine one day under the sun of the living, and under the visible sky. Truly, can we not recognize here the spirit of socialism, which works to bring justice into life itself? (*PTA*, 390–91)

Jaurès has introduced a curious ambiguity here. It is not clear whether the shining justice that he anticipates will be perfect justice. Will the establishment of socialism be like the creation of a new heaven and a new earth, or is socialism the mediation of an ideal that remains as distant as Luther's hidden God? Jaurès's reading of Luther up to this point would suggest the latter. But when he turns to the political implications of Luther's theology, Jaurès chooses not to remind his readers of what he has elsewhere written: that the battle is never wholly won.

Jaurès writes considerably more about Luther than about Fichte, Kant, Hegel, Lassalle, or Marx.[56] The essential ideas of his Latin thesis have already been developed in the section on Luther; he has now to show the way those ideas were worked out through the tradition as a whole.

Kant's contribution to the development of German socialism, Jaurès writes, lies in his dialectical restatement of Jean-Jacques Rousseau's social contract theory (*PTA*, 404–5).[57] Jaurès remarks that Kant's emphasis on liberty is such that one could almost take him for "a French philosophe full of the revolutionary spirit and trusting solely in liberty," except for the fact that Kant accords a "great majesty to the state," as no philosophe would do. Bridging Rousseau and Luther, Kant argues that a social pact—that is, a power outside the individual person—makes a society based on free will possible and that civil society must in turn leave individual liberty intact. Kant shows that Rousseau's idea of a social contract "acquires its maximum force and effective power" in the modern representative republic and in the future prospect of universal peace through a federation of republics (*PTA*, 404–6). In this way, Kant is able to "reconcile the ideals of French philosophy and Prussian monarchy"—that is, the principles of individual liberty and state power (*PTA*, 400). Most French republicans would have been too wary of state power to accept that it could further liberty, but, to Jaurès, this is the most interesting element of Kant's political thought. What Kant has shown, Jaurès writes, is that "individualism and socialism are not opposed to each other as if they were essentially contradictory." Instead, in Kant's dialectical argument "they are brought together and reconciled" (*PTA*, 406–8).

Fichte seems to Jaurès to be an "amplified" Kant. What is only a "germ of socialism" in Kant's work becomes in Fichte's the idea of full-blown "collectivism" and the argument that the state should secure citizens' economic well-being. A social contract must deal with property rights, Fichte argues, but it can make provisions for property rights only if every citizen has a claim on society's wealth—otherwise, some participants in the contract will have to give up something for nothing, violating the precept that Rousseau finds central to the validity of the contract (*PTA*, 409–12). Where French Opportunists and Radicals would be content to let great social inequalities coexist with the Third Republic's democratic institutions, Jaurès wants to take from Fichte the idea that a democracy without substantial social equality is not very democratic after all.

Jaurès admires both Kant and Fichte for making the study of history subordinate to "the demands of justice in the present." To Marx, this would seem a weakness: "Marx justifies the need for collectivism less by its justice than by the historical destiny of social evolution. He is eager to mock those like Fichte, who ceaselessly invoke human dignity and eternal justice." But Fichte understands something that has also become important in Jaurès's own conception of political life. Precisely because Fichte's method of thinking about politics has turned him toward the present and toward questions of justice, he does not rest his hopes on a drastic political change at some point in the future or accept forms of action that might in themselves be unjust. Rather than pushing for "rash action," Fichte understands that "slowness and temporizing do not mean inaction and apathy." For Fichte, Jaurès writes, "one must continue each day to advance toward justice, so that by evening the world is already closer to justice than it was in the morning" (*PTA*, 417–18).

At the same time, Jaurès is careful to point out that Fichte's vision is different from his own. Fichte calls for an all-powerful state, shut off as much as possible from the rest of the world, administering the lives of passive individuals and suppressing any group that tries to assert its particular existence.

Fichte's collectivist state is "an enclosed sphere, a world unto itself," in which a cosmopolitan public life is impossible. This is not a vision Jaurès wants to endorse. But even the claustrophobic nationalism of Fichte's collectivist plan seems to Jaurès to yield a dialectical insight.

Socialists of the 1890s wanted to unite all nations into "one economic society," a federation of all nations. Fichte had argued that only a "closed state" could achieve "a measure of justice" because injustice outside the state would threaten justice inside it. But socialists of Jaurès own generation had realized that internationalism could achieve social justice more securely than Fichte's nationalism ever could: the only self-enclosed society possible in the capitalist era, Jaurès suggested, was one open to all, one that encompassed the globe (*PTA*, 416).

Jaurès finds Hegel's philosophy to be the most creative development in German dialectical thinking since Luther. In Hegel's *Philosophy of Right*, Jaurès writes, "the foundation of right"—that is, the basis of political justice and of legitimate state power—"is freedom." Rather than defining freedom abstractly, Hegel "shows the progression by which freedom gradually takes its full and perfect form." Neither the absolute freedom of the will ("Freiheit des Willens" for Hegel; "liberté de volonté" for Jaurès) nor the individual person's ability to decide freely in a particular context ("Willkür" for Hegel, "libre arbitre" for Jaurès) is a true and comprehensive freedom. The absolute freedom of the will seeks to detach the individual from political bonds with others or even, in some forms of religious contemplation, from what Jaurès had previously called "the sensible world"; the individual freedom to decide in a particular context fails to recognize any standard of morality or justice. Unless freedom is reconciled with "the universal rule" of reason, Jaurès writes, it means nothing but servitude to one's whims. As Luther and Kant argued, this abstract freedom is not so free as it seems (*PTA*, 420–22).

Jaurès sees in Hegel a reconciliation of individual and community, immediacy and universality. Hegel's great idea, Jaurès writes, is that to move beyond an individualistic morality limited to mutual regard for contracts, "it is necessary that each will be enveloped within a certain concrete and natural order, thanks to which it can stretch toward universality—not in an abstract way, but in reality. This is where the family, civil society, and the even the state come from. Only when we begin from a concrete and life-giving moral world do we move from *Moralität* to true *Sittlichkeit*" (*PTA*, 423). Jaurès patiently recounts Hegel's elaborate description of the three spheres within *Sittlichkeit* or ethical life, but what he finds interesting there is simply the idea that life in these overlapping spheres provides a moral education in which the "character of humanity and universality" within each citizen is amplified. The institutional arrangement of ethical life as a whole is what interests Jaurès, to the point that he often seems, in his pages on Hegel, to use the term "state" to indicate not authoritative political institutions alone, but those institutions taken in the context of civil society and the family: "It is in the state . . . that the will of each citizen finds its full freedom in the universality of the law and of civic life. It is the state that gives to man the fullness of life and freedom" (*PTA*, 423).

Many readers of Hegel have noted the way his concepts often come in threes. Within the *Philosophy of Right*, for instance, Hegel moves from his initial conception of abstract freedom to the strictures of morality and from there to the complexity of institutionalized ethical life; ethical life itself, in turn, contains the triad of family, civil society, and state. For Hegel, dialectical thinking means seeing how a two-sided conflict or antinomy can be superseded by a third term or a new stage. Although Jaurès sees something similar in Luther's theology, in the way that grace mediates between God and humanity, Jaurès's definition of dialectical thinking at the beginning of his Latin thesis emphasizes something else: that dialectical thought allows the reconciliation of pairs of elements that are, or seem to be, in conflict. For Jaurès, dialectical thinking usually means seeing how a two-sided conflict can become a two-part harmony, or at least a two-sided dialogue. When a third term enters Jaurès's dialectical patterns, it is most often simply the fact of the reconciliation or harmonization of the first two terms. Hegel is interested in the way an old conflict is obviated by something new; Jaurès is interested in the way a pair of terms can remain distinct while being reconciled. Thus he writes: "What is the Hegelian state? The state is the solid and perfect union of 'individuality and universality.' The state must never impose on citizens anything that can hurt any individuality; on the other hand, the citizens may never demand or expect from the state anything that might be likely to put them outside the universal norm of human nature. In the state the will of each man reaches toward universality, that is to say toward infinity; in the state and by the state, freedom is in the end truly absolute" (*PTA*, 426). This is a reading of Hegel with a distinctive emphasis. Absent here is the often-noted ambiguity of Hegel's key verb "aufheben," which means both "to preserve" and "to abolish": in Jaurès's dialectic, nothing disappears.

Thus the great achievement of Hegel's political thought, as far as Jaurès is concerned, is Hegel's understanding that "civic life" in the context of the law-governed state preserves individuality even while the individual learns devotion to universal ethical principles. Citizens, in this view, are people whose political circumstances prompt them to live for themselves and for others at the same time. Jaurès sees the phrase "Der Staat ist Organismus" as Hegel's most creative symbol for this reconciliation of individual and community. As in an organism, the individual parts of the state-governed community are lifeless without the whole, but being part of the whole does not mean that they are dominated by the other parts. Rather, they each contribute to something they could not have achieved alone. "In an organism there is no organ that can be said to be the foundation of the other members and organs, as if the stomach, arm, or brain were itself the organism. Instead, all the organs taken together are the basis of the whole organism. Likewise, the fundamental basis of the state is not restricted to one or another organ of the state, to executive power or legislative power; the state is the basis of the state" (*PTA*, 427). This reconciliation of individual and community marks, for Jaurès, the point at which socialism emerges from Hegel's philosophy:

> From the moment he compared the state to an organism, this gave socialism a powerful argument for adopting the model of a unitary organism for material goods as well as for the state. Accordingly, Hegel has not placed true and complete liberty either in the individuality of the person isolated from other individuals or in supposed free will, but rather in universality and in the state because only within the state can there be perfect liberty. This is close to socialism. Then, when he put the state above civil society and as something higher than the apparent exterior union of citizens, when he declared that only within the state can there be true religion, true philosophy, he pushed men to submit all their life, that is to say all their goods, to unity, to the law, to the divine reason of the state. (*PTA*, 428–29)

Hegel's thought points toward socialism because Hegel harmonizes individual freedom and political community, and because he does so through political institutions. Jaurès especially likes the elements of Hegel's thought that echo Aristotle. Hegel refuses to set the individual above the community, or vice versa: the state is in a sense the outcome of Hegel's argument, but it is not an outcome that erases or supersedes the preceding steps. As Hegel describes political life, the individual is not lost in the state, but found because membership in the political community orients the individual toward universal concerns and commitments in a way no other membership can. In this view, my rights are secured by the state's laws and law-enforcing mechanisms, and so I can come to see my membership in the state—that is, my citizenship, with all the obligations to and bonds with fellow citizens that it entails, and with the broader obligations toward all rights-bearing subjects that it implies—as something just as fundamental to my personhood as is my freedom. Jaurès endorses these ideas, just as he does Hegel's idea that all important principles at some point become institutions: in this sense, Hegel has inherited Luther's fascination with the Christian doctrine of incarnation, the Word become flesh. In both these ways, Hegel insists on the reconciliation of what others have seen as conflicting: freedom and community, ideas and institutions.

To say that Hegel's reconciliation of these conflicting terms points toward socialism is to say something not only about Hegel but, more important, about socialism, which seems here to mean an exceptionally strong and distinctly modern expression of the ethical principle of freedom reconciled with community—the principle Jaurès has in mind when he uses the term "justice." Expressed in milder ways or in earlier eras, this principle would still be recognizable. Socialism is not the exclusive concern of the labor movement. It is not primarily an economic idea. It is also evidently not a state of affairs to be found only in the future: it has been present in political thought and political life, whether clearly or obscurely, for centuries. If this is so, it must also be present— not just as an idea or an ideal, but as a reality—in Jaurès's own time.

There are moments in Jaurès's discussion of Hegel when he seems to be saying that the principle at stake in socialist politics can be fully realized in some political form, as when he writes of the perfect form of freedom or of the fullness of life. This is not the first time, nor will it be the last, that Jaurès allows himself to hint at an overweening optimism. More often, however, Jaurès remembers his earlier argument that actuality cannot catch up with potentiality, as when he writes that the experience of citizenship directs the citizen *toward* what is universal. Consider his summary of what he wants his readers to learn from Hegel: "From the Hegelian description of the different aspects and moments that make up the progressive march of the Idea and of the Absolute, we can conclude with satisfaction that in the world no form of the Idea, no moment of the Absolute, is self-sufficient or has eternal value" (*PTA*, 429). In this dialectic, nothing is perfect; the absolute is never realized in fact, and the totality is never grasped in thought. Instead, Jaurès's dialectical thinking typically involves a sense of perpetual development, perpetual incompleteness, perpetual tension between principles that may be reconciled but that remain distinct.

Jaurès illustrates this kind of dialectical thinking when he explains Hegel's notorious description of the state as "divine." Hegel does not mean that there are no unjust states, or that we ought to worship the state, but, rather, that the meaning of the state stretches beyond the facts of particular states. Every state, by the encompassing and public nature of its laws and activities, shows that freedom can become something more than abstract individualism, that the detached individual can achieve "his full reality and his whole perfection" by becoming a "substantial person" with a "complete life" in community with others, even while remaining a "private person" with a personal and inward life (*PTA*, 426–27). All this will remain true even if no state fully plays out this potential. The state, as it exists in real political life, is not perfect. Its incomplete justice must be challenged through political agitation, and its thin solidarities must be supplemented by the richer life of smaller groupings with more intense bonds. Moreover, the state is not the answer to the fundamental human questions. Nevertheless, it shows us what the answer looks like; it points toward the perfect reconciliation of public and private, outward and inward, flesh and spirit, even without achieving that perfection. Jaurès says of an often quoted passage in the *Philosophy of Right*: "When Hegel wrote, 'All that is rational is real, and all that is real is rational,' he did not want to justify things themselves simply because they are. Hegel only meant that each event in history, each institution, is one moment of the Idea; each contains truth, however distorted and corrupted. . . . Although the state in and of itself has a divine essence, there may still be many bad states because, in them, the essence of the idea of the state is distorted. The way of history is not the way of the dialectic" (*PTA*, 434). Dialectical thought, Jaurès writes, is not a replacement for the study of history. It does not answer historical questions or allow us to understand history before it happens, except in that it attunes us to the inexhaustible possibility of reconciliation, of freedom-and-community. Instead, the dialectic reveals something about events and institutions that is never fully evident in history.

The most interesting moments in Marx's thought, Jaurès suggests, occur when Marx recalls Hegel's (and Luther's) awareness of impermanence and imperfection. Where "official economists" have treated the key concepts of modern economics—Jaurès lists the examples of capital, labor, and wage work—

as if they were "eternal economic categories," Marx demonstrates that "nothing is eternal except the law of dialectics itself. Contemporary society, far from being a solid and immutable crystal, is an organism susceptible to all sorts of transformations and always eager to take on new forms" (*PTA*, 429). This was not Marx as the French Marxists of the Parti ouvrier français knew him. If there were no eternal economic categories, then the collective property heralded by socialists of Jaurès's generation could not be the permanent solution to human troubles. Marx was supposed to show the transience not of *every* economic order, but of every economic order *prior to* communism; his theories were supposed to guarantee the end to human conflict. But Jaurès writes: "Hegel shows the dialectic proceeding through antithesis and synthesis, and shows how the contradictions of the preceding moments are resolved in a new and more complete moment of the Absolute and the Idea. In political economy, Marx (and Lassalle) show how history reconciles moments that were at first opposed into a new and better order" (*PTA*, 430). A *more* complete moment of the Absolute, a *better* order: whatever victories socialists should expect—and Jaurès does not object to the German socialists' confidence that there will be such victories—they will improve the human condition, but they will not bring about perfect justice or an end to social conflict.

Thus Marx's great contribution, for Jaurès, is his account of what is new and peculiar about the economic and social life of capitalist countries in the second half of the nineteenth century. Up to a point, Jaurès supports Marx's method of thought. Unlike Hegel, who offers an a priori description of the dialectical process, Marx prudently begins by examining facts, "things themselves," and builds a picture of reality a posteriori. Marx takes his place within the sensible world and thus is able to specify the social and material constraints on freedom and human community in a way that no other thinker in the German tradition had been able to do. This leads Marx to an image of socialism unlike Fichte's regimented administrative order: "Through socialism, a new economic order will emerge in which production will be assured as in the Middle Ages and extensive as in modern times, in which man will be master of himself and of things" (*PTA*, 430). For Marx, socialism (or, as he would have written, "communism") means freedom from both want and domination.

However, in good dialectical fashion, Jaurès suggests that when Marx rejects Hegel's "mysticism," he falls into a one-sided style of thought. "Marx opposes economic materialism to Hegelian idealism: things do not flow out of ideas, but ideas out of things. History and political economy do not grow from philosophy, but rather philosophy from history and political economy. Whatever the changes at work in the mind or in human character, they have been brought about through some modification of economic affairs" (*PTA*, 431). Jaurès thinks this view of history is half correct: ideas do follow from events. But events also follow from ideas. When Marx abandons Hegel's notion that the Idea works itself out dialectically, he also abandons any strong sense of human agency. If things in the world are made to change by some fate or force wholly immanent within the world of things, it is not clear that human beings "accomplish anything" or even that human beings "act," rather than merely reacting to the material events that define their existence. Jaurès asks: "What good is it to call for socialism or to organize an army of socialism's soldiers if things themselves will march ahead, step by step, and so make socialism a reality?" (*PTA*, 432).

Jaurès is concerned that Marx has no good answer to this question; he is even more concerned that the Marxists of his own generation also have none. The idea that history marches toward an apocalyptic day of reckoning can inspire courage; it can also justify a principled passivity. Jaurès wants to replace that passive reliance on history with a determined engagement in political life, and this means making an ethical case for socialism. If socialists are to make a public "call" for political engagement, if they are to pull together parties and unions and other groups to advance their principles, Jaurès suggests, they will need to recognize the demands placed on them, now and every day, by the ideal to which they have committed themselves.

Even if socialism could be realized without the motivating power of an ideal of justice, it would not be a socialism worth the name because, without an animating ideal, it would be only a lifeless scheme for administering economic events. Marx opposed Hegel's "mystical dialectic" for good reasons, Jaurès writes, but Marx's own "materialist dialectic," taken by itself, creates even greater problems.

> If everything comes from the movement of things themselves and if humanity cannot be governed by the will and the consciousness of man, then, even when the new society blooms, it will still not be supreme and perfect. It will be new, but still amendable and transitory. If this is so, then socialism will not reflect an eternal value after all! To put it better, where is the evidence that a new form of society produced by a nearly blind necessity will be better and more equitable? In the end, the only thing that gives value to socialism is if it appears to the people as a religion

of justice worthy of adoration, not as the adoration, the cult, of a fact. (*PTA*, 433–34)

That which has eternal value—call it "the potentiality of Being," call it "the ideal of freedom and community"—can only take political form when and to the extent that human beings consciously shape the world according to the ideal. Socialism is not socialism if it does not aspire to the ultimate reconciliation: that of the sensible world and the mind, the flesh and the spirit.

The German philosophical tradition had begun on the border between theology and philosophy. Somehow, Jaurès lamented, the tradition had since lost track of the idea of ideals, of the need for a conscious commitment to something beyond human experience and human history. Hegel's shift toward a wholly immanent account of the Absolute and Marx's materialist turn had in some ways enriched German dialectical thought. However, Jaurès argued, Kant and Fichte, devoted to the idea of justice, had maintained a vital element that had begun to go underground with Hegel and that had disappeared altogether with Marx. Oddly, that devotion to justice had been better preserved—although in a distorted and one-sided way—in French political thought.[58] "Fichte, both by his burning love of pure justice and by the generous instincts of his soul, comes much closer to the French—who in 1789 and in 1848 proclaimed, so to speak, a new gospel of justice—than to those Germans who have accepted the severe historical dialectic of Karl Marx. More important, socialism in Germany will not be able to enter the people's hearts, to leave the schools, to fill the public square, unless it makes equal appeal to the passions and invokes not only the necessities of history, but also 'eternal justice'" (*PTA*, 418).

As much as the German philosophical tradition had to offer the French, the French had something to offer the Germans: their experience of life in the public square. German socialists had never known any political life except that of the self-enclosed school or sect. The members of such a group, kept at the margins of society whether by their own zealotry or by government repression, might well find themselves comforted by the notion that their marginality would inevitably transform itself into triumph. A movement whose members aimed to organize a majority of their fellow citizens, however, would learn the value of appealing to widely shared passions and to the language of justice and injustice.

The politics of the public square, Jaurès suggests, depends on the passions and on the power of the idea of justice in a way other politics do not. Even before the Third Republic, the French had learned how to fill the public square, whether with arguments or with barricades. Was it not the idea of justice that had inspired the republican revolutions of 1789 and 1848? Socialists in a republic, or in a country with a long experience of republican uprisings, ought not to take on wholesale the doctrines of comrades who lived under repressive monarchies. Marx's one-sided materialism, his disdain for "mystical" accounts of history and for the idea of ideals, his notion of historical necessity, and the expectation of absolute transformation that follows from all this are for Jaurès the peculiar products of Germany's exceptionally backward political life.

What German socialism needed, Jaurès proposed, was a deepening of its own dialectical character. Dialectical methods could be applied to the tradition of dialectical philosophy itself. There was no reason why a rigorous analysis of economic history and a fervent devotion to the ideal of justice needed to be sundered from each other. The working-class victory for which socialists labored would be a victory not for a particular part of humanity, but for humanity as a whole; not for self-interest, but for justice. Jaurès ends his Latin thesis with a passage more oratorical than scholarly:

> Dialectic socialism thus accords with moral socialism, German socialism with French socialism, and the hour is near when we will see all spirits, all forces and faculties of consciousness—and also the fraternal Christian communion, the dignity and the true freedom of the human person, and even the immanent dialectic of things, of history, of the world—converge and join together in one true socialism.
>
> In short, to comprehend the German socialism of our day, it is not enough to find it in the particular and transitory form that Bebel and the others give it. We must search out its origins, which is to say, all its sources of intelligence and consciousness. Thus I have examined Christian socialism with Luther, moral socialism with Fichte, dialectic socialism with Hegel and Marx. And I was not displeased to treat these contemporary questions in Latin because this is the language in which the human right of ancient moral philosophy was formulated and in which Christian fraternity was yearned for and sung. Moreover, the Latin language is even today the only universal language common to all

peoples; it fits well with universal socialism. Latin fits well with the "integral socialism" sketched by Benoît Malon, where socialism appears not as a narrow faction, but as humanity itself, where socialism seems to be the image of humanity, of eternity. (*PTA*, 435–36)

Jaurès's reference to Malon is telling. For Malon, "integral socialism" meant the simultaneous pursuit of "material" and "moral" reforms. He proposed policies—worker control of workplaces, municipal ownership of enterprises, a system of social insurance—but he also thought that the experience of citizenship in a republic could foster citizens' solidarity with one another. "There are always more socialists under a republic than under a monarchy," he argued.[59] For Jaurès, socialism has come to mean all that and evidently something more: it appears here as a modern name for the grand reconciliation—or, to use Malon's word, "integration"—of humanity's perennial aspirations for freedom and for fraternity. From the point of view of this kind of socialism, history was a continuous struggle for justice in which the decisive factor had been and would continue to be not an impersonal evolution of social forces but the conscious, collective, daily activity of citizens in the public square. Socialism, for Jaurès, would be the expression within modern political life of humanity's obscure and conscious effort toward a just and beautiful order—an effort that had begun in the ancient world and had never ceased, that could always be carried forward but could never be completed.

DEMOCRACY UNFROZEN

Jaurès successfully defended his two theses and was granted his doctorate in philosophy in February 1892.[1] A few months later, coal miners in the Tarn town of Carmaux went on strike. Jean-Baptiste Calvignac, an officer in the miners' union, had been elected mayor; he asked the mining company for two days' leave each week to attend to his duties; the company refused and then fired him when he took the time anyway. The miners struck, demanding his reinstatement and insisting on his right to serve in public office. Jaurès pushed for arbitration, and when the company would not concede, he toured France to raise money for the strikers.

The strike dragged on for months before the company submitted to the union's arbitration request.[2] In the wake of the strike, the Carmaux socialists asked Jaurès to be their candidate in a January 1893 special election for a seat in the Chamber of Deputies. He accepted, based his campaign on the platform of the Parti ouvrier français, and won the election handily. Returning to the Chamber as one of only a dozen socialist deputies, he arrived on the eve of a change for which most French socialists were not prepared.[3]

Through a coordinated campaign unlike any they had previously mounted and with backing from members of France's growing labor movement—trade unions had tripled their membership since the previous parliamentary elections[4]—French socialists achieved by far their best results yet during the general elections in the autumn of 1893. They won some 600,000 votes, ten times the socialist tally in 1881, and their representation in the Chamber grew to fifty members.[5] Their electoral allies, the Radicals of the republican Center-Left, increased their numbers as well, although not so dramatically. A reluctant alliance between the more conservative republicans (now often referred to as "Progressists" rather than "Opportunists") and the remnants of the old monarchist groups still dominated the Chamber, but now the combined Radical and socialist opposition was stronger, with socialists making up nearly one-third of that opposition.[6] The French socialists were no longer a specter haunting the powerful. They were a substantial political force within the parliament of a republic.

This was a situation in which no socialist party had ever found itself. As a protest movement defined by what it was against, nineteenth-century socialism naturally spoke in terms of opposition and abolition. What would French socialists do now that they had enough power to influence the society in which they lived, but not nearly enough power to demolish and replace it? To some, their old manner of making a stark contrast between the capitalist present and the communist future seemed less useful than it once had been. Jaurès would find an interested audience for his notions of mixing opposites, of reconciling incompatibles, of battles neither lost nor won.

The better to exercise their new power, socialists in the Chamber of Deputies organized themselves as the Union socialiste, meeting weekly and forming committees to address particular areas of public policy. However, the unity of the Union proved to be limited. Twenty or thirty of its members were, like Jaurès, independents influenced by Malon's "integral socialism." Several members of the Union were Radical-Socialists, to the left of the Radicals in their social policies but no more interested in class struggle or in the socialist dream of a fully collectivist economy than the Radicals were. Five were members of Jules Guesde's Parti ouvrier français. Two were Possibilists. Nine belonged to parties committed to direct action in the French revolutionary tradition, whose members considered parliament little more than a sham—namely, the Parti socialiste révolutionaire, founded by Auguste Blanqui and now led by Édouard Vaillant, and the Parti ouvrier socialiste révolutionaire of Jean Allemane, often referred to as the "Blanquists" and the "Allemanists."[7]

Within the Chamber, Jaurès spoke out frequently against the Progressist government's attempts to restrict civil liberties. Despite what even his friends would call a "harsh" and "monotonous" voice, he soon earned a reputation as a forceful orator, an "athlete of the platform" capable of unifying the Left at key moments.[8] Those moments of unity were hard to come by. The Left was divided, and Jaurès was often the spokesman for one particular point of view among the socialists.[9] Such an occasion was the debate between Jaurès and Paul Lafargue in December 1894.[10] A leader in the POF, Lafargue was married to Karl Marx's daughter Laura (translator of the 1885 French edition of the *Communist Manifesto*), and was almost certainly the sharpest writer and thinker among the French Marxists of his time.[11] Before an audience of socialist youth in the northern industrial town of Arras, Jaurès and Lafargue addressed the question of whether socialists ought to adopt the Marxist theory of history. The issue between Jaurès and Lafargue was not how quickly social change would happen: both speakers described the movement toward socialism as a long "évolution"; both expressed their confidence in the eventual victory of socialism. The issue, rather, was whether the idea of justice ought to play a part in how socialists understood their movement. The French Marxists argued that the goals and structure of the working-class movement were dictated by the impersonal forces of economic development. Against this position, Jaurès defended the idea that the socialist movement needed to talk about justice and injustice.

Jaurès spoke first. Marx was right, Jaurès told his listeners, to think that historical change could not be understood without attention to the "social and collective forces" to which human life gives rise. However, Jaurès proposed that "the materialist conception of history does not preclude an idealist interpretation of history" (*OJJ* 6:6–7). Under the material process of social and economic change that Marx had analyzed lay another stratum of human experience, which Marx had ignored. "Before the experience of history, before the constitution of this or that economic system, humanity carries in itself a prior idea of justice and of what is right, and it is this preconceived ideal that humanity pursues. When humanity moves from a lower form of civilization to a higher, it is not by the mechanical and automatic transformation of modes of production but under the influence, dim or clear, of this ideal" (*OJJ* 6:7). The ideal of justice is realized in and through economic and social events, Jaurès argued, and so the Marxist theory of history tells the story of that ideal without realizing it.

Jaurès had returned to the themes of his doctoral theses, although it is unlikely that anyone in his audience knew this. The two elements of history—the aspiration toward ideals and the immanent logic of material and social relations—must not be seen as separate, parallel lines of development: "I do not want to say that one part of history is governed by economic necessity and that another is directed by a pure idea. . . . I claim that they must enter into one another, as do the cerebral mechanism and the spontaneous consciousness in the organic life of man." Just as a physiological term like "brain" and a philosophical term like "consciousness" can each be used to contribute to our understanding of the same phenomena, so, too, Jaurès suggested, materialist and idealist conceptions of history make their distinct contributions without contradicting each other: "You can explain all historical phenomena by pure economic evolution, and at the same time you can also explain them by the permanent, restless desire for humanity to have a higher form of existence" (*OJJ* 6:12–13).

Jaurès buttressed his argument with an appeal to biology—a sort of materialism different from Marx's, but characteristic of his generation's fascination with the idea that Darwinism could be applied to social questions. "Humanity," Jaurès argued, "is the product of a long physiological evolution that precedes its historical evolution." In some ways, human societies change over time, but something remains constant as well: human beings retain a capacity to conceive of particular things in relation to general ideas, a "sense of unity" and of order in the cosmos, and a capacity for language—and thus a predisposition for an "imaginative sympathy" that impels them to ask questions about justice and morality (*OJJ* 6:14–16). As humans, we are by nature capable of recognizing ourselves as parts of a larger whole, and thus we are by nature moved by an appeal to the principle of justice, the idea of a right relationship of parts within a whole.

Accordingly, the question Jaurès poses to Lafargue and other Marxists—the question he suggests they have rendered themselves incapable of posing for themselves—is, "How do you judge the direction of economic change, of human change? . . . Is it evolution, or is it progress?" Jaurès is confident of the direction in which history is moving, but he does not want to suppress the moral questions that this information raises. Instead, he wants to offer the judgment that socialism is not only an irresistible push for change, but also a demand for justice, an aspiration to achieve "full freedom and full solidarity among men" (*OJJ* 6:16–17).

What Jaurès left unsaid is that this turn toward an ethical conception of politics would have consequences for the socialist movement. Socialists had long been accustomed to thinking of socialism as the future outcome of a dramatic and decisive political change, a rupture with the immediate past. To conceive of socialism as a movement to achieve "full freedom and full solidarity" suggested that socialists should begin by achieving some modestly increased measures of freedom and solidarity, that they should replace revolution with amelioration. Whether or not Jaurès saw this yet, Lafargue did. In his response to Jaurès, he argues that if Jaurès were heeded, socialists would fall away from their commitment to an absolute transformation of society. Socialism would even acquire a shade of conservatism. Ideas like "justice" and "morality," Lafargue declares, are empty words that "change their meaning from one historical era to the next," in accordance with the interests of the dominant class, and that lead people to accommodate themselves to the existing social order (*OJJ* 6:26–27). For a political movement to define itself in relation to such ideas would be to shackle itself to the modes of thought dominant in the current social order. Only a thoroughly empirical and amoral conception of historical processes could free socialists from intellectual dependence on the existing society, and thus free socialists for the uninhibited pursuit of the destruction of that society.

For members of the audience, it would have been clear that Lafargue was arguing against a specific political strategy, a strategy Jaurès had already endorsed during his time on the Toulouse city council. Speaking of "liberté" and "solidarité," Jaurès invokes the vocabulary of French republicanism; he redefines socialist aspirations to outline the common ground socialists might share with Radicals and Radical-Socialists. If socialism were to be a strictly working-class movement aiming in the long run at the defeat of every other political force, as Lafargue and other Marxists would have it, then no such common ground could exist, except perhaps as a temporary (and risky) expedient. But if socialism and republicanism shared ideals and merely interpreted them in different ways, a lasting coalition of the Left and Center-Left would be both possible and appropriate.

Beyond the question of coalition strategies, perhaps the most interesting element in Jaurès's debate with Lafargue is the way Jaurès turns away from the imagery of time so central to the imagination of nineteenth-century socialism: he appeals to an idea of evolution, but only to establish a set of human characteristics that he sees as being, for all practical purposes, fixed. Our fixed characteristics, Jaurès suggests—our capacity to argue about justice and morality, to feel sympathy—make us unpredictable and undeterminable. They also create in us a desire for talk and listening, a propensity to disagree, and a need for means of resolving or at least managing our disagreements. If Jaures was right that these capacities are permanent features of the human condition, then socialists would need to think not only about change over time but also about continuity over time, and thus about the spaces, in the present and in the future alike, in which those questions about justice might be asked and answered, in which conflicts might be resolved or managed through talk and listening. This would require a vocabulary and an imagery, not to mention a set of goals with regard to political institutions, that the Marxist tradition could not provide.

The debate between Jaurès and Lafargue revealed just how deep the fissures in the socialist movement ran. Nevertheless, French socialists in the mid-1890s worked steadily to overcome their organizational, if not their doctrinal, disunity. The deputies of the Union socialiste voted together on many occasions. Remarkably, Jaurès was able to persuade the socialist caucus to use its increased clout in an unprecedented way: in 1895, the Union socialiste provided the votes that allowed the Radical deputy Léon Bourgeois to form a government composed entirely of Radicals, against the opposition of the Center and the Right. Appealing to the principle of solidarity, Bourgeois pushed hard for the introduction of a progressive income tax. His government fell after only five months, when the conservative Senate blocked his tax proposal. But for Jaurès and other proponents of a republican-socialist coalition for reform, this interlude seemed to presage the way forward.[12]

As the 1896 local elections approached, socialists considered how they might repeat the success they had enjoyed in the 1893 parliamentary elections.

One cause for hope lay in the labor movement's growing size and cohesion. The 1895 formation of the Confédération générale du travail united craft unions and industrial unions in one umbrella organization. The local workers' centers for mutual aid (*bourses du travail*) had already formed their own national federation three years earlier.[13] Both federations adopted policies of neutrality with regard to electoral politics, but their new strength could only help the socialist electoral campaigns.

In addition to a better-organized base of supporters, the socialists now had a proven electoral strategy as well. Except for the elections of 1885, which used a system of multimember districts in which slates of candidates ran for office together, elections to the Third Republic's Chamber of Deputies were by majority vote within single-member legislative districts. If no candidate received a majority in the first round of voting, a second round would be held. These two-stage elections allowed a large number of candidates and parties to compete in the first round, and then to form multiparty coalitions around a smaller number of candidates in the second round. Before 1893, socialists had occasionally made strategic use of second-round coalitions. But the 1893 elections had seen the most widespread effort yet by various socialist groups to mobilize their supporters around whichever socialist or Radical candidate stood the best chance to defeat the conservatives in the second-round election in each district. They prepared to follow the same strategy in a more systematic way in 1896.[14]

Not surprisingly, socialists made major gains. In cities and towns across France, local coalitions of Guesdists, Blanquists, Possibilists, and independent socialists, often joining with Radical-Socialists and Radicals, were elected to office and set to work to improve public services.[15] Alexandre Millerand—along with Jaurès, one of the leaders of the independent socialist group in the Chamber—convened a conference of elected socialist officials at Saint-Mandé, Paris, in May 1896, to celebrate these victories.[16] Before that audience, Millerand proposed that all the socialist groups adopt a common program. Socialists already agreed that capitalist property should be transformed into collective or social property; they should now recognize that this could only be done through parliamentary means, in a democratic and incremental fashion, relying on the power workers gained through universal suffrage within a republic. Socialists had long declared themselves internationalists; they should also now embrace the principle of patriotism, like the internationalist patriots of the French Revolution. Millerand's Saint-Mandé program received almost unanimous approval from those present. Guesde himself—who before had always held onto the promise of a violent revolution and a dictatorship of the proletariat, and who had long disdained the idea that the republican state was anything other than an instrument of the bourgeoisie—offered a toast to Millerand's program.[17] Socialist unity seemed possible; a durable coalition between socialists and Radicals was not implausible. Socialist strength was growing. That was unmistakable.

In the fall of 1897, Jaurès received a visit from Lucien Herr, the friend who had introduced him to Marx's writings. Now Herr wanted to talk to Jaurès about the strange case of Captain Alfred Dreyfus.[18] An artillery officer—and, as it happened, one of the few Jews in the higher ranks of the French military—Dreyfus had been arrested for espionage in October 1894, after counterespionage officers discovered an inventory of documents (*bordereau*) apparently sent to the German military attaché in Paris by a spy within the French army. The *bordereau* implied knowledge of French artillery, a previously discovered letter had used the initial "D" to refer to a spy, and a handwriting expert claimed that Dreyfus's writing was similar to that in the letter—that was enough to justify the arrest of a man who had few friends among his conservative Catholic fellow officers. In a quick military trial, Dreyfus was found guilty; by April 1895, he was confined on a remote Caribbean island. The convicted man's brother, Mathieu Dreyfus, waged a lonely struggle to bring the case's irregularities to light. For a time, he was largely ignored. But an 1896 newspaper article revealed that Dreyfus's conviction had hinged on secret documents sent by military officers to the judges. Around the same time, behind the closed doors of the military elite, the officer who was asked by his superiors to review the case, a Lieutenant-Colonel Marie-Georges Picquart, came to the unsettling determination that Dreyfus was innocent. By the summer of 1897, although Picquart himself had been transferred to Tunisia, his research had come to the attention of Mathieu Dreyfus's circle of friends. Herr was one of those friends, and his mission in visiting Jaurès was to convince him, too, of Dreyfus's innocence.

Jaurès's first reaction to the Dreyfus case had been to decry the disparity between the prison sentence given to this wealthy officer convicted of treason and the death penalty so often given to working-class enlisted men convicted of lesser offenses.[19] Like almost everyone else in France, he had assumed that Dreyfus was guilty. Now, at the urging of Herr and their mutual friend Léon

Blum, Jaurès began to speak out cautiously about the lapses in normal legal procedure that had marred the case,[20] which would soon become "l'affaire Dreyfus" and would dominate French thought and life for the next two years.

In November 1897, Mathieu Dreyfus wrote a letter to *Le Figaro* alleging that Major Ferdinand Walsin-Esterhazy was the spy behind the *bordereau*. A court cleared Esterhazy in January, but two days later the novelist Émile Zola published a pamphlet titled "J'accuse," accusing the military elite of conspiring to protect Esterhazy and of willfully convicting an innocent man. Monarchists, clerical reactionaries, anti-Semites, and nationalists railed against Zola and his fellow Dreyfusards. Liberal republicans—especially Jews, Protestants, and secularists—began to see Dreyfus's cause as their own. Street demonstrations and public meetings, organized by both sides—and, on the anti-Dreyfusard side, violent riots as well—drew tens of thousands.[21]

Even the socialists were divided. Guesde declared Zola's pamphlet to be "the greatest revolutionary act of the century," but almost immediately the members of the Union socialiste, including both Guesde and Jaurès, issued a statement urging the working class to remain neutral since Dreyfus's foes and defenders were merely two factions within the bourgeoisie.[22] Through the summer of 1898, the Guesdists and Blanquists continued to oppose any socialist involvement in the Dreyfusard cause, declaring that the Dreyfusards and anti-Dreyfusards were "equally enemies of our class and of socialism."[23] Within a few months, however, Jaurès had decided that neutrality was a mistake. Moved by Zola's example and persuaded by Herr's and Blum's arguments and evidence, Jaurès changed his mind. He became one of Dreyfus's leading advocates in the Chamber of Deputies, drawing such wrath from the nationalist Right that on one occasion he was struck by a fellow deputy as he stood at the Chamber's podium. At Zola's trial for libel, Jaurès laid out a careful critique of the conduct of Dreyfus's trial.

Campaigning for reelection in May 1898, Jaurès found himself tarred as an anticlerical extremist. He lost by a large margin. For the last time in his life, he would have a few years in which he could write and speak free from parliamentary duties.[24] Jaurès and his family—his wife, Louise, his young daughter, Madeleine, and, by the fall of 1898, his infant son, Paul-Louis—would remain in Paris. Jaurès took up a position as a writer for Millerand's journal, *La Petite République*. In July and August, after Minister of War Godefroy Cavaignac presented the Chamber of Deputies with new documents purporting to establish Dreyfus's guilt definitively, Jaurès wrote a series of articles for *La Petite*

République, published as a book in September under the title *Les preuves* (The proof), systematically demonstrating the military's reliance on deception and forgery in securing Dreyfus's conviction. Shamed by this public demolition of its case against Dreyfus, the War Office once again reexamined the case. This time, it could not escape the conclusion that key documents in the case had been forged by a Major Joseph Henry, who was arrested, confessed, and then committed suicide in his prison cell. Esterhazy fled the country, in effect admitting his guilt. Cavaignac resigned.[25] There would be more turns in the case, but, in the end, Dreyfus would be exonerated.

Jaurès's painstaking defense of Dreyfus in *Les preuves* contributed to that exoneration. Indeed, Jaurès's role in establishing the innocence of Dreyfus marked one of the few clear-cut victories of his career. In articles directed toward the broad French public, Jaurès offered "a careful examination of the facts, documents, and testimonies" in the Dreyfus case, and argued that no other conclusions could be reached from this evidence except that "Dreyfus has been illegally condemned" and that "Dreyfus has been condemned in error"—that he was both an innocent man and a man deprived of the fair trial to which the citizen of a republic is entitled (*TAD,* 458).[26] Jaurès developed that argument patiently, in article after article.

What reveals most about Jaures's political thought, however, are those parts of *Les preuves* he directed toward his fellow socialists. In one such part, originally published on August 10, 1898, responding to those who believed that their movement had no stake in the Dreyfus Affair, Jaurès argued that socialists ought now to take up the project of defending individual rights inaugurated by the 1789 Declaration of the Rights of Man. The moderate republicans who failed to take Dreyfus's side were all too willing to "surrender the Declaration to the insolence of military power." Defending the principle of individual rights required protecting the integrity of the Third Republic's legal institutions. To those—whether bourgeois republicans or socialist revolutionaries—taken aback by the idea that socialists might concern themselves with "legality," Jaurès proposed a distinction:

> There are two parts in capitalist and bourgeois law. There are the whole set of laws intended to protect the fundamental iniquity of our society; there are laws that consecrate the privilege of capitalist property, the exploitation of the employee by the owner. These laws we want to smash—even, if it is necessary, by revolution. . . . But next to these laws

of privilege and rapine, made by and for a single class, there are others that sum up the paltry progress of humanity, the modest guarantees that it has won little by little, through its long effort of centuries and its long series of revolutions. . . . Unlike the nationalists who want to keep everything about bourgeois law that protects capital and surrender to the generals all that protects man, we revolutionary socialists want to abolish the capitalist portion and keep the humane portion of contemporary law. (*TAD*, 465–66).

Thus, even though Jaurès maintains that his socialism is, in part, a movement of protest and opposition—and despite his claim to be a "revolutionary"—clearly, his socialism is also a movement of conservation, just as Lafargue had charged in their debate. It would be concerned, of course, with economic matters—"the exploitation of the employee by the owner"—but that concern would be embedded in a broader concern with justice. That principle of justice was already visible in the judicial and parliamentary institutions of the Republic. The work of socialists would be to defend—and, eventually, to extend—those institutions, preserving the array of legal rights that structured the relationship of individual citizens to the machinery of government within the Republic.

Socialists have a stake in the Dreyfus Affair, Jaurès writes, because their fundamental commitment is to the principle of justice, and because Dreyfus's case is a clear instance of injustice. Thus when some socialists object that Dreyfus is himself a member of the ruling class, they misunderstand what is at stake in the affair. The divide between social classes, Jaurès insists, is not the only form of injustice. Jaurès writes that Dreyfus "is no longer either an officer or a bourgeois. By his excessive misfortune, he has been stripped of all class character. He is nothing but humanity itself, in the most extreme state of misery and despair that can be imagined. . . . What a mockery to still count him among the privileged!" (*TAD*, 466)

The most provocative of Jaurès's claims comes toward the end of this passage. In what sense might he mean that Dreyfus was "in the most extreme state of misery that could be imagined"? Although undeniably fond of grand phrases, Jaurès was also careful to place emphasis where he wanted to place emphasis—here on the not insignificant fact that Dreyfus had been exiled to solitary confinement and had arrived at this state of isolation by being denied sight of the evidence lodged against him. Dreyfus had been excluded from the spaces and procedures in which a citizen ought to be included; he had been made invisible, and he had been made so because things that should have been visible to him were hidden. He was utterly miserable, it seems, because he was utterly isolated. That is the sense in which Dreyfus's situation raised questions of justice more fundamental than the question of class. The problem with a society divided by class, Jaurès suggests here, is best stated in ethical terms: such a society is unjust. It is unjust specifically because it condemns some (or perhaps, in one way or another, all) of its members to the misery of exclusion, of invisibility, of isolation. Class is one of a number of forms that injustice might take, and those who take on the project of ending the injustice of class, whether or not they realize it yet, have also taken on the obligation of confronting injustice in all its other forms. Thus, Jaurès writes, every "example of human suffering," every "living witness . . . to crimes of authority" becomes "an element of the Revolution" (*TAD*, 466–67).

If socialists had their stake in the Dreyfus Affair, Jaurès suggests, the Dreyfusards had their reasons for needing the support of socialists—or, more precisely, the support of the labor movement. Defending republican legal guarantees cannot be the work of the Republic alone, Jaurès thinks. Political pressure, whether within the Chamber of Deputies or through public demonstrations, would be necessary if the Republic's leading figures were to reopen Dreyfus's case so that his innocence could be established. Such pressure could not be brought to bear by a few individuals, however highly placed in society. What sufficiently large group of citizens would have both the occasion and the organizational wherewithal to stand up for Dreyfus? "Who is the most threatened today by the arbitrariness of the generals, by the ever-glorified violence of military repression? Who? The proletariat. It has thus an interest of the first order to punish and discourage the illegality and violence of the councils of war before they become a sort of habit accepted by all. It has an interest of the first order to discredit and bring down the reactionary army elite that is ready to strike it down tomorrow" (*TAD*, 467). The working class could pursue its agenda only if it arrested the rise of arbitrary military authority, and so to protest the irregularities of the Dreyfus trial was "not only to serve humanity, but to serve the working class directly" (*TAD*, 467). This overlap between the interest of the labor movement and the political needs of the Dreyfusards, Jaurès suggests, might cement the sort of political coalition that the principle of justice requires, but for which the principle of justice alone might not provide sufficient motivation. Members of the labor movement might often decide to take action together out of a sense of shared interest, but, as they did so, they might also come to see the bonds of solidarity that connected them as a set of ethical obligations. If this was the case, the proletariat as an organized class might also be able to recognize an ethical obligation to act in solidarity with all victims of injustice—even a bourgeois army officer falsely accused of a crime.

Whatever the larger implications of this argument, the immediate political consequences of Jaurès's position would have been clear to his fellow socialists. Jaurès was calling on them not only to recognize that Dreyfus's enemies were their own enemies as well, or to take a stand for one particular victim of military injustice. He was also calling on them to see all defenders of the Republic as their potential allies. This was the stumbling block for many of Jaurès's fellow socialists. The idea of cross-class alliances was hardly new. Marx and Engels, after all, had written in the concluding section of the *Communist Manifesto* that the organized working class might, in different national circumstances, make any number of such alliances. In France, Guesdists and Blanquists had joined Jaurès and the independent socialists in supporting Bourgeois's Radical government, and had participated in second-round election alliances and even local government coalitions with Radicals, as Jaurès had in Toulouse. But what Jaurès suggests here is something else: cross-class alliance not as an occasional tactic but as a normal practice, not as a temporary adulteration of the socialist movement's authentic working-class identity but as the movement's proper form. If socialism was committed to deepening the Republic, then it belonged in coalition with any other party committed to preserving the Republic.[27]

Jaurès seems to be trying here to call into existence a movement that did not yet exist. Although this movement would be committed to republican institutions and would see itself as the inheritor of the republican tradition, unlike the existing republican groups, it would seek to transform the economic order and would plant its organizational roots in the working class. It would, in that sense, be distinctly socialist. But, unlike most existing socialist groups, it would be more ethical than economic in character; it would seek to develop in its members and in its country a commitment to justice, to human solidarity. It would be committed to a politics of reform—not of conservation alone or of change alone, but of the two mixed together.

The Dreyfus Affair did not consume all of Jaurès's intellectual attention during 1898. In June, days after the general election, the publisher Jules Rouff asked Jaurès to edit and contribute to a multivolume history of the French Revolution.

In the midst of the affair, alongside his journalistic writings about the relationship between class politics and the claims of justice, Jaurès began what would become his most sustained work of scholarship. By the time the *Histoire socialiste, 1789–1900* was completed a decade later, it would comprise thirteen volumes, the first four (and parts of two others) written by Jaurès and the remainder written by collaborators he recruited and who worked under his editorial direction. Taken as a whole, the *Histoire socialiste* is an impressive work, a gigantic synthesis of political, social, and intellectual history based on extensive archival research. The four volumes written by Jaures—which add up to more than 3,000 pages—examined the events of the French Revolution between 1789 and 1794, from the storming of the Bastille to the death of Robespierre, focusing mostly on the years 1791 and 1792. These volumes were completed before Jaurès was reelected to the Chamber of Deputies in 1902, and they form the backdrop to Jaurès's participation, in those years, in the Dreyfus Affair and in the socialists' subsequent debates about reformism. They are his most complete statement of his way of thinking about the process of political and social change, and contain his most direct tributes to his intellectual influences.[28]

Naming those influences in the opening pages of the first volume, Jaurès reveals something both about his approach to writing history and about the contours of his political thought. The *Histoire socialiste* would be written "under the triple inspiration of Marx, Michelet, and Plutarch" (*HS* 1:10). His readers might be surprised by how "disparate" these three thinkers are, Jaurès admits. But this is just the point. A tidier set of methods would lead to a story that failed to account for the complexity of political life.

Like most French socialists of his time, Jaurès reserved his strongest intellectual affections for the heritage of French socialist thought.[29] Nevertheless, he saw in Marx the invaluable source of a "materialist" understanding of history in which "the march and play of social classes" constitute the story line. This element of the *Histoire socialiste* is more apparent in some parts of the work than in others. There are long sections discussing individual actors, or ideas, or cultural changes far removed from economic affairs; nevertheless, there are also many other sections of the *Histoire socialiste* in which the notion of social class is prominent.

Take, for instance, the introduction to the first volume, in which Jaurès surveys the scope of the entire work. The *Histoire socialiste*, Jaurès announces, will tell the three-act story of the rise of the bourgeoisie and the realization of the conditions for the rise of the working class. First, in the period from the revolution of 1789 to the revolution of 1848, the new bourgeois class defeated the old monarchist regime. The political triumph of the bourgeoisie meant that France's future would be measured against a republican ideal: representative, constitutional government, with legal equality and secure rights for citizens. In this period, Jaurès writes, the emerging proletariat was "a sort of historical complement" to the bourgeoisie, a subordinate ally with no organizations or purposes of its own. But the regimes that came after the 1789 revolution—whether republican or temporary deviations—were like a stream of water in which the workers "saw reflected their poor exhausted faces and were appalled." If a republican government was insufficient to bring happiness to workers, they would need deeper political changes. Thus, by 1848, distinctly socialist ideas had appeared in the works of Fourier, Saint Simon, Proudhon, and others less well known, and worker rebellions had erupted in Lyon and Paris. A working-class political identity had emerged, although working-class discontent was still rarely expressed in the new language of socialism (*HS* 1:3–4).

The revolution of February 1848 and the short-lived Second French Republic marked the beginning of a new period. The working class had "affirmed itself as a class." By this, Jaurès means that workers now had their own political organizations, with their own structures and strategies, and these organizations had, at the same time, adopted a distinctive political idea, socialism, formerly the project only of utopian intellectuals. Nevertheless, after the defeat of the Second Republic, the working class returned to political impotence, and socialism could be no more than a subject of "Platonic discussion." "Not having the power to act," Jaurès laments, "they talked." This period ended with the Paris Commune of 1871, when "the working class took power for the first time"—indeed, Jaurès notes, this was the first time workers had "experienced power" (*HS* 1:4–5).

That new experience, at the dawn of the Third Republic, marked the beginning of the third period of class politics in France. The lesson Jaurès took from the Commune was not (as the Guesdists and Blanquists supposed) that the Republic was not to be trusted, or that the working class could have no reliable allies. It was that, by experiencing power, the socialist movement had reached a new level of maturity. Its task was now to "proceed methodically to the total organization of the working class, the conversion of the reassured peasants, the rallying of bourgeois intellectuals disenchanted by bourgeois power, and the taking of complete power for new forms of property and new ideals." The movement had grown up. It was time to rethink the political theories that had developed in earlier periods and to confront the new problems that came with power and responsibility (*HS* 1:6).

This way of outlining the history of the nineteenth century is like Marx's historical writing in that classes are the actors that move history along. However, even where Jaurès engages in what could be called a "class analysis," he does so in a way different from Marx's. For Jaurès, the turning points in the story are not changes in relationships among classes. Instead, the three acts of this drama open and close with changes in political organizations and institutions; each act begins with the founding of one of France's three republics. Elements that would be peripheral in Marx's writings are here made central. Where Marx treats political institutions, for the most part, as the consequences of class conflicts and class coalitions, Jaurès tells a story in which political organizations and institutions shape everything within and around them.

Although the *Histoire socialiste* would be "materialist with Marx," Jaurès writes, it would also be also "mystical with Michelet" (*HS* 1:8). Where Marx is the hard-headed student of economics and of class conflict, Jules Michelet looks toward the hidden purposes of history. Marx attends to the sensible world; Michelet, to the ideal implicit within it. Like Marx's, Michelet's name would have had an inescapable partisan association for Jaurès's first readers: where Marx represented revolutionary socialism, Michelet stood for democratic republicanism. A writer of grand and impassioned historical works of vast scope, Michelet championed "the people" (*Le peuple* is the title of one of his best-known works) in their conflicts with monarchy, aristocracy, and Church. Michelet's writings claim for France a special place in the development of modern republicanism. To be French, Michelet wrote, meant that one's aspirations for equality and brotherhood pointed not toward "cosmopolitan utopias" but toward one's "patrie" itself since France had "founded for every nation the gospel of equality."[30] For Michelet, the moral meaning of the French Revolution lay in its "utterly pacific, benevolent, loving character"—a character that might seem "a paradox," given the Revolution's bloodier events, but that could be recovered. The Revolution was not to be reduced to the actions of any of its particular leaders or sects—it was not Robespierre's project, or the Jacobins'. It was instead a creation of the French people as a whole.[31]

Jaurès would sound similar notes, and the "mystical" element in the *Histoire socialiste*—the feeling that each moment of history contains within it some movement toward or some element of a transhistorical ideal of justice—

is present on every page. Like Michelet, Jaurès writes history as a moral epic. As he had proposed in his debate with Lafargue, Jaurès aims to relate history in a way that attended not only to class relations but also to the human capacity for imaginative sympathy. What Jaurès draws from Michelet is always tempered by what he takes from Marx, however. The student of history should be aware of the constant presence of the ideal within the real, Jaurès suggests, but must also notice the ways that the content of daily life can either impede or encourage the progress of that ideal. That ideal may be a causal force in history, but so are social and economic relationships—in particular, patterns of class conflict. "We know that economic conditions, the mode of production and of property, are the very basis of history. . . . They determine political forms, social mores, and even the general direction of thought. . . . But we do not forget—as even Marx, confined by his interpretive constraints, never forgot—that it is on men that the economic forces act. Men have a prodigious diversity of passions and ideas, and the nearly infinite complexity of human life cannot be reduced brutally and mechanically to an economic formula" (*HS* 1:6–7). Human beings, Jaurès writes, are enveloped in their social milieus. But alongside this Marxist element to his method of writing history, there is a "mystical" element as well. Human beings also live "in a vast milieu, which is the universe itself." The human soul "vibrates with mysterious and profound forces of eternal life, which move and precede and go beyond human life." Just as it would be "vain and false" to deny the role of "the economic system and the forces of production" in history, so "it would also be childish and crass to explain the movement of human thought, summarily, in terms of the evolution of economic forms" (*HS* 1:7)

This "mystical" element in history is where Jaurès departs from Marx, but his emphasis on economic forces, and thus on class conflict, is where Jaurès departs from Michelet—and, for that matter, from the Radical and Progressist republicans. The *Histoire socialiste* is a republican history as much as it is a socialist history, but it is also a protest against the way that the dominant forms of French republicanism in the 1890s were narrowing the republican horizon.

Michelet once remarked that the French Republic's ideal of fraternity had its source in "antiquity"—that is, in the Greek democracies and the Roman republic.[32] A commitment to fraternity, in an ancient or a modern republic, means a decision to make a priority of what citizens have in common and to take as a central problem of public life the question of how the moral capacity for common purpose might be generated. Modern republics will assert that priority and work out their answers to that problem differently than ancient republics did. Still, Michelet asserted, modern republicans ought to acknowledge and reflect on the classical origins of their political commitments.

When Jaurès claims Plutarch as one of his inspirations, he suggests that he thought much the same thing. Plutarch's *Lives of the Noble Grecians and Romans* traces the role of character and judgment in public affairs, and emphasizes that the qualities proper to political life—courage, moderation, a capacity for reconciliation—are developed through experience. Jaurès wants to be as attentive to political virtue as Plutarch was. "History," Jaures writes, "will never dispense with men of valor and individual nobility." Those socialists who read Plutarch's *Lives* find a "beautiful spirit of inner energy" that allows them to "remain upright in the storm" (*HS* 1:9). Jaurès intends to write history in a way that captures the individual characters—or, better, the character of individuals. Impersonal forces, whether economic or cultural, may be consequential, but so, he suggests, are the actions and judgments of particular people. Accordingly, Jaurès fills the *Histoire socialiste* with detailed portraits of specific actors, from Condorcet to Robespierre to Babeuf. This is, to say the least, an approach quite different from that of Marx, in whose historical writings the main actors are never individuals but always classes.

Jaurès does not comment here on whether the reading of Plutarch might be a sufficient source of inner energy or individual nobility, or on what other sources these qualities could possibly have. That he raises the question of "inner energy" at all is significant, however. Where a Marxist of Lafargue's or Guesde's type could rely on a "scientific" certainty about the future victory of socialism, Jaurès's theory of history denies that kind of certainty. Whatever certainty of purpose might be required of members in the kind of political movement he has in mind, Jaurès suggests that it will have more resemblance to the virtue of the ancients than to the knowledge of the moderns.

The French Revolution was then what it still is: the mirror in which the Left tries to comprehend itself. Jaurès saw in the story of the First French Republic—in the long years of events that led up to it and in the brief burst of activity that was the Republic itself—a vindication of reformist socialism, of left-wing politics defined by democratic methods. The Revolution had its violent spasms and its sudden turns, to be sure, but beneath all that lay a steady flow of continuous change, what Jaurès calls the "uninterrupted progress and nuance of life" (*HS* 1:3). What made the Revolution a revolution was that a new ideal and a new mode of political organization had begun to shape the direction of public life. "The genius of the Revolution," Jaurès writes, "was the masses in motion" (*HS* 4:1684). The power of the mobilized people was sometimes felt directly, through demonstrations, riots, or strikes. However, Jaurès is more interested in the institutions founded by the Revolution. Once elected representative bodies were created, and once an idea of legitimacy restrained government, the Revolution became steadily more inclusive and more egalitarian. Jaurès will often refer to this developmental logic as an "evolution of democracy," and he thinks that, once this evolution has begun, it has a momentum of its own.

Jaurès's "uninterrupted progress and nuance of life" suggests a process that admits of no jolting disruptions. Every social or political change that we might attribute to the Revolution, he argues, had accumulated over the preceding decades or even centuries. The "political rise of the bourgeois class," ostensibly the main event of the Revolution, had begun long before 1789 (*HS* 1:3). Even before the eighteenth century, successive monarchs had consolidated their power, eroding the feudal order and replacing arbitrary authority with something resembling the rule of law. The "generous philosophy" of the Renaissance and the Enlightenment and the conflict between "the spirit of the Church and the spirit of Voltaire" prepared the way for new ideas, first by applying "methods of analysis and deduction . . . to nature" and then by applying those same methods to "reality as a whole, to society as well" (*HS* 1:22, 38, 31). At the same time, the development of rudimentary industry over the course of the eighteenth century made the new business-owning class a "decisive force" in social life even before it won political power, so that the bourgeoisie was "truly ruling" in the new centers of manufacturing even while the king still sat on his throne (*HS* 1:66–67, 96). It took the dramatic events of the Revolution to "tear out the last roots of feudalism," but those roots had been loosened before the beginning of the Revolution proper (*HS* 1:14).

Some of this—for instance, the point about the social and economic power of the bourgeoisie preceding its political victory—is what we would also expect from a purely Marxist history of the Revolution. Jaurès reminds us that the Marxist thread is only part of the story he wants to tell, however. The rise of the bourgeoisie is important not because it leads mechanically to a situation in which the proletariat can rise in its turn, but because in and through the rise of the bourgeoisie, the "evolution of democracy" has been advanced. The rise of the bourgeoisie is in part an economic and social change, but it has political consequences—the end of monarchy, the introduction of representative government, the establishment of legal rights for individuals—and these political developments have consequences in their turn.

What Jaurès means by the evolution of democracy can be seen most clearly by looking at what he says about the origins of socialism. He finds the "greatest and most glorious hour" of the Revolution in the summer of 1789, when the Declaration of the Rights of Man and of the Citizen announced its "highest ideal": "Men are born and remain free, and equal in rights" (*HS* 1:304). This was a bold, grand, eloquent phrase. But there was nothing innovative in it, nothing that had not already been thought (if not always spoken) and nothing that had not already been acted on (if not always in full awareness). Galileo's challenge to the Church authorities was present here, as was the Enlightenment's "fight for free thought," as was the displacement of arbitrary feudal aristocracies with rule-governed administrative states. The Declaration was the modern spirit made manifest (*HS* 1:24, 38–43). Still, the Declaration clarified what before had been obscure, and this clarification of ideas mattered. Almost as soon as the Declaration was written, some in France began to "eloquently appeal to the Rights of Man on behalf of proletarians," Jaurès writes. "It is evident that the working class interpreted the Declaration of Rights as a promise, and that the proletariat had immediately attached its hope to this symbol of the Revolution" (*HS* 1:624).

The suggestion that hope needs to be attached to a "symbol" is interesting by itself, but also interesting is the idea that the text of the Declaration—whether described as a promise or as a symbol—seemed to point beyond itself: after all, in addition to speaking of equality, the Declaration also defended inequality, by naming property as an "inviolable and sacred" right.[33] The Declaration contained an idea of equal rights that proved to be uncontainable, that was capable of developing in new and unexpected ways despite the Declaration's own limitations.

Jaurès sets out to look for the ways that the idea of the Declaration escaped the control of its authors. He sees this dynamic revealed in the National Convention of 1793. The Convention gave institutional form to the egalitarian principle of the Declaration: its members were elected through (nearly) universal manhood suffrage. What took many members of the Convention by surprise was that this new inclusiveness brought conflicts regarding property and wealth into the Convention's own deliberations.

The Convention invited all its members—moreover, it invited all citizens of France, all citizens everywhere—to propose their plans and bring their ideas. As the organization of political power in a democracy touches on all the forms of life, economic as well as political, as the Declaration of the Rights of Man raised the problem of property at the same time as that of liberty, as the institutions created by the will of men necessarily react on the formation and the distribution of wealth, so the whole social question was posed before the Convention. (*HS* 4:1490)

A case could be made that there was no socialism at the Convention: indeed, Jaurès admits that none of the Convention's members took positions exactly like those of socialists of his own generation. Alternately, a case could be made that socialism had been in the air long before 1793: rudimentary ideas of "communism"—of a future society in which property is shared by all the community—had been scattered through the works of several thinkers in the half century prior to the Convention, and in those of a few even earlier.[34] Nevertheless, as far as Jaurès is concerned, the birth of socialism takes place at the Convention because this is the point at which the working-class movement takes up the idea of a republic based on rights and adapts that idea to its own purposes. After this point, the nature of property and the structure of social life would be unavoidable questions of public debate. "Socialist thought awoke," Jaurès writes, when "those who wanted a new distribution of wealth, a new form of property . . . gave to the Declaration of the Rights of Man an interpretation uniquely unsettling for the bourgeoisie" (*HS* 4:1534). François Boissel was only summing up the mood of the moment when he proclaimed in April 1793: "Robespierre, yesterday you read the Declaration of the Rights of Man, and now I am going to read the declaration of the rights of the *sans-culottes*." That workers might have, as Boissel asserted, a right to "the enjoyment and use of the goods of the earth" was to draw the "social question" within the compass of political life (*HS* 4:1562).

Jaurès gives Boissel a great deal of credit for bringing socialism to birth, but he sees François-Noël Babeuf (nicknamed "Gracchus," after the hero of the Roman plebs) as the figure in the 1790s who united definitively the protests of the "masses in motion" and the idea of rights. With Babeuf, Jaurès writes, "communism ceases to be a bookish doctrine; it enters into history and it adapts to history's laws." Although Babeuf's doctrines are not the same as those of later socialists—he is more interested in a wide distribution of property than in collective or social property—he demonstrates that "none of the political institutions created or valued by the Revolution could function or produce their full effect if they did not tend toward equality of fact" and not just equality of legal rights (*HS* 4:1537–38). Babeuf knew something that later revolutionary socialists would forget: "The very evolution of democracy pushes toward its logical consequences: that social equality will result. It is by this fusion with the nascent democracy that communism leaves abstract and utopian regions and enters into the movement of life. Thus political democracy is a socialism unaware of itself, which only becomes conscious of itself little by little" (*HS* 4:1542). Socialism, we might say, is a democratic understanding of the possibilities opened up by democratic institutions. If this is so, then the day-to-day functioning of democratic institutions must contain a covert aspiration toward socialism. Jaurès notes approvingly that Babeuf was "interested in the mechanism of deliberation in the assemblies." This, he remarks, should serve as "a great lesson for the doctrinaires of theoretical socialism, who affect indifference and disdain for the play of parliament" (*HS* 4:1542–43). For Jaurès, the origin of socialism is found not in the Revolution's extreme or violent moments, but in the humdrum practices of its representative bodies at work. Those who want an image of socialist politics should look past the Revolution's street barricades to its parliamentary procedures.

Accordingly, Jaurès proposes that, for socialists, the great hero of the Revolution should be not a protocommunist like Boissel or Babeuf, but the leader who, more than any other, deserves credit for upholding the institutions of the new republic: Maximilien de Robespierre. In Jaurès's portrait of Robespierre, we are more likely to see a resemblance to Lincoln than to Lenin. Jaurès argues that the key to understanding Robespierre is to recognize that he was, in his context, a moderate. Robespierre knew that his Republic was fragile, shadowed by the danger of counterrevolution. His ability to preserve the Republic for as long as he did was remarkable and due in large part to his policy of modulating the use of violence. Jaurès does not accept the Jacobin claim that state terror can foster civic virtue, and he argues that Robespierre instigated the Terror reluctantly, as a temporary emergency measure to save the new Republic from its aristocratic and clerical enemies. Robespierre meant executions to be occasional examples rather than routine policy, and he opposed the extreme policies of the Hébertists, who wanted a more systematic application of terror and a more thorough (and violent) campaign of de-Christianization.

His aim was to restore normal constitutional government as quickly as possible. Caught between counterrevolutionaries and ultrarevolutionaries, Robespierre's turn toward terror was, Jaurès argues, a measured and unavoidable use of violence in defense of institutions meant to replace violence with debate (*HS* 4:1676–95).

Robespierre's prosecution of the Terror clearly makes Jaurès uncomfortable; his apology for Robespierre is strained at times, and he admits that Robespierre's judgment, at least in his last days, was damaged by "doubt, blindness, and vertigo" (*HS* 4:1820). But the moments when Jaurès does express an uncomplicated enthusiasm about Robespierre reveal something about his own thought. The issues of greatest concern to socialists—wages, profits, property— were not Robespierre's preoccupations. Why, then, Jaurès asks, should socialists be so interested in Robespierre's leadership? His answer is that, when Robespierre defended representative institutions and mobilized mass political participation, he provided socialists with the political and intellectual model they would need for the twentieth century. The echo of the Dreyfus Affair is audible: Robespierre's lesson is that the representative and legal institutions of a republic are worth preserving, and that both their preservation and the pursuit of their democratic potential require "the masses in motion." "For Robespierre," Jaures writes, "democracy is at the same time the end and the means."

> O, socialists, my companions, do not be scandalized! If socialism were a sect, if its victory had to be the victory of a sect, it would have to pass a sectarian judgment on history; it would have to give its sympathy to the little groups whose formulas seemed to best anticipate the sect's own formulas, or to those fervent factions that seemed to undermine the regime we want to abolish by raising the people's passions nearly to delirium. Socialism, however, begins not from sectarian exasperation but from the power of a broad evolution of democracy. That is the reason why, with each moment of the French Revolution, I ask: What is the politics that best serves the Revolution as a whole, the democracy as a whole? (*HS* 4:1620)[35]

Thus, most of the time, Jaurès's sympathies lie with the groups that led the Revolution through its successive stages. First the Gironde established the "broad outlines" of the "political and social theory" of constitutional government (*HS* 4:1465), then Robespierre's Jacobins extended the Constitution of

1791 into the more thoroughly democratic government of the subsequent years, becoming the champions of universal manhood suffrage, representative democracy, separation of church and state, secular public education, and the rights of the lower classes. The Jacobins, and their larger Montagnard coalition, became the party of democracy and of "social equality" (*HS* 4:1548). As important as it might be to note the moment from which socialism emerges, that moment must be set in its proper place, as one moment within the broader evolution of democracy, within the Revolution as a whole.

It is all the more striking, then, that there is one major theme of Girondist and Jacobin politics to which Jaurès takes exception. The third clause of the Declaration of the Rights of Man states: "The nation is essentially the source of all sovereignty; nor can any INDIVIDUAL or ANY BODY OF MEN be entitled to any authority which is not expressly derived from it."[36] This idea, derived from Rousseau's notion of the general will, came to be central to the political thinking of the French Revolution. Here was French thought at its most undialectical: for both the moderate and the radical republicans of the 1790s, the unity of the Republic was inviolable. For the nascent French labor movement, the consequences were disastrous. A 1791 law sponsored by a member of the Constituent Assembly named Isaac-Réné-Guy Le Chapelier proclaimed: "The elimination of every kind of organization that joins together citizens with the same condition or profession is one of the fundamental bases of the French Constitution." Groups of workers were thus forbidden to "nominate presidents, secretaries, or agents; keep minutes; pass resolutions; undertake deliberations; or adopt policies regarding their supposed common interests." All attempts to bargain collectively were declared to be "contrary to the principles of liberty and of the Constitution" (*HS* 4:1605–6). The citizens of the nation were to have no representatives save those that assembled to represent the nation as a whole. By the logic of the Le Chapelier law, a class that attempted to organize itself was violating the unity of the nation and attempting to usurp for itself a share of the nation's sovereignty. This was the spirit that still animated mainstream French republicanism in the Third Republic; it was the republicanism from which Jaurès had dissented when he joined the labor caucus during his first term as a deputy in the Chamber.[37]

The Le Chapelier law offered the appearance of symmetry—employers were also forbidden to form any sort of syndicates—but it was clear that, overall, workers would be hurt by it and employers would benefit from it (*HS* 4:1606). If the working class could not organize, class conflict would hardly disappear. The consequence, instead, would be that class struggle could take no organized or institutional form: the labor movement would be a movement of desperation rather than legality. Although the Revolution's impulse toward unity was not wrong, Jaurès thought it was a mistake to see any institution as a perfect representation of the general will. If deeper justice and more authentic unity were to be pursued, organized groups of citizens would need to challenge the imperfect unity and incomplete justice of the state. Because a republican state aspires to represent the unity of the nation, it needs to allow for pluralism and make room for open conflict. The nation needs its representative institutions, but so do classes and communities within the nation.

Despite its flaws, the Revolution of 1789 to 1794 was "great," Jaurès concludes, because it "affirmed the idea of democracy in all its fullness" and "gave to the world the first example of a large country governing itself and saving itself with the force of the whole people" (*HS* 4:1821–22). Nevertheless, that period of revolution was "necessarily limited." In the last pages of volume 4, the last full volume he wrote for the *Histoire socialiste*, after describing the fall of Robespierre, Jaurès muses: "Perhaps it was not possible for a single generation to strike down the old regime, to create a new right, to rouse a proud and shining people from the depths of ignorance, from poverty and misery, to fight against the united world of tyrants and slaves. . . . It took a century for France—after the Revolution, after innumerable trials, relapses into monarchy, awakenings of the republic, invasions, dismemberments, coups d'état, civil wars—to arrive at last at the organization of the Republic, at the establishment of legal liberty by universal suffrage" (*HS* 4:1820). The Revolution was still incomplete at the beginning of the twentieth century. The Revolution's first generation had asserted a "new right," a democratic conception of justice. A century after Robespierre's fall, the work socialists had before them was to find the forms of republican organization that could preserve that "new right" and extend it into those areas of life still untouched by republican principles. Above all, this meant an expanded application of the principles of popular sovereignty and individual rights.

> Socialism asserts and depends on this new right. Socialism is a party of democracy in the highest sense, because it seeks to organize the sovereignty of all in the economic order as in the political order. It founds the new society on the right of the human person, because it wants to give to all persons the concrete means of development that alone will permit

them to fully realize themselves. . . . I am convinced that democracy is a great achievement for the proletariat. It is at once a decisive means of action and a model according to which economic relations as well as political relations must be organized. From this comes the impassioned joy with which I have noted the molten rush of socialism flowing from the furnace of the Revolution and from the establishment of democracy. (*HS* 4:1822)

The heart of socialism, Jaurès asserts here, is the realization of popular sovereignty within the economic sphere. Socialism would be a movement not against the legacy but in the tradition of the Revolution. The Radicals and Progressists of the Third Republic also claim to inherit the project of the Revolution, but they distort its meaning. Unlike the moderate and conservative republicans, Jaurès writes, socialists

have not immobilized and frozen democracy and the Revolution. We do not claim to keep human society rigidly within the economic and social formulas that prevailed from 1789 to 1795, which were a response to conditions of life and conditions of production that have since been abolished. Too often, bourgeois democratic parties limit themselves to collecting some fragments of cooled lava at the foot of the volcano, to gathering a few extinguished cinders around the furnace. The molten metal must be cooled in new molds.

The problem of property is no longer posed, can no longer be posed, as in 1789 or in 1793. Individual property appeared then as a bulwark for human personhood. With great capitalist industry and the social association of producers, universal enfranchisement requires that the major means of work become common and collective property. And to drag the Revolution away from what is outdated and retrograde in the bourgeois conception of democracy, a strong class action of the organized proletariat is necessary. (*HS* 4:1822)

Democracy is a project, not a finished thing. With the development of capitalism, the democratic ideas of the Revolution need to take new institutional forms. A democratic republic under new conditions could not simply imitate older republics. It would instead need to adapt older democratic and republican ideas to confront new problems. The great danger was that either the ideas or the institutions of democracy would freeze in place. To remain fluid, to keep the democratic project lively and responsive to its conditions—that was the challenge posed by the Revolution.

The *Histoire socialiste* poses a specific challenge for Jaurès's fellow socialists. The work of expanding bourgeois democracy, he emphasizes, would have to be the work "of a class and not of a sect since the proletariat must organize the whole democracy, all of life, and it can only organize democracy and life by mixing itself with them. Great and free action under the discipline of a clear ideal. The politics of democracy and the politics of class: these two terms are not at all contradictory. The power of the proletariat moves between them, and history will combine them one day in the unity of social democracy" (*HS* 4:1822). This mixing was exactly what some socialists had declined to do during the Dreyfus Affair. When they tried to maintain an exclusive attention to the needs of the working class, Jaurès suggests, they failed to engage in the "politics of democracy" and had become a mere sect. Class politics ought to open out into democratic politics, into a strategy of coalition building and into the broadest imaginable commitment to individual rights and human solidarity. At the same time, those moderate republicans who had no interest in the "politics of class" were misunderstanding the legacy of the Revolution: that a republic was a living thing, and a republic in the twentieth century would wither if it attempted to simply reiterate the doctrines of private property and individualism that had guided revolutionaries of the eighteenth century, or if it denied the need for open conflict within the nation. Under the new conditions of twentieth-century capitalism, the politics of democracy would be rootless and lifeless unless grounded in the politics of class.

Jaurès calls for "motion," but he is not unaware of the need for "molds" as well: note his references to organizations, organizing, and unity. His two metaphors here—the flow of lava and the organism—point in different directions, on the one hand, toward an expansive fluidity; on the other, toward an internally coherent entity, bounded in space and limited in life span. This inconsistency in Jaurès's imagery is frustrating, but it is also suggestive. If a surging democratic impulse and secure democratic institutions are both necessary, it would seem that the democratic project can never take a final or definitive form.

Jaurès suggests much the same thing in volume 1 of the *Histoire socialiste*. Imagining, almost offhand, what would occur if the working class somehow achieved complete power immediately, Jaurès comments that, even in the socialist society that followed, important conflicts would arise. "Some would want to strengthen and expand the central action of the community; others would want to guarantee the broadest possible autonomy to local groups of workers. To regulate the new relationships among the nation, the trade union federations, towns, local groups, and individuals, to establish for the first time both perfect individual liberty and social solidarity, to give legal form to the countless ways that social property and individual action might be combined, an immense effort of thought would be necessary, and in this complexity there would be disagreements" (*HS* 1:6). These do not sound like the sort of disagreements that necessarily lead to bloodshed or enmity, but they are disagreements all the same. The work of constructing organizations and institutions and of resisting their tendency to become rigid—all that would be permanent. The friction between individual and community, between the community and its neighbors, between the smaller community and the larger would continue to be the basic stuff of political life. Socialism would not mean the abolition of any of this.[38] Jaurès wants to replace brutal social conflicts with survivable political conflicts: an ambitious project, but a far cry from the "final struggle" in which most nineteenth-century socialists thought they were engaged. What Jaurès wants to say is that the work that defined republican and socialist politics in his own time would not, at some point in the future, be replaced by some other kind of political work. The Revolution, as Jaurès understood it, would remain unfinished.

A SOCIALIST STATE OF GRACE

In September 1898, as Jaurès was beginning to work on the *Histoire socialiste*, the leaders of the Paris labor unions decided that the time was right to spark a revolution. Workers in the building trades were already on strike, and the railway workers' union had decided to go out in solidarity with them. Like many in the Confédération générale du travail, the Paris CGT leaders were influenced by the ideas of revolutionary syndicalism—in particular, by the idea that the way to end capitalism was to foment a simultaneous strike by workers in all or nearly all sectors.[1] This seemed to them to be the right moment for a general strike, and the Confédération leaders circulated a secret letter suggesting that France's unions prepare for one.[2]

Not surprisingly, the letter did not remain secret for long. The government responded to the strike proposal by sending the army to occupy Paris. Rumors spread of an impending coup d'état; indeed, anti-Dreyfusard leaders had been calling for a coup for months, while their supporters rioted in the streets.[3] Although neither coup nor revolution took place, the Republic appeared fragile in this crisis, and even Jules Guesde and his fellow Marxists found themselves appreciating it in a way they had not before. Led by the Guesdists, the socialist groups—including the smaller revolutionary parties, the Blanquists and Allemanists—formed the Comité d'entente socialiste, which organized public meetings and demonstrations across France in support of the Republic, sometimes in conjunction with Radicals and moderate republicans. In 1899, the country saw, for the first time, a unified May Day march that included all the socialist groups.[4]

No longer a member of the Chamber, Jaurès was free to take a leading role in the Comité d'entente.[5] In January 1899, he published an article calling for a general congress of socialist groups for the purpose of founding a new, united party. Socialists were already moving toward closer cooperation, Jaurès wrote, and, to cement their unity, they needed an organization that could coordinate their electoral and parliamentary efforts. From the Union socialiste to Alexandre Millerand's Saint-Mandé program to the Comité d'entente, the trajectory was clear. A unified party would not have to achieve uniformity, he proposed; it could, instead, harmonize the varied strains of French socialism. Jaurès also issued what must have sounded like a warning. The congresses of a unified socialist party, he insisted, would need the freedom to discuss "all questions of doctrine, method, and tactics." "The thought of a great party cannot be immobilized without dying. . . . It is not enough to respond to all problems with the same two or three basic formulas. The adaptation of these formulas to the movement of life, the endless confrontation of these formulas with facts, requires that thought always remain awake. . . . For these questions to be resolved in accordance with life, all living forces of socialism and of the proletariat must be called to deliberate them."[6] About the "two or three basic formulas" Jaurès had in mind, there would have been little mystery to his readers. But he did not take this occasion to restate his arguments against the idea that socialists should have an exclusive focus on class struggle, or against the dogmas of the materialist theory of history, or against many socialists' certainty that their battle would someday be fully won. Such formulaic thinking froze thought, Jaurès suggested, and made its adherents less able to respond to new facts, or to facts newly perceived. Rather than substituting new comprehensive explanations for old comprehensive explanations, Jaurès sought to cultivate a different intellectual sensibility among his comrades: he argued that the way to develop this sensibility was to create the kind of institutional space appropriate to them. A party structured to allow for "all living forces of socialism and of the proletariat" to "deliberate" upon that party's doctrines and methods would develop its members' capacities for political judgment.

Although, within months, there would indeed be a debate among socialists about "all questions of doctrine, method, and tactics," it was not the debate Jaurès envisioned in his January article. Rather than defining the common ground shared by members of the socialist movement, the debate would divide socialists even more bitterly than before. That debate was precipitated by a governmental crisis.

After President of the Republic Félix Faure, a conservative who had opposed any reconsideration of the Dreyfus case, died suddenly in February 1899, the Chamber of Deputies and the Senate elected as his replacement Émile Loubet, a moderate republican known to be sympathetic to the Dreyfusards. Nationalists and monarchists soon renewed their murmurings about a coup d'état. After an appeals court ordered a retrial for Dreyfus in June, an indignant monarchist broke into President Loubet's box at the Auteuil racecourse and swung his cane at the president, denting his top hat. When a joint rally of socialists and republicans protested this affront to the Republic, police used violence against the protestors. Challenged in the Chamber to explain police conduct, Prime Minister Charles Dupuy failed to receive the vote of confidence he requested. He and his cabinet resigned.[7]

The Third Republic had never allowed any of its prime ministers a long term in office, and negotiations over the formation of new cabinets, or the reshuffling of old ones, were an almost constant feature of French government in the late nineteenth century. But the political crisis that followed Dupuy's resignation was without precedent. For ten days, President Loubet was unable to find anyone who could form a ministerial coalition capable of winning approval in a parliament where no plausible coalition of parties and factions held more than the slimmest of majorities. With the Republic's governing institutions in a state of frightening instability and passions over the Dreyfus Affair still at a high pitch, the possibility of a right-wing coup d'état had never seemed more real.[8]

The crisis ended on June 22, when René Waldeck-Rousseau, a Progressist senator with Dreyfusard sympathies and close ties to big business, presented his proposed new government to the Chamber. Waldeck-Rousseau's creative stroke was to choose as the most prominent ministers in his cabinet two men who in the eyes of many represented opposing political forces. One of the two was General Gaston de Gallifet, who as both a committed republican and a senior officer was perhaps the only potential minister of war who could stifle antirepublican sentiments within the officer corps; to the Left, Gallifet was the reviled "butcher" of the Paris Communards in 1871.[9] The other surprise was Waldeck-Rousseau's proposed minister of commerce: Alexandre Millerand.

With Jaurès out of office, the author of the Saint-Mandé program was now the acknowledged leader of the socialist group within the Chamber. Throughout the ministerial crisis, Millerand had been writing in *La Petite République* that the solution was "a cabinet of republican concentration" representing the full spectrum of republican groups, including socialists.[10] The day before Waldeck-Rousseau's announcement, Millerand had asked at the weekly meeting of the Union socialiste what the caucus members thought, in principle, about the idea of a socialist entering such a cabinet. Waldeck-Rousseau had approached him about this possibility, Millerand told his colleagues, but the negotiations had fallen apart. No one objected to what Millerand presented as a hypothetical scenario, and he seems to have taken this as tacit approval for him to accept a subsequent ministerial offer without further consulting his socialist colleagues.[11]

Millerand's acceptance of this office marked a new level of socialist influence, and some socialists were pleased. With more seats in the Chamber of Deputies than ever before, and more unified than ever before, socialists had become a force the Republic's most powerful figures felt compelled to accommodate. Millerand's new position, and the leverage on labor law and social welfare policy that might come with it, seemed the natural outcome of the socialists' new situation.

Many other socialists were shocked, however, by Millerand's entry into a government of any kind, but, above all, by his entry into a government that included Gallifet. Within days, the Blanquists and Guesdists, the two socialist groups most committed to the idea of revolution and least interested in what Jaurès had called "the play of parliament," withdrew from the Union socialiste in protest. Jaurès endorsed Millerand's participation in what he called a "fighting government," arguing that socialists needed to rally to the defense of a fragile Republic and to support a coalition government that could continue the work begun by the Dreyfusard coalition.[12] The period of tentative unity among French socialists had ended.[13] Before long, the "cas Millerand" had become the occasion for a fierce debate about what was soon labeled "ministéri-elisme": the question of whether, or under what conditions, it might be accept-able for a socialist to become a minister in a coalition government dominated by "bourgeois"—nonsocialist—parties.

The division between French socialists was clear—and, as never before, binary. The Guesdists and Blanquists were "antiministérieliste." The independ-ents and the remnants of the Possibilists were "ministérieliste." The Alle-manists had long maintained their loyalty to the principles of both "révolution" and "république" but now felt compelled to choose between them; their party split into antiministerialist and ministerialist factions.[14] The antiministerialist group, in a July 1899 joint statement, declared that Millerand and his support-ers wanted to replace "the class and hence revolutionary political method of the militant proletariat" with a "counterfeit socialist political method, consist-ing of compromises and deviations" and insisted that socialism remain a movement of "intransigent opposition" to the existing society. To the dismay of the revolutionary socialists, the ministerialist deputies remaining in the Union socialiste joined their Radical-Socialist, Radical, and Progressist col-leagues in a formal coalition, the Bloc des gauches (Coalition of the Lefts), dedicated to keeping the Waldeck-Rousseau government in power.[15] Although there were scattered precedents for the ministerialists' actions—recent local coalition governments and the socialist Louis Blanc's service in the short-lived government of the Second French Republic—the ministerialists' inability to counter the antiministerialists' initial criticisms reveals their discomfort. Something was different here; the identity of the socialist movement was at stake now in a way that it had not been when socialists supported Radical governments without claiming for themselves the power to formulate laws, or before the Dreyfus Affair and the rise of a new kind of right-wing movement had raised the question of whether the Republic would survive into the new century.[16] Socialists who supported Millerand and the government to which he belonged argued that, in such a time of crisis, there could be no political priority higher than preserving the Republic, and that to use parliamentary power—with all the compromises it involved—was thus a legitimate activity for socialists. Whatever this new ministerialist socialism would lead to, it would certainly not be intransigent opposition.

Since they had no members in the Chamber of Deputies at the time, the Possibilists were somewhat above the fray; at their urging, the socialist factions agreed to meet in a general congress that December. Unlike the congress Jaurès had envisioned in January, the goal of this assembly would be not to create a new united party but, more modestly, to calm what the Possibilists called the "fratricidal conflict" among socialists. Specifically, the congress was to address two questions: whether Millerand had acted appropriately in joining a coalition government and on what basis socialist unity might still be achieved (the second question added to the agenda at Jaurès's suggestion).[17]

The First General Congress of French Socialist Organizations met in Paris in early December.[18] Jaurès joined ministerialists such as Aristide Briand and René Viviani in defending Millerand's participation in the Waldeck-Rousseau government. As he had earlier in the year, Jaurès argued that ministerial participation followed from decisions that socialists—even Guesdists and Blanquists—had made long before. Together, the socialist groups had supported Léon Bourgeois's government; they had governed towns and cities; they had increased their numbers in the Chamber of Deputies to the point where their votes could determine whether progressive or reactionary governments took office. Moreover, the need to defend the institutions of the Republic as part of the longer project of building a "social republic" meant that socialists had responsibilities they ought not to shirk. He insisted that there could be room for significant reforms even within a bourgeois government: "Citizens," he declared, "once we had to cut through the false teaching of the iron law of wages, which would have discouraged the workers from struggling to improve their conditions; now we have to cut through the equally false notion of the iron law of the state." The Marxist idea that capitalists would never accede to workers' demands for wage increases had turned out to be false, and so would the idea that socialists would have to wait until they had a parliamentary majority (or a revolutionary dictatorship) for their growing political power to have real effects. This meant a commitment to using as effectively as possible the fragments of power that socialists did hold—if necessary, by being the junior partner in a political coalition with republicans of the Center and Center-Left. In the end, there was no practical alternative to the work of accumulating small reforms, little by little, since no one could "predict exactly when and how capitalism [would] collapse."[19] Paul Lafargue, speaking for the antiministerialists, responded that Millerand's entry into the Waldeck-Rousseau cabinet was not a continuation of past socialist tactics but the "point of departure of a new method of political action."[20] Jaurès would soon cease to deny that he was advocating a "new method."

After passing one resolution offering support for ministerial participation under "exceptional circumstances" and another offering unqualified condemnation of ministerialism, the General Congress then voted—with little discussion, and despite the congress's limited mandate—to form a new Parti socialiste français (PSF), with Millerand's Saint-Mandé program as its platform, to be governed by a general committee. The socialist caucus in the Chamber of Deputies was reunited in name, but hardly in spirit.[21] For the first time, French socialists had, or told themselves that they had, a single nationwide party. It should not have been a surprise when, within weeks, tensions developed between the new and assertive PSF General Committee, on which antiministerialists held a majority, and the Chamber caucus, in which the ministerialist majority was unimpressed by the General Committee's claims to authority.[22] Already, the Parti socialiste français seemed about to split apart.

While French socialists argued about ministerialism, German socialists were engaged in a similar conflict, and, by 1900, the two debates began to converge.[23] The German situation was markedly different from the French, however: unlike the intellectually heterogeneous (and, in German eyes, incoherent and haphazard) French socialists, the German Social Democratic Party was unified and disciplined, with the political thought of Marx and Engels as its common doctrine. The German party was also rapidly growing: between 1887 and 1898, the SPD's vote share in the Reichstag elections had more than doubled.[24] On the other hand, Germany was a constitutional monarchy, in which the Reichstag had only limited power to check that of the emperor. Thus, despite their success in organizing members and mobilizing voters, German socialists had negligible influence on legislation. What sustained their party was the expectation that, at some point in the future, the time would be ripe for revolution. Not just yet, however. As German socialist leader Karl Kautsky, nicknamed the "Pope of Marxism," would later write, the SPD of his day was "a revolutionary party, but not a party that makes revolutions."[25]

In January 1898, a respected SPD leader named Eduard Bernstein—Engels's literary executor and a friend of prominent British socialists like Sidney and Beatrice Webb—had published a two-part article in the socialist journal *Neue Zeit* that shocked members of the SPD in something like the way that Millerand's entry into government would shock French socialists in 1899. Bernstein wrote that the time had come for socialists to shift their attention from the future to the present. "Wherever the socialist party has achieved political significance, the same phenomenon tends to recur: the party undergoes an internal change. Earlier excesses of phraseology and argument are shed; the enthusiasm for generalization abates; and there is less speculation about how the spoils are to be divided after Armageddon. People are, indeed, very little preoccupied with this interesting event. Instead, they study the details of topical problems and look for ways and means of using them to push the development of society in a socialist direction."[26] And, in a turn of phrase that would make him infamous: "I frankly admit that I have extraordinarily little feeling for, or interest in, what is usually termed 'the final goal of socialism.' This goal, whatever it may be, is nothing to me, the movement is everything. . . . What Social Democracy should be doing, and doing for a long time to come, is organise the working class politically, train it for democracy, and fight for any and all reforms in the state which are designed to raise the working class and make the state more democratic."[27]

Met with furious criticism from Kautsky and other SPD leaders, Bernstein tried to soften his rejection of the socialist "final goal": what he had really meant was that "the movement is everything to me because it bears its goal within itself."[28] Nevertheless, many in the German Social Democratic Party thought that Bernstein had lost touch with the essence of socialism. After the SPD formally condemned his views at its 1899 congress in Hanover, Bernstein elaborated his ideas in a book, *Die Voraussetzungen des Sozialismus (The Preconditions of Socialism)*.[29] Here he "revised" fundamental parts of Marx's economic theory. Marx was wrong, Bernstein wrote, when he argued that the development of capitalism would lead inevitably to a decisive economic and political crisis. The growth of intermediate classes between the bourgeoisie and the industrial proletariat and the surprising capacity of a capitalist economy to adapt to workers' demands for higher wages belied Marx's expectation of a catastrophic collapse of capitalism. Without that collapse, there could be no revolutionary moment of transition to a wholly new form of society—nor would there need to be. To recognize this was not to depart from Marxism, Bernstein argued, but to make what Engels had labeled "scientific socialism" more thoroughly scientific—that is, to open Marx's theories to revision in light of new evidence. Marx had constructed a "science of society," but his work was obscured by a "scaffolding" of utopian sentiment and Hegelian obfuscation that could be stripped away if Marxism was made to more closely resemble the natural sciences.[30] The Marxist theory of revolution was not a theory in the scientific sense, but empty words; socialists needed to replace the mindless "cant" of socialist tradition with the critical spirit of Kant.[31]

The conflict between a hardening Marxist orthodoxy and a critical reformist spirit was not confined to Germany and France. The years between 1890 and 1900 had seen the founding of new socialist parties and the growth of old ones, and during this period Marxism had increasingly become the common language of the socialist movement, in no small part thanks to gifted popularizers like Kautsky and to the attractiveness of the organizational model offered by the proudly Marxist SPD for socialists outside Germany.[32] Even within France, many Blanquists and Allemanists, who had long disparaged Marxism as a German import inferior to the French revolutionary traditions, found their interest in the Guesdists' brand of Marxism increasing as their alliance with Guesde's Parti ouvrier français grew stronger. Especially among anti-ministerialists, but outside their circles as well, Marxism had become prominent in France to an extent that would have surprised the French socialists of the previous decade. Increasingly, Marx's ideas now provided the common lens of observation and the common criteria for political judgment that allowed the scattered and precarious socialist organizations to understand one another's grievances and aspirations and to see one another as parts of a single international movement. Marx's writings also provided the common stock of slogans: international socialist gatherings met in rooms hung with banners that quoted the *Communist Manifesto*: "Workers of the world, unite!"[33] Without Marx, it seemed, there could be no such thing as "socialism" in the singular.

By 1900, however, discontent with Marx's doctrine of history and a new willingness to make coalitions with parties of the Center and Center-Left were apparent within every socialist or labor party. Bernstein and Jaurès were not alone in espousing a reformist socialism: Filippo Turati in Italy, Victor Adler in Austria, Émile Vandervelde in Belgium, Hjalmar Branting in Sweden, and other less-known figures had begun to do much the same thing, while British socialism had long displayed a reformist tinge, whether in the ethical socialism of Keir Hardie's Independent Labor Party or in the vision of technocratic social planning proffered by the Fabian Society, in which Bernstein's friends the Webbs were leaders.[34] The fixity of the orthodox socialist view and the dissent from that orthodoxy seemed to grow in proportion to each other.

Although this pattern was repeated in country after country, the unprecedented nature of the French political situation and the intellectual prestige of the German socialist party gave the ministerialism and revisionism debates special prominence. In February 1900, Jaurès would bring these two debates together, putting the Millerand case in an international and theoretical context that it had, so far, been lacking. In a speech at the Paris Hôtel des sociétés savantes, later published under the title "Bernstein et l'évolution de la méthode socialiste" (Bernstein and the evolution of socialist method),[35] Jaurès took up Lafargue's charge that ministerialism represented a "new method of political action." Admitting that there was something new afoot, Jaurès asked his audience to think through the consequences and requirements of the "method" that he and other ministerialists were engaged in. Jaurès made clear which parts of Marx's political thought he now accepted and which he now did not, explaining what was new and what was not new in his politics and confronting more directly than before the problem of how a battle that would be neither won nor lost could be sustained. His speech on Bernstein is as good a place as any from which to watch the way that social democracy emerges out of older forms of socialist thought and begins to become a distinct way of engaging in and reflecting on political life.

"In the controversy that has arisen between Bernstein and Kautsky over the principles and the method of socialism, I am, in the end, with Kautsky," Jaurès announces. No doubt the antiministerialists in his audience were both pleased and puzzled to hear this leader of French ministerialism open his speech by disowning German revisionism. But in his next sentence, Jaurès praises the "immense service Bernstein has rendered to our party" by "obliging us all to reexamine our fundamental ideas and, above all, to adjust those ideas more precisely to reality." Moments later, he adds another qualification to his endorsement of Kautsky: "There is in Kautsky a little of Bernstein, and so when I approve fully of Kautsky, I also approve partly of Bernstein" (*OJJ* 6:119). Jaurès's position was beginning to sound more complicated than it had at first.

"What I want to say," Jaurès explains, "is that we have to make a new socialist politics, in some ways a more active politics. We have to modify our attitude regarding certain problems. But we can do this without violating the common traditions of international socialist democracy" (*OJJ* 6:119). The problem with the old socialist politics—Kautsky's, Guesde's—is that in pinning its hopes on a future revolution, it became a politics of excessive patience. The old socialist politics could not account for the "active" approach that Millerand had taken; the Guesdists' vacillations—disdaining the Republic, supporting the Republic; pursuing socialist unity, rejecting unity—suggested that they had not found a coherent way to think about the new situation to which Millerand's action responded. The problem with Bernstein, Jaurès suggests, is not that he has the wrong attitude regarding the salient problems but that he has violated the common traditions of the movement: he has broken a connection that does not need to be broken. When Jaurès says that he is, "in the end, with Kautsky," this seems to mean that, to him, the common traditions to which Kautsky holds do not sound like mere cant, as they do to Bernstein. Jaurès's "new socialist politics" will speak in an old language.

That old language was Marxism. Jaurès wants to preserve socialists' ground of unity, and thus their "common traditions." He insists, however, that what socialists inherit from Marx is not a closed catechism but a method of thinking that "contains the means of fulfilling and renewing itself" (*OJJ* 6:119–20). Interestingly, the elements of Marx's thought that Jaurès praises are not those to which Bernstein objected, and his efforts to "renew" Marxism bear more than a little resemblance to Bernstein's efforts to "revise" it. Marx's theory of value, Jaurès argues, is essentially correct: what the capitalist gains at the end of the worker's day is best understood not as a set of physical products but as the incarnated labor power of the worker. The importance of this theory of value is that it reveals the fundamental conflict between the employer and the worker in a capitalist economy, a conflict that cannot be resolved simply by redistributing the products of work.

As if he were making a minor point, Jaurès comments that Bernstein may have been right that this conflict can be managed so that it never leads to a crisis. For instance, capitalists might accept workers' demand for a shorter workday because they expect to be able to raise productivity levels within that shorter workday. In that case, the political crisis Marxists expect would be averted. The conflict between classes would persist, but it would be kept within bounds.

But this is not a minor point at all. Bernstein's rejection of Marx's crisis theory was at the heart of his revision of Marxism and among his most controversial arguments. What Bernstein gets wrong, Jaurès suggests, is not his understanding of economics but his finding the ministerialist call for immediate action to be "irreconcilable with the Marxist theory of value." Properly interpreted, Jaurès insists, Marxism does permit the worker a "power of immediate action" (*OJJ* 6:121–23). Like Bernstein, Jaurès wants to accept some parts of Marx's doctrine and to reject others, but where Bernstein describes this mixed response to Marxism as a fundamental revision, Jaurès describes it as a qualified acceptance: the common traditions can be interpreted in new ways; even when introducing a new thought, there is no need to turn away from the old conversation.

When Jaurès turns to Marx's theory of history, his effort to translate Bernstein's revisionism back into the Marxist vernacular becomes more subtle still. Marxist materialism, Jaurès argues, allows more flexibility than Bernstein recognized. The essence of Marx's theory of history, Jaurès explains, is that "men's conception of the world, of justice, of government, of law, of right is modified according to the economic system in which they live, and the general movement of human history is determined by the economic system's slowly or suddenly changing form" (*OJJ* 6:124). This is already more flexible a formulation than Guesde, Lafargue, or Kautsky would have accepted. "Modified" is not a strong verb, and "the general movement of history," whatever that phrase may mean, is evidently not the whole story. Jaurès is quick to endorse Marx's claim that economic relationships are "the basis" (*le fond*) of history. Tellingly, however, he soon introduces other images alongside Marx's. Several times during the speech, he uses the words "la force" or "le ressort" to describe the power of the factors that shape history. "La force" has most of the connotations of its English cognate, including the sense in which "force" is used in physics. "Le ressort" has a physical referent, too—it can mean a spring in the sense of a piece of wound metal—but it can also mean a moral or spiritual motive power, or the source of such a power.

This new imagery matters. History might have only one *fond*, yet be moved at the same time by any number of outward *forces* or inward *ressorts*. For example: "There are forces [*forces*] that are called science, the Church, democracy. Each of these forces has its internal logic, its own law of development that drives it toward an end that one can name in advance, if its development is not frustrated or inhibited or pushed farther by the dominant economic forces. Thus science has its law that is to some degree independent of economic phenomena" (*OJJ* 6:125). Or: "Thus it would be absolutely childish to try to explain each historical phenomenon—each human phenomenon—plainly, exclusively, abstractly, according to one sole motive [*ressort*], according to one category isolated from other trends and forces. Society is not like a watch where one single central spring [*ressort*] determines the movement of the hands moment by moment; various motives [*ressorts*] command it, and if we study only the effects of one, even if it be central and dominant, we will never know what time it is" (*OJJ* 6:127). Trying to show his listeners how one force can be dominant even while it and other social forces have "reciprocal" effects on one another, Jaurès compares economic forces to a wind that shakes the leaves in a forest. Each tree responds, but each responds in its own way, while the wind itself "is dispersed, and its direction altered" by the forest (*OJJ* 6:124, 127).

One of these various *forces* and *ressorts* is of particular interest to Jaurès. "Democracy," Jaurès tells his audience, "has its law, too. Clearly, it tends toward introducing the greatest possible equality among men, so far as it is not thwarted by adverse economic forces, and to the degree that this equality allows the fundamental privilege of property to remain" (*OJJ* 6:126). Some socialists, Jaures points out, complain that any immediate effort to circumscribe the power of the Church, to advance science, or to strengthen democratic institutions will fail since such efforts leave capitalism in place. But this analysis misses something. "Since democracy, the Church, and science each have their own logic, their own internal drive, their particular force of development, we must act directly on each of them—either by developing them, if they work toward the economic changes we want, or by pushing against them, if they work against us" (*OJJ* 6:128). Neither the Marxists' disregard for the independent logic of political life nor the radical and moderate republicans' unwillingness to challenge capitalist property relations is warranted. Jaurès pushes his audience to recognize that, although the logic of democracy may be circumscribed by the power of capital, the power of capital can also be qualified by the logic of democracy.

To treat the logic of democracy and the force of capitalism as being of equal power would constitute a "vain eclecticism," Jaurès admits. In a few limited ways, the logic of economic relations dominates everything else: however democratic and energetic the state might be, Jaurès argues, the power of capital cannot be counterbalanced without a labor movement. Economic power must be met with economic power; thus, even while socialists attend to electoral and legislative politics, they must also understand that their "fundamental work" is to organize a movement based in the workplace (*OJJ* 6:128). Nevertheless, the development of the labor movement has a logic or a *ressort* of its own that is as much political as economic: the logic of democracy, it seems, is at work in both "the masses in motion" and "the play of parliament." Marx was right that "workers are going to organize within industries where the concentration of capitalist industry naturally suggests to them the idea of grouping themselves," Jaurès notes. "But they must also learn to unionize, to group themselves, where capitalist industry is dispersed. Their action must go farther and faster than the action of capitalism." Workers organize not only because the nature of their work pushes them to do so, but also because they decide to do so, whether or not they have been pushed, and because they learn something from the process of organizing itself, from the political experience of grouping themselves (*OJJ* 6:130–31). This is why the process of organizing has the potential to go "farther and faster" than the development of a capitalist economy might dictate. Organizing, like other aspects of democratic politics, tends to build on itself.

So far, much of this speech reworks themes that Jaurès had developed earlier in the decade, themes that were by this time common currency among French ministerialists, German revisionists, and their counterparts elsewhere. Adherents of a "new socialist politics" would not wait for a moment of crisis to carry out a revolution but would be active right away, in unions and in legislatures, working to extend the logic of democracy into the economic sphere. They would be unapologetic about the imperfection of their achievements, using their small share of political power to win what they could, as Millerand was trying to do within the Waldeck-Rousseau government. All this would have been evident to the members of Jaurès's audience, from the first moments of his speech. But Jaurès follows the idea of a reformist socialism through to its moral consequences and inward *ressorts* in a way few others did.

Reluctant to jettison the Marxist language of revolution, Jaurès has nevertheless committed himself to a gradual process of political "evolution." How to reconcile these two elements of his political thought would seem to be no easy task. What Jaurès does here is to use words like "révolution" and "communisme" in a way that shifts their meaning. Within the old language inherited as the common tradition of socialism, a new way of thinking about politics takes shape. Consider some of the passages in this speech where Jaurès comes closest to endorsing the idea of a fundamental change in the structure of society at a future point in time. "There is a revolution in a society only when that society carries within itself a contradiction that it cannot resolve without passing to another form of society. Just this is what dooms capitalism. . . . Little by little the workers perceive that since they produce in common, they could very well possess in common, and so communism appears as the means of resolving the internal contradiction that capitalism carries, and that capitalism itself cannot resolve without perishing" (*OJJ* 6:129). Perhaps capitalism's "internal contradiction" cannot be *resolved* permanently except by a transition to communism, but Jaurès has already suggested that this contradiction might be *managed* indefinitely. If this is so, a "revolution" that brings about "communism" appears here as a hypothetical proposition, as an illustration of the socialist critique of capitalism's "internal contradiction" but not as an expectation regarding a future form of society. Workers perceive not that they "will," but that they "could," "possess in common." Jaurès suggests that the process by which workers gradually organize themselves must somehow be defined in relation to the ideal of communism, but he gives no reason why socialists ought to expect to arrive at that hypothetical end point. Similarly, when discussing Marx's "dialectic" theory of history: "The dialectic does not imply that the ultimate reconciliation will yield one single concept or be achieved at one single moment. There can well be intermediary concepts, many intermediary forms of society, that lead gradually up to the complete solution of the fundamental contradiction that imperils society. We can thus keep the dialectical method, the power of the dialectical interpretation of history, without renouncing that positive, graduated, immediate, effective action which is today, more and more, the law of militant socialism" (*OJJ* 6:129–30).

There are two ideas at stake here. One is the idea of a "complete solution" of social contradictions, a state of perfect harmony between individual and society. The other is the idea of an abrupt and qualitative change in the form of society, a rupture with the present. These two ideas were at the center of the old socialist politics. In Jaurès's new socialist politics, however, both of these ideas are softly displaced. The "complete solution," in this passage, slips from its old position at the forefront of socialist consciousness, as Jaurès suggests that the life of the socialist movement takes place and will continue to take place within the "intermediary forms of society," neither fully capitalist nor fully socialist. The work of "militant socialism," socialism active in the real world, will yield incomplete solutions, and socialists should do this work knowingly.

As to whether a moment of rupture with the present order of society will ever arrive, Jaurès remains carefully agnostic.

> It is certain that every great social revolution happens both through a slow economic preparation or evolution and through the decisive intervention of the oppressed class, when that economic evolution is advanced enough to allow an effective revolutionary intervention. . . . But it is difficult for men to know at what moment a new society is possible. There are sure signs of maturation for crops or fruit, but it is much more difficult to know if a new society is ripe since very often the maturity of the human harvest is measured by the inner feelings of the harvester. There is really no sure sign that the hour for a decisive revolutionary

intervention has come. But that is not a reason to deny that there is always the possibility of a point in history where sufficiently developed economic evolution and decisive intervention by the oppressed class meet to produce a great historic shift. (*OJJ* 6:130–31)

Who can say with certainty that there will never be a dramatic break in the continuity of history? Jaurès seems to shrug his shoulders here. But one thing is certain: even if such a moment awaits us, there is no way to know when it is at hand, and so Jaurès argues that the labor movement ought not to retain old ways of thinking that tend to "immobilize it in a hallucinatory expectation of the future society." Speculation about a moment of rupture is at best unimportant; at worst, it makes socialists less able to comprehend what is going on around them, and less able to respond prudently to the circumstances in which they find themselves. What is important is the attitude socialists take toward the question of "method" in the present. Thus Jaurès admits that, whatever their other differences, he heartily joins Bernstein in endorsing "the action—the direct, immediate, daily, continuous, reforming intervention—of the organized proletariat" (*OJJ* 6:131).

What Jaurès has done here is to transform the communist "solution" from a literal expectation to a symbol. Jaurès has assured his listeners that their common language need not be abandoned, even though he has also suggested that the words of that language can be used to say new things. What Jaurès seems to understand, and what Bernstein seems not to have understood, is that the cohesion of their movement depends on continuity with its own past, even— perhaps especially—at a moment when a new way of thinking is introduced.

Bernstein had been warned of just this point by Ignaz Auer, an elder of German social democracy, who wrote in a letter: "Do you think it is really possible that a party which has literature going back fifty years, an organization going back forty years and a still older tradition, can change its direction like this in the twinkling of an eye? For the most influential members of the party to behave as you demand would simply mean splitting the party and throwing decades of work to the winds. My dear Ede, one doesn't formally decide to do what you ask, one doesn't say it, one *does* it."[36] When Jaurès acknowledges his respect for the common traditions of the socialist movement, he is recognizing that, within the movement itself, as within the polity, change can (and ought to) occur without rupture. In both the "evolution of socialist method" and the "economic evolution" of society, the new appears continuous with the old. Gradually, as a result of many preparatory changes, socialism has arrived at a point where a policy of intransigent opposition can and should be eclipsed by a method of democratic reform. Gradually, as a result of many preparatory changes, France has arrived at a point where the Declaration of the Rights of Man can and should be interpreted not as a justification for a capitalist—and therefore a stunted—republic but as a demand for an enlarged, richer, expansive form of republican life, in which democratic procedures are extended to the economic sphere and in which the full dignity of citizenship is extended to the working class. Just as the Left can enter its new era of maturity still speaking its old socialist language, so France can make room for socialism while still keeping its old republican traditions.

When Auer warned Bernstein against proclaiming his revisionist ideas in public, he seems to have worried that, without confidence in the "final goal of socialism," the movement's members would simply give up. To tell party militants that the moment of revolution was not near, that the ideal of communism might be no more than a symbolic solution for all-too-literal problems would be to undo years of party building. Who would risk life and limb in a strike or demonstration, who would risk imprisonment or exile—or, for that matter, who would devote countless hours to the tedium of meetings and organizing—for a movement that did not promise to bring about a wholly new form of society? Bereft of their common goal, what would keep union and cooperative and party activists talking with one another? The moral price of reformism, Auer saw, would be the loss of the revolutionary hope that made possible a cohesive and growing movement. Better to engage in reformist politics without admitting out loud that one was doing so.

Jaurès sees the danger Auer saw, but he wants to say out loud what he is doing. He has introduced a new socialist politics as smoothly as he can, but nevertheless he has also admitted that there is something new here. At the root of Jaurès's politics, we find a commitment to the immediate work of political reform. Everything else distinctive in his political vision stems from this decision regarding "socialist method." This commitment gives rise to a problem, and because Jaurès has announced this commitment, he cannot avoid the problem. The kind of political hope that can sustain this new socialist politics will have to arise from within the socialist method itself.

In one of the more remarkable passages in his speech on Bernstein, or in any of his speeches, Jaurès takes up to the moral question raised by the new method.

> Some say to me, "In preaching to the proletariat immediate action, trade union action, cooperative action, daily effort, the reforms that little by little must lift the proletariat up to the level of power where it can indeed fulfill the revolution—in preaching all this you seem to grant capitalist society too long a life, too distant a limit. Be careful when you recommend to the workers a reformist organization and a reformist method because, even though this method will in the end amount to revolutionary action, you still seem to see the collectivist or communist order as a remote paradise of which one can only dream, while in the meantime you counsel the proletariat to settle on the capitalist earth."
>
> I do not understand how this question of date could divide us. It is not for any of us, on either side, to prophesy. Bernstein puts off the transformation of society to an indeterminate period, floating in the hazy future. Kautsky declares that he does not think it imprudent to say that if German socialist democracy progresses in the next thirty years like it has in the past thirty, there is a strong chance that the social revolution will be achieved then.
>
> But I think all these calculations of dates are pointless and vain, and if someone says that we are postponing the socialist ideal, that we are making a sort of paradise out of it, then as for me, I say that this paradise could be as close to the believers as they believe. I say that if they believed it truly, this paradise could be for them the deepening of their momentary existence—or rather, it could be present in their very existence, if they had the feeling that each of their acts, each of their thoughts, each of their words respond to it, hold to it, and shape future events, high and low. Well, then, I ask the socialists not to specify the date when socialism will be able to triumph; that is impossible to determine. I say to them to live always in a socialist state of grace—I mean, to always work, in each minute, in each hour, to bring about socialism and to rediscover in it all the effort, all the action, all the power of their thoughts and of their lives. This we can do now, from today onward, because we have what I would call a victorious certainty. We are certain that, whatever may be the date of the event, all humanity will be waiting for it when it comes. We know

that things follow such a course, that economic evolution and the march of the proletariat have such a direction, that no revolution will be made in the world, whether political or religious or social, if it is not *ours*. (*OJJ* 6:134–35)[37]

The first charge against him, as Jaurès relates it, is that he has made the communist ideal insufferably distant, rendering it incapable of inspiring personal sacrifice or political loyalty. Curiously, he does not deny a second and corresponding charge that he has asked the labor movement to accept the longevity of an unjust and conflict-ridden social order. His response, instead, is to invert the first charge: the ideal is already present, here on the capitalist earth. Gone is the ambiguity of his writings about Luther: Jaurès's hope now is not for a socialist paradise but for a socialist state of grace. What Jaurès recommends to his listeners is that they not think of their day-to-day political work as a means to the end of a new society in which that political work will become unnecessary, but that they see in that work itself the presence of the socialist ideal—the ideal of freedom and fraternity—within the world. Socialism is not a state of affairs to be realized at some future point in time, or even an abstract ideal against which actions are to be measured. It is here, now—the secret meaning within or underneath every small task that makes up the movement's work, a new appreciation of a quality or dimension that can be felt at every moment in the political life of a socialist.

Thus, even when Jaurès uses imagery of future events in the passage above, he does so in a way that seems more than anything else like a symbol for an experience in the present. Rather than invoking a "certainty of victory," he invites socialists to feel "a victorious certainty." Rather than saying "our revolution will be made," he says that "no revolution will be made . . . if it is not *ours*." The important thing is not the content or the timing of future events; it is that socialists can live "now, from today onward" in such a way that they find "all the power of their thoughts and of their lives" as if for the first time.

Bernstein had written that the movement carries its goal within itself. Jaurès's idea here is similar, up to a point. What Jaurès adds when he makes socialism analogous to a state of spiritual grace, however, is a sense that the movement's goal is at the same time realized and unrealized, present and absent, tangible and untouchable. Jaurès shares the view he had attributed to Robespierre: that democracy should be taken as both means and end. He sees a likeness between the socialist means and the socialist end, but this is not the same as saying that no distinction can be made between them. The end is present within the means, for Jaurès, but in a mediated way: the full glory of the ideal end remains hidden. Thus there is a self-critical edge to Jaurès's socialism—or, better, a current of doubt within Jaurès's socialist belief. To experience grace, after all, is not the same as seeing God face to face. We see socialism whenever we recruit union members or go on strike or advocate for social welfare legislation or attend a meeting of a socialist party subcommittee, Jaurès seems to say—but we see it through a glass, darkly. Something remains out of sight, and to forget that would be to reduce socialism to the immediate organizational needs of the unions and parties and other organizations that make up the movement.

Jaurès's choice of words like "believers" and "grace" to convey this notion must have surprised his audience; it certainly seems to have moved them since they interrupted him with applause three times during this part of his speech.[38] When Jaurès refers to socialists as "believers," he reveals that he does not want to reduce his politics to the pursuit of a particular set of policies or to the use of a particular strategy. The revolution he has in mind, he says, might be "political or religious or social." It is not quite clear what a religious revolution means, but the phrase certainly suggests some inward transformation, some renovation of inner life. This was not, in itself, a new notion for socialists. The generations of militants who had built the labor movement from nothing, enduring the oppression of empires and monarchies, must have experienced an inward transformation as well. Adherents of the old socialist politics would have needed to acquire an uncommon confidence in the coming total victory of their movement. Adherents of the new socialist politics, Jaurès thinks, will need to acquire an uncommon affection for the process of political activity itself. They will need to be receptive to the ways that a sustaining hope might well up within democratic political life, every day.

How to understand the daily work of politics—that was the root of the ministerialism and revisionism debates. At the beginning of his speech, Jaurès aligns himself with Kautsky against Bernstein. At the end, when he turns to that root problem, he distances himself from both. Jaurès is certain that there is no disagreement between Bernstein and himself on the need for "practical action" (indeed, if Bernstein were French, Jaurès suggests, he would also have supported Millerand). The difference between them arises from the fact that Bernstein thinks practical action to be incompatible with Marxist theory and thus with the idea of class struggle, whereas Jaurès does not. Thus, according to Jaurès, Bernstein has called not only for "cooperation" between but the "melding" of the labor movement and its liberal—or, in France, republican— allies. Kautsky, for his part, has accepted some cooperation between labor and the liberal bourgeoisie, but only reluctantly; he wants the proletariat to keep as much as possible to "the integrity of its isolation." Or, as Jaurès explains:

> In this, I agree with neither Kautsky nor Bernstein. Contrary to Bern-stein, I hold that the classes are radically distinct, radically antagonistic. But, contrary to Kautsky, I hold that it is not necessary to fear the mul-tiplicity of meetings and contacts between the working class—mistress of its own consciousness and action—and other classes. Here is why: it is impossible for one class to act without enlarging the surface of contact between it and the rest of human society. To act is necessarily to mix itself in the universal movement. There is no form of action in which the proletariat will not be exposed to collaboration and cooperation with elements of another class. (*OJJ* 6:138)

Jaurès wants to allow for both the fact of conflict and the possibility of coop-eration; he thinks that Kautsky and Bernstein each hold to one of those ele-ments while neglecting the other. Political life may be a quest for harmony, but that quest is necessary because antagonism is real. That antagonism, after all, is why Jaurès holds on to parts of Marx's social theory: class conflict needs an explanation. For all his generous humanism and passion for reconciliation, Jaurès retains a realism about conflict that he accuses Bernstein of lacking. As long as politics is a struggle for power, a group that seeks to engage in that struggle will need its own organizations. But even though the working class needs distinct organizations to express its distinct interests, it is not alone in the world. Relations between the labor movement and the organizations of other classes sometimes take the form of conflict, but not always. When Jaurès says that the classes are "radically antagonistic," he means that they have opposed interests. But because they have common interests as well, their antag-onism need not be a fight to the finish.

Although Jaurès joins Kautsky in appreciating the labor movement's importance as a distinct political force, he charges Kautsky with misunder-standing what labor actually does. Kautsky sees the unions and parties and other groups that make up the movement as "secondary instruments for win-ning short-term and temporary results" (*OJJ* 6:136–37). This view assumes that the labor movement's primary purpose is to do something utterly different, with permanent consequences, at some point in the future—that is, when the revolutionary moment arrives. A shared certainty of victory, in Kautsky's view, binds the movement's members together. But Jaurès has already expressed his skepticism about that victory and made clear that his intention is to help socialists think through the activities they are engaged in now. When he calls for members of his movement to "live now in a socialist state of grace," he is asking his listeners to conceive of their movement's "daily effort" in a particular way. To be "mistress of its own . . . action," the labor movement will need its own organizations; to be "mistress of its own consciousness," it will need to understand those organizations not as "secondary instruments" but as the substance through which the movement's ideal is made present. The kind of movement Jaurès wants to evoke here will define itself by its method: socialism, for Jaurès, is a set of practices that turn the logic of democracy against the logic of capitalism, that make room on the capitalist earth for freedom and solidarity. The members of such a movement will share an ideal not in the sense that they await the same future event, but in that they have adopted a common norm by which to align their various present activities.

Outside a political state of grace, such variety would undo a movement. Electoral campaigns, legislative debates, union organizing, strikes, cooperative workshops, *bourses du travail*, journalism, scholarship—these activities are quite different from one another, and those who engage in each will tend to jealously defend the importance of what they do. Thus, when Jaurès tells socialist "believers" that "each of their acts, each of their thoughts, each of their words" echoes a single common ideal, he is making a counterintuitive claim. A more intuitive claim, made by the syndicalists, on one side, and certain of Millerand's (or Bernstein's) supporters, on the other, would be that socialists would need to choose between union militancy and parliamentary compromise. Jaurès refuses that choice; he wants socialists to be able to further the logic of democracy in any number of divergent ways while still seeing one another as fellow socialists. A "state of grace" is inward and personal, but those persons who live in it are joined together, assembled into a particular kind of community: their inward experience turns them outward, away from what Jaurès had in his French thesis called "the mean and egoistic self," toward one another, and beyond. When Jaurès invokes a socialist state of grace, then, he means in part that, despite the inevitable tensions among the movement's components, each contributes to a common project that will be intelligible only if "each of their acts" is felt to mediate—in its particular and incomplete way—a common ideal.

Accordingly, to explain why he thinks Kautsky fails to appreciate the real significance of the labor movement, Jaurès exchanges the imagery of time for the imagery of shared or public space—imagery more closely associated with the republican tradition than with Marxism. Political life consists of antagonism, Jaurès says, but also of meeting and mixing. The meaning of ministerialism is not that the working class has begun to dissolve its organizations into those of the liberal bourgeoisie, but that the "surface of contact" between the working class and other organized groups has increased as the internal coherence and external power of the working class have grown. The work of socialism, Jaurès suggests, consists and will continue to consist of activity within spaces—nations, cities, the buildings and rooms of governing institutions— that are shared with other movements and classes. Activity in shared spaces inevitably entails some antagonism, but it also entails some "collaboration and cooperation." People in a crowded room bump elbows, but they also look one another in the eyes and hear one another's voices. This complicated mixture of antagonism and cooperation is not a temporary inconvenience, to be abolished later on. It is political life itself, and any revolution in a sense that Jaurès can accept will occur within it.

Interested as he is in the contours of actual political life, Jaurès wants to convince his listeners that ordinary forms of political cooperation, like an electoral alliance or a multiparty governing coalition, have a moral significance beyond their immediate achievements. Nearing the end of his speech, Jaurès declares: "Either the proletariat will refrain from action, or it will constantly mix with the action of other classes. The essential thing is that throughout this mixing, this tumult of elements, it always acts according to its class consciousness, with its distinct and organized power. And if, as a distinct party, it extends its surface of contact with other classes—as for me, I will not object. We want the revolution, but we do not want eternal hatred" (*OJJ* 6:139). If there are times when the labor movement finds itself in unlikely alliances with its sometime enemies, this should not be seen as merely a pragmatic accommodation to the contingencies of power. Such accommodation can be properly comprehended only if it is understood as the mediation of an ideal: such a moment points in the direction opposite to eternal hatred. "Ah, what joy there is for men who have hated and detested one another to recognize one another in these moments of convergence, in these instances of cooperation.

Consequently, what joy—what sublime, universal, eternal joy—there will be on the day when we see the ultimate convergence of all men!" (*OJJ* 6:140).[39]

No one who had listened closely to Jaurès could at this point think that he expected this ultimate convergence to occur on a real day. He might—with more precision but less emotive power—have put these two ideas the other way around: we can imagine a time of ultimate reconciliation, and consequently we can rejoice in moments of proximate reconciliation. We can find moral sustenance in events that, to an observer who looks only at the surface of things, might seem to have no meaning beyond their usefulness within a political strategy. Thus, at the end of his speech, in calling on his listeners to build a unified socialist party, when Jaurès asks them to offer France and the world an example of "socialist fraternity" that can stand in contrast with "the divisions of bourgeois society" (*OJJ* 6:140), he is proposing more than a program of action. He is also proposing that the prosaic activities of party building be seen as the manifestation of a fraternal impulse that no organization or institution can exhaust.

THE QUESTION OF METHOD

As Jaurès himself acknowledged, his "new socialist politics" required new ways of thinking about political action and about the moral dynamics of political commitment. Jules Guesde also sensed something new emerging through the ministerialism debate. In September 1900, he published an article in an antiministerialist newspaper, the *Petit Sou*, retracting his previous support for the Third Republic's institutions and declaring now—as he had in the 1880s—that it made no difference to the socialist movement whether it carried on its struggle within a republic or under a monarchy.[1] Like the leaders of the other revolutionary socialist groups, the Blanquists and Allemanists, Guesde had slowly accustomed himself to parliamentary work and tacit cross-class coalitions, but now he and they recoiled from them. His *Petit Sou* article rejected Jaurès's method of reform and denounced Jaurès's idea that socialism meant a rehabilitation of older democratic and republican ideas. Guesde spoke for many antiministerialists who now realized, as had Jaurès, that the debate over Alexandre Millerand was a debate over more than Millerand.

It was also a debate with resonance outside of France. Since 1889, delegates from the world's socialist and labor parties had gathered from time to time to express their solidarity with one another and to discuss the direction of their movement. This loose network of organizations, variously referred to as "the Socialist and Labor International," "the Socialist International," or more simply "the International," had been the site of deliberations about questions such as the strategic uses of mass strikes, the proper relationship between trade unions and socialist parties, and the ethics of revolutionary violence. The International had made the first of May a day of annual worldwide demonstrations and had served as the forum for communication among parties and labor organizations that might otherwise have remained isolated within their national borders.[2] It was evident that the ministerialism controversy would find its way onto the International's agenda before long, just as German revisionism had found its way into the French socialists' own discussions.

The Fifth Congress of the Socialist and Labor International was held in Paris in September 1900, immediately followed by the Second General Congress of French Socialist Organizations. Guesde submitted to both gatherings resolutions condemning ministerialism. The ensuing debate at the International congress was fierce, with French delegates prominent on both sides; British delegate Henry Hyndman wrote that he witnessed expressions of "Gallic fraternity [that] could scarcely be distinguished from a keen disposition for mutual slaughter."[3] Now, however, the French ministerialists and German revisionists marshaled delegates more successfully than they had at their own party congresses the previous year. Despite the efforts of Guesde and his allies, the International congress passed a compromise resolution—written by Karl Kautsky, as orthodox a Marxist as anyone but too shrewd a political operator to invite an unnecessary split in the movement—which treated ministerialism as a tactical question, not a question of principle. This was hardly an endorsement, but it gave reformists the doctrinal breathing room they wanted, and it was understood by everyone as a defeat for Guesde.[4] At the French congress, the Guesdists recognized that they were outnumbered and walked out before any votes took place, clearing the way for a resolution praising the ministerialist deputies in the Chamber. The Guesdists had, in effect, quit the Parti socialiste français.[5]

When Jaurès and Guesde met that October in Lille to debate their opposing "méthodes," each accused the other of weakening socialism.[6] The mood of this debate was contentious, with each speaker interrupted more than once by hecklers or critics in the audience. Jaurès argued that, by training socialists' attention on the prospect of a revolutionary crisis in the future, Guesde was in effect calling for "abstention" from the exercise of political power in the present. The movement's method ought to entail "entering into action and taking part in events," and that had to include "parliamentary action," which would inevitably draw socialists into coalitions with other parties (*OJJ* 6:202). The growing power of French socialism revealed something that had not been obvious to most socialists of an earlier era: that a society is not a monolith. Jaurès declared: "All the world's great revolutions have been made because the new society, before blooming, has put down roots into all the fissures in the soil of the old society"(*OJJ* 6:206). As long as socialism took the form of an oppositional movement, a protest against the existing society, socialists would tend to think of that society as an undifferentiated solid mass. But the experience of having a small share of political power had taught socialists to see their society as porous, penetrable, variegated. Guesde, in turn, argued that any political power short of the power to make revolution was an illusion. He charged that ministerialism disarmed socialists because it rendered them unable to take a consistently oppositional stance, stripping them of the revolutionary aims that had made their politics distinctive. Guesde and Jaurès agreed that something had changed in the character of the socialist movement as it had grown. Their difference was that Jaurès endorsed this change, whereas Guesde wanted to recover from it.

At the third French socialist congress, held in Lyon in May 1901, the Blanquists and their allies walked out after the congress voted down their proposal to expel Millerand from the PSF. With the Guesdists and Blanquists both departed, the Parti socialiste français now had an unshakable ministerialist majority. A few smaller antiministerialist groups left the PSF within that year; by the spring of 1902, the party was ready to reconstitute itself. It adopted a new platform, most likely written by Jaurès, which defined socialism as the effort "to transfer into the economic order the democracy that has already been in part realized within the political order," and which took hope from the "tendency of political democracy to enlarge itself into social democracy." The new PSF platform included a perfunctory reference to the "total transformation of society" and allowed for "the possibility of revolutionary events" but affirmed that the heart of the party's project was the effort to mobilize "the great strength which the conscious, organized proletariat can employ within democracy." "Too often the workers neglect to profit by the means of action which democracy and the republic put into their hands. They do not demand from trade-unionist action, co-operative action, or universal suffrage all that those forms of action can give. No phrase, no device, can enable the working class to dispense with the constant effort of organization and education."[7] The question for socialists, then, was precisely how they should engage in such a "constant effort," in a reformist project with no revolutionary end in sight.

Later that year, the Guesdists, Blanquists, and other antiministerialist groups would found the Parti socialiste de France (PSdeF), a self-described "party of revolution" emphatically opposed to any alliances between socialists and bourgeois parties. The split within French socialism appeared to be complete. Jaurès was now the leader of a party explicitly committed to a method of democratic reform.[8]

During the late summer and fall of 1901, as it became clear that the break between the reformist and revolutionary socialists could not be prevented, Jaurès wrote a series of articles for *La Petite République* that were published as a collection later that year in Charles Péguy's *Cahiers de la Quinzaine*, and published again the next year by Éditions des Cahiers as the book *Études socialistes.*[9] Before this, Jaurès had commended to socialists the "daily effort" of reformist politics. He now wanted to say something about what that effort would be like. If political life was not a mere reflection of or consequence of economic life, if politics could reshape society, then adherents of Jaurès's new socialist politics would need to have a new way of thinking about the dynamics of political life. In some of these "études," Jaurès uses the writings of unimpeachably orthodox German Marxists, such as the recently deceased and much-loved Wilhelm Liebknecht or even Marx and Engels themselves, to argue that his reformist position was not a departure from the socialist tradition.[10] But even though Jaurès still wants to preserve his connection with that tradition, he is also more willing than before to take a frankly nonrevolutionary position. Thus, in other essays, he argues forcefully against the revolutionary socialists and devotes more attention than before to understanding the logic of reform itself.

In "Le socialisme et la vie" (Socialism and life; *OJJ* 6:353–60), Jaurès asserts that socialism stems from the central principle of modern French politics: individual rights within the context of a republic.[11] This republican understanding of socialism (or socialist understanding of republicanism) is premised on an ethical commitment. The Third French Republic gives institutional form to the ideals of liberty, equality, and fraternity, Jaurès suggests, but those ideals can take only truncated forms within any capitalist republic. Fuller freedom, substantial equality, firmer and more inclusive solidarities—that is, a more complete realization of justice—require the kinds of economic and political reforms that socialists characteristically champion. Thus socialism is not only a concern of workers: "To be socialist is, for everyone, an obligation derived from the principle of justice" (*OJJ* 6:353). The responsibility of the labor movement is to awaken the French Republic to a more authentic recognition of principles it already holds.

> I know well that the revolutionary bourgeoisie slipped a tone of oligarchy, a spirit of class, into the Declaration of the Rights of Man. I know well that they attempted to consecrate for all time the bourgeois form of property, and that within the political order they began by refusing the right of suffrage to millions of the poor, making them passive citizens. But I also know that, from the start, democrats appealed to the rights of man, of all men, to demand and to win the right of suffrage for all. I know that, from the start, the workers depended on the Rights of Man to buttress their economic demands. I know that the working class, even though it had only a rudimentary existence in 1789, did not hesitate to put the Declaration of the Rights of Man into practice, to broaden it by giving it a proletarian meaning. They proclaimed, starting in 1792, that the right to one's own life is the first of all rights, and that the law of this highest form of property must be asserted over all others. (*OJJ* 6:353–54)

In the *Histoire socialiste*, Jaurès argued that socialism began with the confluence of the labor movement and the idea of rights. He repeats that argument here: "Socialism emerged from the French Revolution from the combined action of two forces: the force of the idea of right, and the force of the action of the nascent proletariat" (*OJJ* 6:356). But his emphasis now is on the moral claim that socialism makes on every person who admits an obligation to seek justice—that is, every person who acknowledges the moral meaning of citizenship in a republic.

> So, magnify and embolden the meaning of the word *life*. Understand it not only as subsistence, but as the whole of life, as the development of all human faculties, and it becomes clear that the proletariat grafts onto the Declaration of the Rights of Man nothing less than communism. Thus, from the start, the human rights proclaimed by the Revolution had a deeper and broader meaning than that given them by the revolutionary bourgeoisie. That given meaning—a narrow and oligarchic justice—was not the full extent of human rights: the bed of the river was broader than the river, and there had to be a new stream, a proletarian and human swell, for the idea of justice to be fulfilled at last.
>
> Socialism will restore the meaning of the Declaration of the Rights of Man, and will be the full realization of human rights. (*OJJ* 6:354)

The theory of justice encapsulated in the Declaration of the Rights of Man points to the ideal of communism, that is, to the image of a society in which economic production serves, and is under the control of, the community as a whole. For the communist consequences of the principle of individual rights to become evident, all that is necessary is that the individual's right to full human development be understood as the source and measure of all other rights. But, by itself, all this is merely "vague philosophical speculation," Jaurès writes. Only "through the action of the workers" can this communist interpretation of the idea of human rights become "a party, a living force." Everything the labor movement does—organizing, propaganda, mutual aid, demonstrations, strikes, bargaining with employers—reveals that existing property arrangements impede human development. As this injustice becomes apparent to all, the moral obligation to reform property arrangements becomes apparent as well. Socialists had their moral and strategic reasons for accepting cross-class political coalitions; bourgeois republicans, for their part, had a duty to ally with the Left, whether or not they had yet accepted this.

This is more complicated than simply mixing idea and active force, principle and interest. The idea of rights may have always had communist implications, but in fact these implications were little remarked upon until the working class asserted itself, Jaurès points out. The labor movement, in turn, might have self-interested reasons for reinterpreting the idea of individual rights, but by picking up the idea of rights it did more than acquire a rhetorical tool. When the labor movement began to use the idea of rights to structure its demands, it also began to think in a new way. By claiming rights, it admitted obligations. Thus when Jaurès begins "Le socialisme et la vie" with the claim that everyone has an obligation to be socialist, he is reminding the labor movement of the controversial claim he had made during the Dreyfus Affair: that the labor movement has an obligation to every victim of injustice. When the idea of rights and the action of the labor movement are mixed, both are changed.

Jaurès is concerned here with the notion that organizations and ideas shape each other. In his speech on Bernstein, Jaurès had argued that democracy has a force or a logic of its own. The process of political reform, it seems, exhibits that logic. Each change in organizational or institutional life tends to foster a change in ideas or consciousness—and the other way around, as well.

In the two "études" that most directly challenge the theories of his revolutionary counterparts, Jaurès expands on the democratic logic through which ideas and institutions influence one another. In "Grève générale et révolution" (General strike and revolution; *OJJ* 6:331–43), Jaurès responds to the doctrine of revolutionary syndicalism.[12] He begins by granting the syndicalists their premise that a general strike was plausible. What then, Jaurès asks, are the conditions under which a general strike might be successful? There are three, he proposes:

1. The working class must have a real and profound passion for the objective it has declared.
2. The greater part of public opinion must be prepared to recognize the legitimacy of this objective.
3. The general strike must not seem at all to be a disguise for violence; it must be simply the exercise of the legal right to strike, although in a broader and more systematic way and with a marked class character. (*OJJ* 6:332)

The initial problem for advocates of the general strike, Jaurès argues, is that the passion and courage required to carry out such an action can be elicited "only by an interest that is both very great and very near, by an objective very important and immediately achievable." In his speech on Bernstein, Jaurès had proposed that socialists see their "activity" as the mediation of their ideal; here he is interested in the way the movement's ultimate end is mediated by its proximate ends, by the specific reforms that it might win: for instance, the groups of workers that are "best organized" and "most conscious" might become passionate about a concrete demand like the eight-hour day, old-age or disability pensions, or unemployment insurance. Perhaps they would engage in a mass strike for such "encompassing and well-defined objectives, for extensive, clear, and immediately achievable reforms" (*OJJ* 6:332). But Jaurès warns that

> the working class will not rise up for a general formula, like the coming of communism. The idea of the social revolution will not be enough to carry them along. The socialist idea, the communist idea, is powerful enough to guide and order the successive efforts of the proletariat. It is to draw nearer to that idea each day, it is to realize that idea gradually that the proletariat organizes and struggles. But, for a great movement to be aroused, the idea of the social revolution must be embodied in specific demands. . . . It is not enough to say: "Communism!" because the workers will immediately ask: "Which communism? What will tomorrow be like if we win?" Great movements are not made for objectives that are too general, with blurry outlines. They must have a solid fulcrum, a specific mooring. (*OJJ* 6:335)

The only way syndicalist leaders might spark a general strike, then, would be by using specific demands to motivate workers' action in the hope that the strikers would, to their own surprise, find themselves in a revolutionary situation, fighting for the introduction of a new social order they had not anticipated. Thus the worst thing about the syndicalist leaders, Jaurès writes, is this: "THEY TRICK THE WORKING CLASS" (*OJJ* 6:335). Jaurès sees this as a moral outrage. He also argues that it is a strategic error. For how can the workers remain committed to their movement when they realize that its goals have changed in ways they did not want or expect? Although syndicalism sees itself as an anarchistic movement, in the end, it depends on leaders' making decisions on behalf of their passive and malleable followers. If those followers turn out not to be so malleable, the movement is liable to collapse as soon as its leaders ask their followers to do things for which they are not prepared.

Even if syndicalists could overcome workers' tendency to "recoil before an enterprise so vague and hollow" as a revolutionary strike (*OJJ* 6:336), they would face further problems. Jaurès maps out in some detail the strategic moves and countermoves of a hypothetical revolutionary situation, considering the roles of cities, railroads, food supplies, communications, the army, whatever armed force the revolutionaries might put together, whatever armed groups might be formed by citizens opposed to the revolution, and the geographic dispersal of strikers' workplaces, to conclude that a general strike would result in civil war, extensive sabotage, and the isolation of localities from one another. The revolutionaries would be driven into actions that would undermine their purposes.

> The only recourse left to the forces of the working class, astonished by their powerlessness at the moment of their apparent victory, will be destruction. . . . We can see clearly that the revolutionary tactic of the general strike has the objective and the effect of breaking economic and social life to bits. To stop locomotives, halt steamers, deny industrial machines their coal is to replace the single common life of the nation with the scattered life of innumerable local groups. This chopping up of life IS THE EXACT OPPOSITE OF THE REVOLUTION. . . . Every great revolution exalts life, and this exaltation is possible only through the consciousness of an encompassing unity, through the ardent communication of strengths and enthusiasms. (*OJJ* 6:341)

A serious effort to think through the idea of a general strike, Jaurès concludes, reveals that "there is only one ruling method for socialism today: winning the support of a majority through lawful means." No other method can at the same time express, preserve, and deepen the "encompassing unity" of the nation (*OJJ* 6:343).

Jaurès has turned the syndicalist dream of the general strike into an illustration of the logic of reform. As an exceptionally demanding form of political action, the general strike serves Jaurès's argument well because it throws into relief dynamics that are present less dramatically within more modest forms of political action. The essential point is that conscious commitment to political action requires comprehensible goals. To hold in one's mind the relationship between the risk one takes immediately and the goal one hopes to achieve requires that the goal in question not strain one's imagination, that it not require too distant a leap of faith. With an incomprehensible, imagination-straining goal—like the idea of an actual transition to communism—one is left only with the possibility of a political movement whose members are less than fully self-aware, a movement that depends too much on the guidance of leaders and too little on the deliberation and intention of ordinary members.

Strengths and enthusiasms "communicate," Jaurès notes. The organizational strength of a political movement depends on the enthusiasm of its members, we might say, and that enthusiasm, in turn, depends on the members' confidence that their movement is strong enough to attain the goals it has set—that it has set goals within the limits of its strength.

Thus progress toward the increased strength of a movement and progress toward its increasingly ambitious goals happen in tandem. The only way to build a movement organizationally strong enough and internally enthusiastic enough to achieve profound social change is to seek, at every step, proximate and modest goals. Those goals represent the fragmentary realization of the ideal that guides and orders the movement; that ideal has the power to inspire enthusiasm because it comes down to earth in the movement's immediate tasks and small achievements. In the end, Jaurès wants to say, there is no feasible method of establishing justice except the method of seeking one proximate goal after another—that is, the method of reform.

If this part of Jaurès's argument holds true, then even though the enthusiasm of movement members need not be shared by all members of their society, they will still need to draw outright opposition from as few of their fellow citizens as possible and to win at least tacit support from as many as possible. Jaurès had written two weeks earlier, in an article titled "Majorités révolutionaires" (Revolutionary majorities; *OJJ* 6:301–6):[13]

> Those great social changes that we call revolutions cannot, or can no longer be, the work of a minority. To achieve the Revolution, at least in modern societies, a revolutionary minority, however intelligent and energetic, is not enough. It requires the participation and support of a majority, of an immense majority.
>
> It might be—it is a historical puzzle difficult to solve—that there have been some periods in some countries where the human multitude was so passive and formless that the strong will of a few individuals or groups could mold it. But since the constitution of modern nations, since the Reformation and the Renaissance, there has been hardly any individual who is not a distinct force. There is hardly any individual who does not have his own interest, his attachment to the present, his views regarding the future, his passions, his ideas. Thus for some centuries, within modern Europe, every human individual has been a center of energy, of consciousness, of action. And so in periods of transforma-

tion when the old social bonds are unraveling, since every human energy is of equal power, it must obviously be the law of the majority that decides matters. (*OJJ* 6:301)

The power of the individual—which stems, Jaurès seems to suggest, from both the breakdown of outward social hierarchies and the development of new forms of inward self-determination—is what makes modern political life modern. Although the emergence of socialism was in part a product of the modern rebellious spirit, socialists themselves had not yet learned the lesson that followed. The same great social and moral transformation that had given each member of the working class the capacity to defy the social order had at the same time given all other members of society (not to mention all other members of the working class) the capacity to either accept or object to the working class's collective demands.

Jaurès is arguing against both the Blanquist and the Marxist strains in French revolutionary socialism—strains of thought that had converged as the Blanquist and Marxist parties merged into the Parti socialiste de France, though they were still distinguishable. If Jaurès was right about the new power of the modern individual, then Auguste Blanqui's dream of a conspiracy of revolutionary leaders was folly: the masses would not follow as passively as the revolutionary elite would require. Marx and Engels's claim that the unique position of the working class in the process of economic production gave it a unique capacity to bring the social order to a moment of revolutionary crisis could not hold in these circumstances. Indeed, Jaurès denies both parts of this claim. Modern politics is necessarily the politics of majority rule because every member of society is a potential member of any number of possible coalitions. Moreover, the working class has no guarantee of a starring role in history. The labor movement's power is derived not only from its members' roles in economic production, as important as those roles might be, but also from its politics—from its electoral and legislative strategies and its conscious effort to organize workers. The members of the labor movement have only one reliable method of action, Jaurès argues: to try as best they can to earn the support of a majority of their fellow citizens through the slow process of organizing, coalition building, and the pursuit of one concrete, realizable goal after another.

Thus, however little Jaurès has to say about the third condition for a successful general strike—the use of legal and nonviolent means—it is a logically necessary component of his argument. Political organizations and institutions, whether union locals or national parliaments, impose boundaries on behavior. To win either the passionate participation of movement members or the quieter support of the wider public is to enter into a range of organizational and institutional relationships, each of which entails certain constraints. And if the power of the labor movement is necessarily the power it builds through its own organizations and its coalitions with other organized groups, its power will necessarily be both enabled and constrained by the rules and limits governing the various institutions it shares with other members of the political majority it seeks to pull together.

What began as an argument about whether a successful general strike is feasible has become an illustration of the logic of reform. The labor movement, Jaurès suggests, will be perpetually limited by the same factors that make possible its growing power. The organizations of a mass labor movement and the institutions of national politics that allow large numbers of people to join together in support of socialist reforms at the same time limit those people, and thus socialism itself, to means compatible with the survival of those organizations and institutions. There is no way to transcend the limits of the political consciousness of the movement's members or the limits of the political organizations and institutions that gave the movement form without arriving at the dead end of an isolated sect, a club of leaders without willing followers. A genuinely revolutionary moment might arrive—as such moments did in, say, 1789 or 1848—but if it does, it will only be a sped-up version of the normal process of continuous change. It cannot be the radical rupture that Marxist or syndicalist theory imagines.

This is no tragedy, in Jaurès's view. Gradual change is change all the same: the mutual influence of consciousness on organizations and institutions and of organizations and institutions on consciousness shows that a modern society has a capacity for profound self-transformation. That is the logic of reform. Jaurès thinks there is something educational or pedagogical about the day-to-day work of socialism, not only in the trivial sense that the work of any movement includes informing supporters and training leaders, but also in the sense that the "ardent communication of strengths and enthusiasms" generates a dynamic of political learning that changes the quality of movement members' commitments. The nature of an organization—what means it uses, what goals it sets, what opportunities for deliberation it provides, what gains it makes— affects the political consciousness of its members (and, for that matter, of bystanders); it shapes the hopes they entertain and the commitments they undertake. Reforms strengthen the organizations that seek reforms, and thus lead to further reforms—a pattern Jaurès refers to several times in the *Études socialistes* as "revolutionary evolution."

The preface Jaurès wrote for the *Cahiers de la Quinzaine* collection of these essays, titled "Question de méthode" (The question of method; *OJJ* 6:239–66), contains the sharpest critique of Marx and Engels's political thought he had yet offered.[14] Jaurès cites Marx's *Capital* and his earlier work *Critique of Hegel's "Philosophy of Right"* as well as Engels's *Condition of the Working-Class in England in 1844*, but he reserves most of his attention for the *Communist Manifesto,* the Marxist work most likely to have been read by French (or other) socialists at the time.

The fact facing the socialist movement at the dawn of the twentieth century, Jaurès writes, is that "the working class is growing in number, in cohesion, and in consciousness" (*OJJ* 6:242). The question of what the movement ought to do with its newfound power thus becomes unavoidable. This new situation is disorienting—all the more so because, accustomed to marginality, the movement clings to an outmoded explanation of what it is and what it is doing. The problem with Marxism, Jaurès charges, is that it fails to offer a useful answer to the "question of method." Indeed, its account of what socialists should do next had been rendered irrelevant by the growth of the socialist movement itself.

Marx's "decisive merit"—in fact, the only one of Marx's ideas that had "fully stood the profound test of time"—is that he "connected and combined the socialist idea and the working-class movement" (*OJJ* 6:243). Jaurès recognizes that Marx was neither the first nor the only person to have made this connection, but, here again, he is solicitous enough toward Marx's devotees to balance his criticism with praise: Marx refuted both "the empiricism of the working-class movement" and "the utopianism of socialist thought." Jaurès thinks that Marx was right to propose that the labor movement needed to give an account of itself and its ends, and equally right to link the socialist ideal to a "concrete and historical force," but he went wrong when he tried to predict the future of the labor movement. Marx's "method of revolution" failed because it "proceeded from exhausted historical hypotheses and imprecise economic hypotheses." The "rhythm of revolution" Marx sensed in his study of history established the pattern for his own revolutionary expectations, Jaurès tells us.

In France in 1793 and 1830—and, we might add, in England in 1648 and America in 1776—the working classes had been subordinate partners in coalitions led by and dominated by the nascent bourgeoisie. Working-class hopes had been raised and then dashed by these revolutions, but next time it would be different, Marx argued: the working class would seize the upper hand. The problem with this argument, Jaurès writes, is that it assumes that the proletariat will be strong enough to win on its own. There is no precedent for such an uprising, and as the prospect of a one-class revolution comes to seem less and less plausible, Marx's followers become desperate (*OJJ* 6:244–46).

The Marxists of his generation, Jaurès charges, want to find a shortcut through history: in despair at history's refusal to cooperate with Marx's expectations, they want to leap beyond the slow process of revolutionary evolution. Indeed, he argues, it is hard to imagine a revolutionary scenario that does not tempt the proletariat into tactics of "violence and surprise" through which the movement would try "to organize its 'dictatorship,' and to 'conquer democracy' by force." Jaurès left no doubt that he found such a route ethically objectionable, but his argument here is that the Marxists have projected a historiographical error into the future, seeking rupture where they should look for continuity instead. The dream of a revolutionary moment is the fantasy of the powerless: "What the *Manifesto* proposes is not the revolutionary method of a class sure of itself, whose hour has at last come; it is the revolutionary expedient of a weak and impatient class that wants to artificially hasten the course of events" (*OJJ* 6:247–48). French socialists in the era of ministerialism could see what German socialists, hemmed in by the Kaiser's regime, could not imagine: that such expedients were not only ugly and unnecessary, but also unrealistic.

Jaurès comes back to a theme he had broached in his speech on Bernstein, and, without exactly changing his position, he alters the emphasis of his argument in a significant way. Jaurès had argued in that speech that Marx's concept of crisis was not central to his *economic* theory, and thus that one could still be loyal to the Marxist tradition while setting aside that particular idea. Perhaps this was so, but what Jaurès now wants to say is that the concept of crisis is central to Marx's *political* theory, a theory that falls apart because it depends so completely on the conviction that a moment of crisis will be brought about through the contradiction between capital's continued expansion and the workers' continued immiseration. Marx's economic analysis might have been derived through a posteriori methods, but his theory of revolution had an ending chosen in advance. Marx could not admit the possibility that the working class might improve its condition by degrees, thus forestalling a political crisis, because his entire edifice of thought took its outlines from a sort of inverted theology, "a Hegelian transposition of Christianity."

> Just as the Christian God abased himself to the lowest level of suffering humanity in order to wholly redeem humanity, just as the Savior, to save all men, had to reduce himself to a nearly animal state of lowliness, a level below which no man can be found, just as that infinite abasement of God was the condition for the infinite restoration of man, so in the dialectic of Marx the proletariat, the modern Savior, must be despoiled of all security, deprived of all rights, lowered to the lowest historical and social nothingness, so that, by lifting itself up, all humanity will be lifted up. And as the God-Man, to continue his mission, had to remain poor, suffering, and humiliated until the triumphant hour of his resurrection, until that singular victory over death that freed all humanity from death, so the proletariat must hold to its dialectical mission so that until its final uprising, until the revolutionary resurrection of humanity, it carries the weight of the essential capitalist law of oppression and depression like an ever-heavier cross. From this, it seems, comes Marx's basic difficulty in facing the idea of the partial relief of the proletariat. (*OJJ* 6:259)

What Jaurès objects to is not that Marx draws on religious precedents, but that he does so in implicit (perhaps even unconscious) and thus unaccountable ways. Because Marx does not acknowledge the theological structure underlying his theory of the labor movement, he is stuck with the consequences of that structure even when a more careful reading of history would suggest a different line of thought. Once Marx adopted this "Hegelian transposition of Christianity," the political conclusion—an immiserated proletariat, a moment of crisis, the absolute transcendence of the future over the past—was settled, long before he began to gather the historical and economic evidence with which he would buttress his theory. Thus Marxists could not adequately acknowledge the "partial relief" the working class was able to win through union organizing and legislation because to do so would be to admit that the proletariat had refused to play the role in which Marx had cast it, the role of the crucified and soon-to-be-resurrected Christ.

Just as important, the part of Christian theology on which Marx's thought is modeled is not the part that Jaurès finds most valuable. In *De la réalité du monde sensible*—which he would cause to be republished about the same time as the *Études socialistes* were published in book form[15]—he had written: "God is present in all struggles, in all sadness. . . . The world is, in a sense, the eternal and universal Christ" (*PTA*, 154).[16] For Marx, the image to borrow from Christianity is that of the "singular victory," the once-and-for-all crisis through which the new order overcomes the old. Jaurès, instead, adopts the paradigm of incarnation: everywhere he looks, he sees, or searches for, the immanent presence of potentiality within actuality, of the infinite within the finite, of the ideal within the real.

The political implication here is that where Marx looks forward to a particular point in time at which the socialist ideal will triumph, Jaurès looks forward to a struggle with no definite resolution, to a continuous, complicated, never-perfected process. The "question of method" is for Jaurès not a question of how a revolutionary moment might be prepared for or even how a nonviolent substitute for revolution might be found, but is instead a question of how the socialist ideal might become flesh and dwell on the earth. What Marx's work was missing, in other words, was a sufficient appreciation of how political bodies work. Marx's historical analysis and his economic projections both failed in the end, Jaurès argues, because Marx had an impoverished theory of organizations and institutions, and thus his social and economic theory was not able to anticipate the consequences of the labor movement's political development:

> Each degree of power the proletariat realizes is embodied in specific forms: universal suffrage, unions, cooperatives, the various forms of public power and of the democratic state. We cannot consider proletarian strength independently of the forms in which it is already partially organized, and of the mechanisms it has partially appropriated for itself. Thus, today, it is not utopian to search carefully for the method by which socialism will be realized, the mode through which it will be achieved. To do that is not to return to utopianism and break off from the life of the proletariat. On the contrary, it is to remain within the life of the proletariat, to advance through it and to define oneself through it. The life of the proletariat is no longer "the spirit floating over the waters." It is already embodied in institutions, both economic institutions and political institutions. (*OJJ* 6:244)[17]

In his speech on Bernstein, Jaurès had asserted that, however much economic forces might matter, the logic of democracy matters as well. Here we see more of what he meant. That the socialist ideal will be "realized" is not in question: the growing power of the working class determines that it will be. In a sense, the work of organizing the labor movement and winning labor's proximate goals *is* that realization. But the socialist victory is always mediated by, and thus limited by, the specific organizational and institutional forms through which working class power is made real. What is interesting here is that Jaurès suggests—still somewhat gently—that the "communism" realized through the institutions he lists will not be a regime of perfect justice and permanent social harmony. To be embodied, after all, is to occupy a finite physical space and to be mortal.

Although, at some points in the *Études socialistes*, Jaurès still uses the old image of the "final goal," in his telling, the realization of that goal will be neither final nor permanent. "Communism," as Jaurès uses the term, is the ideal of human reconciliation, and that ideal is mediated in the world through imperfect methods of managing and limiting conflict. Thus he writes in "Le socialisme et la vie" that the socialist goal is not to replace capitalism with "the ponderous monotony of a central bureaucracy" but with "countless instruments—towns, cooperatives, unions—that will allow the freest and most supple movement of social property, that will harmonize social property with the mobility and infinite variety of individuals' powers" (*OJJ* 6:359). Because the ideal is to be embodied in any number of ways, none of its embodiments will be definitive, and so the various institutions that embody the ideal will not necessarily operate as a harmonious ensemble.

This is not a vision of plurality dissolved into unity, of public power that has lost its political character, of mere administration. What Jaurès describes here is an architecture of organizations and institutions each of which holds a fragment of power and each of which will continue to present the desires of different constituencies. This architecture will inevitably give rise to tensions, but in a way designed to make those tensions survivable. It will be subject to continual renovation: it has a shape, but not a fixed and perfected shape. This is a vision consistent with the oldest ideas of republican politics: a vision of common life as political life, as institutionally mediated disagreement about problems that can never be fully resolved but that need never render common life impossible.

It is not that Jaurès wants socialists to fit new reformist means to old revolutionary ends. Rather, he wants them to "remain within the life of the proletariat," to work with the "specific forms" in which that life has been "embodied"—to look at the labor movement's parties, unions, and cooperatives and to think through the logic of what they are already doing. If this means wholeheartedly pursuing "partial relief" or "partial reforms" (*OJJ* 6:261), then new ways of thinking about the socialist or communist goal must follow.

As much as he has marked out a wide area of disagreement with Marxism and other varieties of revolutionary socialism, Jaurès is still intent on maintaining both the common traditions of the movement and the symbol of a communist destination. As in his speech on Bernstein, however, Jaurès is equally intent on making room within the common traditions of socialism for a commitment to political life in the present. He writes toward the end of "Question de méthode":

> Some of our critics always say that this method of evolution, subject to the law of democracy, risks weakening and obscuring the socialist ideal. Quite the opposite. It is the routine appeal to violence, the quasi-mystical expectation of a liberatory catastrophe, that excuses men from sharpening their thought, from defining their ideal. But those who set themselves to lead democracy along the straight wide road toward full communism, those who are not able to count on quick-spent enthusiasms and feverish illusions, are obliged to define with absolute precision the form of society toward which they want to lead men and direct events, and the set of institutions and laws by which they hope to achieve the communist order. As the socialist party fully accepts democracy and legality, it becomes part of the nation, and the more it does so, the more precisely it draws its plans. (*OJJ* 6:263–64)[18]

Awakening from the dream of revolution, socialists become aware that their actual political activities follow a democratic logic. Jaurès wants to specify the "institutions and laws" that he seeks, not to draw a blueprint of a postcapitalist society, but to identify proximate reforms worth pursuing. The "straight wide road" stretches to the horizon, but it begins at our feet. "Through a less turbulent atmosphere the final goal stands out more clearly. If it is not to get lost in the most vulgar empiricism or dissolve into an opportunism without norms and without object, the socialist party must order all its thoughts and all its action in light of the communist ideal. Or, rather, this ideal must be always present and always discernible in each of its acts, in each of its words. . . . Communism must be the visible guiding ideal of the whole movement" (*OJJ* 6:264). Heady talk of revolution is useless; movements need concrete goals. But to drop all reference to purposes beyond the next piece of legislation or the next election or the next union action would be disastrous. The movement's norms, its motivation, its wellspring of hope lie in its ideal. Jaurès refers to "communism" first as a direction of movement but quickly drops this metaphor for others: "communism," he says, is a "light" that illuminates; it is a "visible" ideal; it is "present and discernible." Like the socialist state of grace he had spoken of in his speech on Bernstein, the communist ideal Jaurès writes about now is here with us—on the capitalist earth, within the sensible world. An "ideal" in the usual sense of the word is an idea hovering above the "acts" and "words" of human beings, judging them as if from afar. Jaurès's "ideal" is something different: it is known *through* real acts and words, even though those acts and words never reveal it in full.

Jaurès writes in "Question de méthode" that the *Études socialistes* represents "only a fragment of—or, better, a preparation for—a longer work, more systematic and substantial, wherein I would like to define precisely what socialism is for the beginning of the twentieth century: its basic idea, its method, and its program" (*OJJ* 6:241). Instead of turning to this longer work, he was soon plunged into new parliamentary responsibilities. The elections of April 1902 returned Jaurès to the Chamber of Deputies (he would never again lose an election) along with thirty-five other members of the Parti socialiste français and four independent socialists allied with the PSF, compared with twelve members of the Parti socialiste de France. The Bloc des gauches as a whole had increased the margin of its majority to about eighty seats. René Waldeck-Rousseau stepped down as prime minister, perhaps because he saw that the composition of the Chamber had shifted to the left. The informal Délégation des gauches that coordinated the parties of the Bloc des gauches, and to which Jaurès belonged, was quickly converted into a more permanent steering committee for the Bloc. The Délégation gave the strengthened Bloc des gauches majority a coherence no previous governing coalition in the Third Republic had achieved. Within three days of Waldeck-Rousseau's resignation, the Délégation saw to it that the Progressist president of the Chamber was replaced by the former Radical prime minister Léon Bourgeois and that the

Radical senator Émile Combes was installed as the new prime minister. No socialist joined Combes's government, but Jaurès used his position within the Délégation des gauches—and, from January 1903 to January 1904, his position as a vice president of the Chamber—to make the socialists a pivotal force within the governing coalition.[19]

The policy of "republican defense" that had justified socialist support for Waldeck-Rousseau, Jaurès asserted, should be replaced by a policy of "republican offense." Indeed, in no small part through the contributions of Jaurès, the Combes government was to be a period of social reform without equal during the Third Republic. At last, Radicals achieved the aims to which they were most passionately committed: the definitive separation of church and state and the thorough secularization of primary education. Combes's government also won the abolition of certain middle-class draft exemptions and the reduction of mandatory military service from three years to two, as well as the adoption of a maximum ten-hour day for many workers and an eight-hour day for miners, along with some modest public assistance for the elderly, the disabled, and the chronically ill. Jaurès was instrumental in these victories, influencing the content of legislation and keeping the factions within the Bloc united.[20]

What Jaurès could not do, though, was to turn the Combes government toward an energetic pursuit of a progressive income tax—Combes thought such a move too likely to upset his business supporters—or the completion of the labor law reforms Millerand had initiated during the previous government.[21] With Jaurès's support, Millerand had sought to institute a system of tripartite bargaining through a national council including union, employer, and government representatives and to encourage arbitration of labor disputes. Jaurès hoped to revive Millerand's proposals during the Combes government, and perhaps to establish further rights for workers—such as a comprehensive system of pensions—but at these projects he would fail. Syndicalists in the labor unions wanted to intensify, not moderate, the conflict between employers and employees, and rejected Millerand's labor law proposals. Most Radicals in the Chamber had long since shed whatever sympathy for unions they had felt in previous decades and would now have preferred workers to assert their interests as individuals.[22] Thus Combes refused to put labor law reform on his government's agenda. At the same time, the Parti socialiste français was riven by an increasingly bitter divide between its right wing, which wanted to drop all talk of class struggle, and its left wing, which still harbored revolutionary dreams and accepted a reformist strategy only as an expedient.[23] Chiding members of both wings for trying to make politics too easy, Jaurès defended what he called a "complex politics" that refused to abandon its commitments to either democracy or the class struggle.[24]

Frustrated by Combes's political caution and distracted by the need to mediate conflicts within the PSF, Jaurès managed for a time to hold together his party and the coalition to which it belonged, but the extensive reforms he wanted remained on the horizon of the possible. This period was to mark the pinnacle of his political influence. It was also to mark the pinnacle of the Socialist International's debates about reformism.

When the Sixth Congress of the International met in Amsterdam's Concertgebouw in 1904, the debate about "tactics" dominated its agenda.[25] Worried by the growing strength of the ministerialists and revisionists, defenders of orthodox Marxism like August Bebel and Karl Kautsky were no longer averse to a direct confrontation between the socialist movement's two branches.[26] The German social democrats and Guesde's Parti socialiste de France introduced a resolution based on one the SPD had adopted at its Dresden congress the previous year. The Austrian socialist leader Victor Adler and the Belgian socialist leader Émile Vandervelde, allies of Jaurès, joined to propose a substitute that differed from the Dresden resolution by only a few words. Where the Dresden resolution condemned "the revisionist attempts to change our proven and glorious tactics based on class struggle," Adler and Vandervelde's alternative affirmed those same proven and glorious tactics without any mention of revisionism. Where the Dresden resolution declared that "socialist democracy will accept no participation in the government of bourgeois society," the Adler-Vandervelde text spoke only of the "dangers and inconveniences" of such participation.[27]

However subtle these differences in wording, delegates to the Amsterdam congress understood what was at stake. In the words of Rosa Luxemburg, perhaps the most eloquent champion of the revolutionary socialists: "The Dresden resolution is the symbol of the victory of revolutionary socialism over reformist socialism."[28] As Jaurès saw it, either the congress would pursue "socialist reconciliation" by tolerating the presence of reformists within the movement's ranks, or it would have to "excommunicate" its dissidents.[29]

Although participants in the Amsterdam debate introduced few new ideas on either side, speakers and audience alike seemed to have sensed that this congress was unusually momentous. As the debate reached its peak, the meeting hall became crowded and stiflingly warm. Listeners perched on a mantelpiece and pressed so closely around Jaurès that his fists struck their heads as he gesticulated.[30] Heckling and interruptions, sometimes violent in tone, broke out frequently. Nevertheless, despite the conflict of principles and the physical tension at the Amsterdam congress, in reading its proceedings, one is struck by how comradely the tone of that conflict so often remained.

Thus, at one point, Jaurès takes the floor just after Luxemburg has excoriated the French ministerialists' choice of class collaboration over class struggle. The person who is to translate Jaurès's rebuttal into German is none other than Luxemburg herself, and Jaurès quips: "In a moment, citizen Rosa Luxemburg is going to translate my words, and this will be clear proof that one can combine struggle and collaboration." Later, moments after the congress has erupted in protest at Jaurès's frank criticism of the German party, he is granted more time to speak by apparently overwhelming approbation.[31]

Jaurès's rhetoric had rarely carried so much urgency. Day after day, along with a small group of reformist leaders from other countries, he defended the reformist option, first in the resolutions committee, where he faced off with Guesde, then on the floor of the congress, where he debated Bebel and Luxemburg—both of whom, like Guesde, insisted that socialism must be defined solely by its opposition to the existing social order and by its commitment to class struggle.[32] Although Jaurès admitted that the method of reform might not meet the approval of socialists in every country, it was justified in France because of its results: the reformists' pursuit of coalition politics had "helped to save the Republic."[33] Reformism had staved off, for the present, the threat of a new and powerful reactionary force, a conglomeration of "Caesarism," clericalism, militarism, anti-Semitism, and nationalism. It had opened up the possibility of further social and labor legislation. Not least, it had won genuine mass support, electing socialist deputies from several cities. Should these achievements be tossed aside and this progress be brought to a halt? Had not the reformists demonstrated that they knew how to build a powerful movement, when to compromise and when not to, how to make common cause with bourgeois Radicals and liberals even while breaking with those allies to support labor militancy and policies of "social justice"? Could the movement afford to impose a single method of action on every country, he asked, when, in some countries, the method of reform was proving so fruitful?

Jaurès wanted to defend more than the record of his own party. His object, he said, was to protect the "freedom of tactics and of action" of every party. It would be "imprudent to bind the universal proletariat with such strict tactical formulas" as the Dresden resolution demanded "just when it is about to face new questions." The proper response to the different patterns of "political and social evolution" in different countries was to think through the unique situation in each time and place, to develop the movement's capacity for clear-eyed observation of circumstances and for nuanced judgment. A more prudent socialism, he suggested, would be defined not by a doctrine about the future, but by a commitment to understanding what it was actually doing—to identifying the moments that best exemplified what the movement ought to be, and then building on the lessons of those moments. That would mean acting differently, and talking differently, in different countries and at different times. Jaurès was met with loud protests from the floor of the congress when he charged that the German social democrats succumbed to a "deadly illusion" when they imagined that their own "conception of politics and of socialism could serve as a single norm, an inflexible rule, a uniform standard to be imposed on the action of the socialism of every country."[34]

> By universalizing, by internationalizing their Dresden policy, [German socialists] pass on to international socialism the spirit of uncertainty and hesitation with which they are themselves filled at the present time. At this moment, what weighs down Europe and the world, what lies heavy on the security of our peace, the security of public freedom, the progress of socialism and of the proletariat, what holds back all social progress in Europe and in the world, is not the supposed compromises or reckless experiments of the French socialists, who have united with French democracy to save the liberty, progress, and peace of the world. What holds back everything is not this. It is the political powerlessness of German socialist democracy.[35]

This was a shocking claim. Had not the SPD won 3,000,000 votes in the 1903 Reichstag elections? Did it not have more members than any other socialist party?[36] If the measure of a socialist party's strength was the extent to which it had constructed a vehicle for revolution, it would seem obvious that the German socialist party was the strongest in the world. But Jaurès argued here that to prepare for a future revolutionary event and to engage in the work of socialist reform were two different projects. The German party was weak despite its apparent strength, Jaurès told his German comrades: the "two essential means of proletarian action elude you: you are capable of neither revolutionary action nor parliamentary action." The German working class "has not, historically, had a revolutionary tradition. It has not won universal suffrage on the barricades, but has received it from on high." A movement that began with social uprisings, as had the French Left, is capable of rising up again, because the structure of its organizations and the character of its members' political commitment carry traces of that history, and its gains are more secure for this. But a movement is shaped not only by its own organizational history but also by its institutional context and by the strategic options available to it. Thus it matters immensely that the Reichstag is only a "quasi-parliament," Jaurès argues. Unable to translate its mass support into real power because of the subordination of the Reichstag to the emperor, unable to come to terms with its situation because of its "imprudent" application of old Marxist dogma to a new situation, the German party is immobilized. Powerless, it is unable to seriously consider "how it might institute democracy in [its own] country." To adopt the Dresden resolution as the uniform policy of the International would be to make the German party's inability to think politically a permanent feature of the socialist movement.[37]

To reject the Dresden resolution, accordingly, would mean to accept what Jaurès had written in his *Études socialistes*: that political power is always embodied in specific forms. At bottom, Jaurès's argument at Amsterdam is that political institutions, like living bodies, have differing powers and limitations, and that these differences matter. A representative constitutional regime like the Third French Republic opens up possibilities not available in other kinds of polities, and the International ought to allow member parties to pursue such possibilities. Likewise, the various organizations of the labor movement open up possibilities that a republican state, without labor's pressure, would be unlikely to realize. However simple this claim might be, as Jaurès had by now come to recognize, to accept it would have complicated consequences. Socialists might share an ideal of social justice, but that ideal would take shape in different ways in different countries, and in various ways within any one country. The realization of that ideal would necessarily remain incomplete, and it was time, Jaurès thought, that socialists recognize all this.

A new way of thinking about the politics of the Left had emerged through the socialists' debates about reform. The new reformism retained much of the traditional language of socialism, but its adherents were nevertheless trying to say something new: that every political body has its limits, but also that the life of political bodies has a dynamic not reducible to economic forces—in other words, that politics can shape society. Socialists could let go of the nineteenth-century dream of abolishing politics, Jaurès and his fellow reformists announced. They could replace the powerlessness of a revolutionary movement that did not make revolution with the modest but real power of a movement consciously committed to the method of reform—and willing to face the consequences of this commitment.

LIFE IN COMMON

Jaurès's speech at the 1904 Amsterdam congress earned "prolonged applause and lengthy acclamations," but "Jaurèsism" went down to defeat.[1] The Adler-Vandervelde resolution failed in a 21–21 tie vote, after which the Dresden resolution passed by a vote of 25 to 5, with 12 abstentions. A resolution calling for socialists in each country to form a single party—in effect, a demand that the Parti socialiste français merge with the Parti socialiste de France—was approved unanimously.[2] The reformism debates were over, and the reformists had lost.

Although at Amsterdam they had supported the unity resolution, back in France the leaders of the PSF did not concede immediately. Jaurès at first proposed that the two French socialist parties seek an alliance rather than a full merger, and when the PSF did finally enter merger talks with the PSdeF, its negotiators yielded ground reluctantly. But yield ground they did. By January 1905, the two sides had agreed that their new party would declare itself to be "not a party of reform, but a party of class struggle and revolution." Its deputies would be not merely a *distinct* bloc in the Chamber (a formulation the reformists could have accepted), but a bloc *opposed* to all others (a formulation that precluded anything like the Bloc des gauches). Socialist deputies would be permitted to vote in favor of particular pieces of legislation, but would be forbidden to cast any vote—such as a vote for a government's proposed budget—that might draw them into a relationship resembling a coalition with another party. Socialist elected officials and socialist journals would be subject to the governance of party congresses. The only concessions the reformists could wring from their new partners were a limited autonomy for local party branches and an agreement that, in "exceptional circumstances," the party could reconsider its rule against cooperation with other parties.[3]

When the new Parti socialiste, section française de l'Internationale ouvrière (Socialist Party, French Section of the Workers' International, or SFIO) was officially formed in April 1905, several leading members of the Parti socialiste français either conspicuously declined to join or withdrew almost right away. Among them were some of Jaurès's closest allies and associates: Aristide Briand, with whom Jaurès had founded the journal *L'Humanité* the previous year; René Viviani, who had contributed a volume to the *Histoire socialiste*; and, not least, Alexandre Millerand himself.[4] It would not be hard to imagine Jaurès joining them. Outside the SFIO, he might have been able to pull together a small group of like-minded reformists, and might soon have been in a position to hold ministerial office himself, as would both Briand and Viviani less than two years later.[5] Inside the SFIO, he would be denied the chance to support (let alone serve in) any reform-minded government that might be formed in the near future. Worse, he would no longer be so free to think in public about the method of reform and its consequences. He would be reduced to taking the approach Ignaz Auer had recommended to Eduard Bernstein: doing the things a reformist does without saying what he was doing.

Jaurès chose socialist unity. When the SFIO was formed, he thus found himself in an uncomfortable position. He had advocated unity for years, but this was not the socialist party he had wanted. His talents made him the unified party's chief orator, writer, and parliamentary tactician, and the deep personal respect his warmth and integrity had earned him, even among those socialists who disagreed with him, meant that the job of reconciling the party's disparate factions fell in large part to him. But the SFIO's doctrine of revolution was a rebuke to the views for which he had been the chief spokesman. By joining the SFIO, Jaurès became the leader of a party that had been founded through his own defeat.

Why did he do this? Accepting unity meant membership in a growing party rather than in a small sect, and it gave Jaurès a continued bond with the International. These could not have been insignificant considerations. Perhaps unity would not have to mean the end of the reformist project. One sympathetic commentator wrote in 1906: "Jaurès is too wise a politician not to know when a partial surrender will lead to final victory. His belief in the Reformist method is of course unshaken, but he is willing to wait and be politic."[6] This is plausible enough. Certainly Jaurès succeeded, over time, in leading the SFIO into a gradual acceptance of reformist tactics. Within months of its founding, an SFIO congress gave tacit approval for local party groups to make district-level second-round election alliances with the Radicals or other bourgeois parties, and this limited form of multiparty collaboration was given explicit license at subsequent party congresses.[7] In 1910, the SFIO even permitted participation in multiparty governing coalitions at the local level, although its policy of opposition to such alliances at the national level would remain firmly in place throughout Jaurès's lifetime.[8] Between 1905 and 1914, the SFIO's election programs increasingly emphasized positions the Socialists shared with the Radicals, such as support for social insurance programs and progressive income taxes.[9] In 1913 and 1914, the SFIO even gave tacit—but decisive—support to a Radical government.[10]

This quiet movement toward a renewal of the Bloc des gauches or something like it could only go so far, however. Not only was the SFIO doctrinally opposed to ministerialism, but a wave of strikes between 1905 and 1907—over 430,000 French workers struck in 1906, the greatest number of strikers France had ever seen in a single year—and a 1907 controversy over the unionization of public school teachers made it impossible to ignore the divide between the Socialists and the increasingly antiunion Radicals.[11] At the same time, the continued rise of syndicalist ideas within the unions—the Confédération générale du travail formally distanced itself from all political parties in a 1906 declaration—made impossible the kind of union-party cooperation that was leading some other European socialist movements toward political pragmatism.[12] Nevertheless, the possibility of something like reformism remained. Working informally with Radicals and other allies—including ex-Socialists like Briand, who became prime minister in 1909—the SFIO deputies helped to pass a number of public assistance and pension laws between 1905 and 1910.[13]

The SFIO acted more and more like a party of reform, but Jaurès's public rhetoric was severely constrained. Where before he had sometimes been able to use his speeches and writings to help reformist socialists recognize and think through what they were doing, Jaurès now wrote and spoke for (and to) a party in which the toleration of the reformist minority by the revolutionary majority always seemed provisional. Jaurès could caution his comrades against revolutionary impatience, as when he warned the delegates at the SFIO's 1908 Toulouse congress that "neither a sudden act of violence nor the sudden act of a majority" could dispense with the need to proceed "gradually, through a series of efforts and institutions," but he had to be careful at the same time to pledge his fealty to the teachings of "all our masters" and to the policies set by "all our national and international congresses." The SFIO might be involved in "reformist action," but Jaurès acknowledged that it had a "revolutionary spirit," and he seems to have known that there was little he could do to change this. The room for creative reinterpretation of a common tradition had shrunk, and, as the leader of an avowedly revolutionary party, Jaurès now spoke often and with little qualification about the prospect of violent insurrection, about the total abolition of capitalism, and about the certainty of a proletarian victory.[14]

Leaving the Amsterdam congress after his defeat there, Jaurès told Émile Vandervelde: "I am going to study military questions."[15] These questions had a new salience. Although it had been nearly thirty years since the last major war between Europe's great powers, the first years of the twentieth century had seen a marked increase in military and colonial expenditures. An international conference at the Hague in 1899 had tried to establish arms control agreements, rules of war for future conflicts, and a system of arbitration for international disputes. These principles would be reaffirmed by the second Hague conference in 1907, but it was by no means certain how meaningful they would prove to be if tested. The European powers were expanding their colonial holdings in Africa and Asia, and the Boer War of 1899–1902, though a relatively minor engagement, seemed to presage larger conflicts.[16] Socialists had traditionally opposed offensive war, had often been critical of the harshness of European colonial policies (although not necessarily critical of colonialism per se; some thought colonialism would benefit European workers), and had generally endorsed the rudimentary forms of international law pursued by the Hague conferences. But these had not been issues of high priority in the previous decades, and the International's resolutions on such matters had been vague, even by the International's standards.[17] Socialists, like other Europeans, now found themselves worrying about the prospect of a war sparked by colonial disputes or great-power rivalry.

Jaurès found that, despite his precarious position within the SFIO, he had considerable freedom to speak out on foreign policy. The years from 1905 to 1909 were marked by a series of crises in Morocco, where successive French governments risked war with Germany, perpetrated cruelties against Moroccans, and sparked a civil war within the French colony in their efforts to expand France's colonial holdings in northwest Africa. Jaurès became a persistent and prominent critic of French policy in Morocco.[18] The prevention of war become a central theme at the International's congresses at Stuttgart in 1907 and Copenhagen in 1910, as well as at the SFIO's own meetings, and at those gatherings Jaurès became the leading proponent of a policy in keeping with his old call for a "more active" socialism. Orthodox Marxists like Jules Guesde and Karl Kautsky argued that capitalism would inevitably generate war, and that nothing therefore could be done in the short term to prevent war. In contrast, syndicalist-influenced antimilitarists like Gustave Hervé (a former schoolteacher who had been the leader of the PSF's left wing) thought socialists should threaten to call general strikes in any country that was involved in any war, even a war of defense. Against both, Jaurès proposed that the labor movement might be able to prevent war if workers everywhere pledged to engage in a general strike in any country that launched an *offensive* war.[19] The reformism debates had ended, but still at every congress of the International or of the SFIO Jaurès called on socialists not to wait until after capitalism had been abolished to work for the realization of solidarity.

The idea of a general strike to prevent offensive war was probably more useful as a device to shame the orthodox Marxists for their political passivity than as a plan for stopping a war. The International simply did not have the capacity to bring about the kind of continent-wide mass strikes that could conceivably stop a war among the great powers: unions affiliated with the International comprised scarcely half of the *organized* European working class, while many workers remained entirely unorganized. In the one instance where something like Jaurès's proposal was tried, it failed: an Italian mass strike in response to Italy's 1911 declaration of war on the Ottoman Empire was followed shortly by an Italian attack on Tripoli. Moreover, the kind of international arbitration system that might make it possible to clearly distinguish offensive from defensive war did not exist.[20] In retrospect, what seems most consequential about Jaurès's contribution to the socialist debates on the prevention of war was that, by insisting on the illegitimacy of offensive war, he emphasized the legitimacy of defensive wars. On its face, Jaurès's defense of national defense was not a new or unusual idea: except for a few antipatriots like Hervé, most socialists had never doubted that the military conquest of one country by another was unacceptable.[21] But Jaurès pushed the widely shared idea that defensive wars were legitimate farther than any other leader in the International when he decided to take up the question of *how* national defense and international peace might be effectively pursued at the same time.

To answer that question, Jaurès revived one of the oldest demands of the European Left: the replacement of standing armies by citizen militias. From the Greek city-states and the Roman republic, eighteenth-century republicans like Jean-Jacques Rousseau and Thomas Paine had taken up the idea of the citizen-soldier, and in the nineteenth century that idea had become the common currency of republicans in France and of socialists everywhere. In Jaurès's time, a citizen militia was part of the political doctrine, if not the actual policy, of the Third French Republic—it provided a strained justification for the military draft—and had been established as a standard plank in socialist party platforms: the Guesdists' 1880 platform, written in consultation with Marx himself, had called for a citizen militia, as had the 1902 platform of Jaurès's Parti socialiste français.[22]

Few socialists had thought much about the application or implications of the militia idea. In 1907, however, Jaurès began a long study of military organization and strategy. He read extensively at the Bibliothèque nationale and consulted with a sympathetic army captain, Henry Gérard. In 1911, he published the results in a book, *L'armeé nouvelle* (The new army), in which he presented a detailed plan for a citizen militia—or, to use the French term, a "nation armée" (nation in arms).[23]

L'armée nouvelle was to be the first installment of a series of reform proposals which together would constitute a plan for "the socialist organization of France."[24] The "new army," Jaurès writes, "will not be an isolated fact" but "will necessarily be part of a comprehensive social policy program" (*AN*, 358). Jaurès would never develop the rest of this program, and the program he does outline in *L'armée nouvelle* is oddly unbalanced: some of the secondary ideas are eminently practical, whereas the central concept was outdated even when Jaurès published it, as some critics pointed out at the time, and became utterly irrelevant with the invention of new weapons and war equipment in the subsequent decade.[25] Nevertheless *L'armée nouvelle* remains the most revealing of Jaurès's later political writings. It ranges far beyond the topic of its title, and suggests much of what Jaurès's broader program might have contained: it is the closest Jaurès came to a comprehensive statement of his political thought.[26] Jaurès finds in this book a forum in which to present, in its fullest form yet, his conception of reformist socialism, a forum denied him at party congresses and in Chamber debates, where he had to act as the leader of an avowedly revolutionary party. Here, however, the common tradition on which he draws most is not the Marxism of the socialist movement but the republicanism of France and of the writers of antiquity who had been his first intellectual loves. Beginning with the notion of a citizen militia, Jaurès plays out the claim that the old ideas of the republican tradition might be worth revisiting.

The premise of *L'armée nouvelle*, in keeping with that republican tradition, is that national defense is a worthwhile objective. It is telling that Jaurès considers this a principle in need of justification; he is evidently worried by the emergence of a bitter antipatriotism within the circles of the French socialist party and labor movement influenced by Hervé and by revolutionary syndicalism. Working by analogy, Jaurès argues that, for anyone who has already accepted either republican or socialist principles (which, for Jaurès, of course, are not separate sets of principles to begin with), opposition to domination of one kind ought to entail opposition to domination of other kinds. Here is a characteristic summation: "To revolt against the despotism of kings or the tyranny of bosses and capital and then to submit passively to the yoke of conquest and the domination of foreign militarism would be a contradiction so childish, so pathetic, that at the first sign of it all one's reason and instinct alike should rise up and sweep away the very notion" (*AN*, 361–62). Monarchy, capitalism, and lack of national self-government are objectionable on the same grounds, and those who object to any of these threats should object to all of them, Jaurès suggests. This is not so simple as it sounds, and no doubt this parallelism would have been unsatisfying to Hervé and other antipatriots. To define a problem is to define the group for whom that problem is a problem: to speak of the despotism of kings is to identify *the people* as a group with a common grievance, just as to speak of the tyranny of bosses is to identify *the working class* as a group. Likewise, the domination of foreign militarism is a problem only if *the nation* is understood as a group with some meaningful commonality. The similarity in these three cases is that someone is dominating someone else. This is significant, in that it suggests the commitment to freedom that underpins Jaurès's entire argument, but the differences among the three forms of domination Jaurès mentions are also significant. Although Jaurès does address the idea that the members of a nation have something substantive in common with one another, his primary concern is with a more immediate question: if republican and socialist principles require national defense, what method of securing national defense is most compatible with those principles?

His answer, of course, is a citizen militia. The existing arrangement, which set a large reserve force alongside the active force, allowed the Third Republic to pay lip service to the notion of a citizen army, but Jaurès writes that the Republic paid a price for its incompletely republican military: the professional active army—sequestered in its barracks, governed by an officer corps with distinct values—was cut off from the life of the nation, and so developed interests and a culture separate from those of the nation as a whole. In contrast, a citizen militia would mix the military into the life of the nation. A militia would not be prone to illiberal conspiracies in the manner of the Dreyfus Affair, and would be unlikely to pursue power for itself through a coup d'état. It might also be unwilling to fire on demonstrators or striking workers, a point of special interest to socialists (*AN*, 344–58).

The professional army's isolation from the nation worries Jaurès not only because of the risk that the army will seek to dominate the civilian government or civilian organizations, but also because the professional army badly educates the citizens who serve in it. Classical republicans had wanted the citizen's experience of shoulder-to-shoulder combat to infuse his peacetime political life with a soldierly solidarity. Suspicious of the sensibilities learned in modern warfare, Jaurès wants a militia for quite a different reason: he wants the army to be infused with the sensibilities of civilian life. Thus he proposes that every able-bodied male citizen between the ages of 20 and 34 be assigned to a local militia unit corresponding to his place of residence. In Jaurès's militia plan, based in part on the Swiss model, each citizen-soldier would spend only six months in barracks-based training and would attend eight three-week training periods spread out over the remainder of his period of service, with only occasional local marching and rifle practice sessions while he was not on barracks duty. Once he reached the age of 35, he would have minimal obligations. Thus, for thirteen years and two weeks of his fourteen years of military service, the citizen-soldier would live at home (*AN*, 549–57).

Unlike a centralized national army or a military composed of rootless youths, a local militia unit of men whose median age was around 30 would be characterized by what Jaurès calls the "bonds of affection"—toward families, friends, neighbors, fellow union members—that defined their lives outside the barracks (*AN*, 45–46). Citizen-soldiers would need some time in the barracks to acquire certain specifically military skills. But such time should be kept to a minimum, Jaurès argued. In the Third Republic, the so-called active army was in fact passively obedient and dispirited. Its soldiers could handle weapons or march with a certain "sterile formalism." But, once those basic skills had been learned, the subsequent years of barracks life to which active-duty soldiers were assigned and during which basic skills were drilled endlessly had no purpose but to reduce soldiers to machines retaining no "mechanism to confront the questions of life and death that the ever-changing drama of combat poses to combatants" (*AN*, 24). Mute obedience and rote performance, Jaurès suggests, are not as useful for soldiers as military authorities presume. Moreover, they are not the proper attributes of republican citizens. The citizen-soldiers of the militia, in Jaurès's plan, would return to civilian life before they unlearned their capacities for judgment and their civilian affections.

Just as he wants rank-and-file soldiers to retain the moral education of civilian life, Jaurès also wants officers, who necessarily spend more than a few months in full-time military duty, to be shaped more by the shared life of the nation than by the peculiar life of the military. Thus, in Jaurès's militia plan, no more than one-third of the officers could be career soldiers, and extensive provision would be made to ensure that men of all classes had opportunities for training and promotion to the officer ranks. Officer training would be conducted within the liberal arts and sciences faculties, rather than in separate military academies: officer-trainees would read Plutarch as well as Clausewitz (*AN*, 553–56).

Because soldiers and officers in the militia would retain the characteristics of citizens, they would have an attachment to home and an aversion to violence that would render them ill suited for any but defensive wars. Citizen-soldiers, Jaurès speculates, might even resist deployment in a war of "conquest and pillage" that would take them far from their families and familiar surroundings

(*AN*, 45–46). Jaurès finds this an appealing prospect: here was yet another means to reduce the threat of war between the great powers of Europe.

Jaurès has not forgotten his promise to address the question of national defense, however. The greatest advantage of a citizen militia, he argues, is that, despite the common assumption to the contrary, a militia would be better able than a professional army to conduct a war of defense. The defensive advantages of a citizen militia would be especially important in the case of France. France's most likely enemy in a future war was Germany, and Germany had a massive army—not surprisingly, since its population was half again that of France. For all their immersion in "military science," Jaurès writes, France's military leaders had not grappled with the glaring fact that the Third Republic's active army was too small to resist a German invasion.[27] What France inevitably lacked in "military force" it would have to make up for in "moral force."[28] Where Germany, with its professional army and its "hierarchical and feudal" social order (*AN*, 55), could count only on the kind of power that could be measured in quantities of soldiers and military equipment, a France with a citizen militia would have a power of a different kind, a power invisible to those who think about politics in terms unsuitable for republican life. Military authorities insisted on the need for a professional army, Jaurès argues, because they had forgotten how to think, and how to see, like citizens.

> Just as minds shaped by the habits of life under a monarchy can recognize the majesty of power only when it is concentrated in a family or in a man . . . so minds shaped by our military tradition can recognize the power of the army only in a distinct, self-directing, self-contained institution. . . . Just as there is no power more majestic than law that gives form to the will of all, so there is no army so strong and brilliant, so able to give moral authority and full respect to leaders who are truly in harmony with it, as one that is the nation itself, passionately committed to its independence and organized for its own defense. (*AN*, 39)

The nation in arms, Jaurès writes, has the "moral force" that appears when "all souls thrill to a common will" (*AN*, 8). Like the civic virtue lauded by classical republicans, Jaurès's "moral force" is a characteristic of citizens, not of institutions. It is an interior capacity that manifests in action. Jaurès is careful to point out that the moral force with which he is concerned must be "summed up and concentrated in an idea" (*AN*, 9). Although it can be partly described with words like "emotion," "passion," and "inspiration," the moral force Jaurès wants is also a matter for the intellect; it is a subject for arguments among citizens. If all souls, or even many souls, are to have in common the will to realize this idea, they will have to be persuaded of the idea's validity, or at least of its attractiveness. This must be an uncertain endeavor. Jaurès does not comment on the fissure he has opened up here between the need for a common will and the need for reasoned persuasion. We might note, however, that this sort of problem is not new for Jaurès: here, again, he wants to hold at the same time to the principles of solidarity and freedom, to common feeling and rational critique, despite the impossibility of doing so in a perfect way.

France will be strongest, Jaurès proposes, when it realizes the potential power of impassioned and organized citizens. The alternative to this approach, the intellectual enemy against which he directs his fire, is the model of military organization developed by Napoléon Bonaparte. Although the Napoleonic model of a large, professionalized, centralized army designed for offensive strategies represented "a compromise between the Roman monarchical tradition and the French Revolution," the latter was "reduced to being no longer a principle, but merely an energy than can be subordinated and made use of" (*AN*, 101). The Napoleonic model adopts some distinctively modern techniques of mobilization and organization, Jaurès writes, but it rejects the best fruits of the Revolution. The French Revolution's "boldest and most sweeping" innovation was that it attempted at the same time "to inspire passion and also to impose discipline throughout a mass of combatants, through the power and enthusiasm of an idea." That idea, which summed up the moral force of a citizen army, was "the great love of the Republic, the great enthusiasm for liberty and for human dignity." Napoleonic soldiers might be effective up to a point, but they shared neither passion nor inspiring idea with one another, or with those who directed their activity (*AN*, 85).

The merely military force of a Napoleonic army, Jaurès fears, will not be sufficient to defend France against an attack by Germany's inevitably greater military force. This would be all the more true given the Fabian military strategy Jaurès recommends in the event of an invasion: an invading army, he proposes, should be allowed to gain French territory; local militias should constantly harass the invading army, but should avoid decisive battles until the time and place were right for the nation in arms to mass itself and strike (*AN*, 140–41). This strategy would, no doubt, require great patience and solidarity on the part of militia members and civilians alike. A large and well-equipped army lacking moral force might conceivably win a conventional offensive war. But only an army and a populace with redoubtable moral force could follow as pure a defensive strategy as Jaurès recommends.[29]

One of the most striking features of Jaurès's argument for a new army is that so little about it is distinctively military. Jaurès begins his argument for the new army by acknowledging the need for national defense, but before the end of *L'armée nouvelle* he will introduce other state functions, besides defense, that he considers essential to a modern republic. Napoleonism, as Jaurès describes it, is not only a form of military organization, but also a certain model of the modern state: centralized, professionalized, remote from daily life. Clearly preferring a republican model, Jaurès seems to suggest that the citizen militia's principles of service and participation might be applied outside the military, with any number of legislative and executive activities benefiting from an infusion of moral force. But this is a question he does not explore.

How, then, was any part of the modern state to elicit moral force? Not in the ways used by premodern societies. The method of military organization (or, more broadly, of social and political organization) used by "monarchies and oligarchies, governments of brutality and plunder" is to demand mechanical obedience, Jaurès writes (*AN*, 47). Jaurès sees a "new spirit of autonomy" as the hallmark of the modern era, and he thinks that this spirit has worked its way into "all social relations and all institutions," albeit partially, through the political activity of the labor movement. The consequence: "It is not possible to impose the old forms of obedience, discipline, and patriotism on men who now demand full political and social liberty" (*AN*, 7).

Thus the moral force of a modern republic cannot come from the old sources: traditional hierarchies, established religion, the glory won by rulers (*AN*, 10–11). Modern republican patriotism has a subtler source and more radical political implications. The moral force of the modern "patrie" is "inseparable from organic habits, from the manner of speaking, looking, walking, smiling, thinking, from the countless memories, happy or sad, by which the life of each person in a human group, at once delimited and vast, is mixed with the life of all" (*AN*, 451).[30] A society without traditional means of instilling a common will cannot achieve the "tremendous surge of shared passion" required for a militia defense "without a foundation of common experiences formed in the imperceptible depths of consciousness through many days of familiarity" (*AN*, 450). These "common experiences" are found in public life, in places where society's members stand in rough equality with one another.

It is "by shared environments, the community of language, of work and of festivals, by all the turns of thought and feeling common to all the individuals within a group, under the multiple influences of nature, history, climate, religion, war, or art," Jaurès writes, that people are made into citizens of a common "patrie" (*AN*, 449–50). The "patrie," we might say, is constituted by its citizens' awareness of and love for what they have in common: after all, patriotism entails fraternity, as surely as the sons of a common "pater" are each other's "fratres."

Notably, the commonalities Jaurès is concerned with here involve immediate, face-to-face experiences; they happen in public spaces that fall within the compass of the senses. The idea that the patriotism of a large nation-state might arise from local commonalities—or, for that matter, that the moral force of the nation in arms might grow out of local bonds of affection—is as much a problem as a solution. Jaurès is still convinced, as he was when he wrote his doctoral theses, that the parts find meaning within an ordered whole, but he is also aware that the parts might trouble the harmony and limit the unity of the whole. Will local affections be a "hidden root of sorrow" within the "patrie"? Although Jaurès does not say, he has given us reason to think that local affections and broader loyalties will exist in tension with one another, but that this tension will be worth fostering and its attendant sorrows worth enduring.

Whatever problems might follow from this shared public life, the existence of that public life is itself a problem; it cannot be taken for granted. In a rare autobiographical moment, Jaurès writes:

> I remember that it was about thirty years ago when I arrived in Paris, just a youth. Alone in the immense city one winter night, I was overcome by a sort of fear for society. I thought I saw thousands upon thousands passing each other by without recognition, an uncountable crowd of lonely ghosts unmoored from all human connections. And I wondered with a sort of impersonal dread how all these beings accepted the unequal distribution of good and ill, why the enormous social structure did not crumble and fall. I saw no chains on their hands or feet, and I said to myself: by what marvel do these thousands of suffering and harrowed individuals endure all this? Of course I could not see: the chain was on the heart, but a chain the burden of which the heart itself could not feel. Thought was bound, but by a bond that it did not know. Life had imprinted its forms in their spirits, and habit had fixed those forms in

place. The social system had shaped these men, and had somehow become their very substance. They did not rebel against reality because they had wrongly identified themselves with it. (*AN*, 365)

Jaurès has not forgotten his earlier comments about the insuppressible modern "spirit of autonomy." Indeed, he goes on to note that some members of this society—most especially, members of the labor movement—have, "through a prodigious effort of the spirit," become able to "glimpse, beneath the present social order, the possibility of a new order" (*AN*, 365). These few have been emboldened to "rebel against reality"—or to see beyond actuality to potentiality, as a younger Jaurès might have written. But the image of the "uncountable crowd of lonely ghosts" remains. The figure of the isolated individual appears often in modern literature and social criticism. Jaurès emphasizes something, however, that not all prophets of modern discontent have noted, namely, a circular relationship between loneliness and inequality. The lonely ghosts are not only "unmoored from all human connections" but also suffering from "the unequal distribution of good and ill." Loneliness has the inward consequence of rendering individuals less apt to question their social positions, and thus less likely to challenge inequality. Inequality, in turn, makes impossible the genuinely common outward experiences that are the alternative to loneliness. Loneliness undermines the moral force that makes possible effective national defense, and thus republican self-government—or, perhaps, it simply marks the absence of such moral force.

Aside from its consequences, loneliness is, for Jaurès, important in and of itself because it is an element of or aspect of injustice. He turns briefly to this theme in a later passage. "Even for someone exploited and subjugated, a human group in which he has at least some defined place—some hours of peaceful sleep at the bottom of the palace steps—is worth more than all the world outside, filled with absolute hostility and total insecurity. . . . The slave, says the great Homer, has only half his soul. Even this half, however, he risks losing if he becomes separated from the social milieu where he has at least some shelter, some reciprocal bonds of affection" (*AN*, 449).[31] To be a slave is certainly to experience the injustice of domination. But to be lonely is also to experience an injustice not reducible to any other. Jaurès never settles on a single name for the state of being not lonely or not isolated—the nouns "fraternité," "solidarité," "communauté," and "harmonie" (which all share the meanings of their English cognates) and the verb "concilier" (which I have generally translated as "reconcile") all appear frequently in Jaurès's writings—but the resonance with the old republican emphasis on the common good, and the older Aristotelian theme of friendship, would be hard to miss. The student Jaurès had written that the ideas of the Greeks and Romans could "refresh and revive" modern minds. What he is trying to do in *L'armée nouvelle*, it seems, is to figure out what resources drawn from classical republicanism might help him, and his readers, to comprehend and to confront the problems of political life in a new era.

Jaurès has made clear that he wants to prevent domination of France by other nations through effective national defense. He also wants to prevent monarchical, clerical, or capitalist domination within France. And—alongside and not reducible to anything else—he wants to confront the problem of loneliness. The heart of *L'armée nouvelle* is Jaurès's contention that these concerns fit together in a coherent whole: "The nation in arms necessarily means the just nation" (*AN*, 48). Early in the book, Jaurès had argued that socialists should support the transition to a new army. In later chapters, he argues that the idea of the new army itself points toward socialism—that is, toward an unmistakably reformist and decidedly nonrevolutionary socialism.

Jaurès adds two new elements to the arguments for reform he had made prior to the founding of the SFIO. First, drawing on what he had written earlier in *L'armée nouvelle* about moral force and loneliness, Jaurès says something about the ends—and not only the proximate ends—of his kind of socialism. If moral force requires common experience, and if a capitalist society tends to render its members lonely by undercutting the possibility of common experience, then there ought to be public policies that counteract the "despair" of the people by "lessening their misery" because this in turn allows for the relief of their loneliness (*AN*, 358–59). Accordingly, Jaurès sketches out a program of social insurance, public education, public housing, workplace rights, and public health measures—what later generations would call a "welfare state."

> Insure the workers against the consequences of illness, unemployment, disability, and old age, so they do not resort to striking with their hearts already embittered by excessive suffering. . . . Make sure the child of the worker can attend school and remain long enough to gain something that cannot be lost: a hunger for greater knowledge, for a methodical and reflective way of life. By a legal limit on the working day, give work-

ers enough leisure so they can live, and can have the two things that make for serenity and balance: enough family life and enough life out of doors. . . . Give the working masses—too often crammed into slums or exploited by the exorbitance of rents—sufficient and decent lodging at a price that will not overwhelm them. Institute a minimum wage in all the household industries . . . which are like shadowy hollows where ignored miseries, silent despairs, and implacable grudges accumulate. Have the courage to prohibit the poisonous liquors that agitate the people's nerves. . . . Add to the schools medical services to monitor children for the first signs of inherited disabilities, and respond to their effects with appropriate aid. Fortify, thus, the nervous balance of the working class. (*AN*, 359–60)

Notice the purposes of Jaurès's policy program. The welfare state protects against bitterness, fosters enlightenment, allows for a life of "serenity and balance," ends the geographic segregation of the poor. Exploitative home industries are to be reformed not only because they generate "miseries" but, just as important, because they hide those miseries from public view and sympathy. Poor health threatens the "nervous balance" of the working class. Jaurès is concerned with material wealth, economic security, and bodily health because exclusion from them leads to a kind of moral deprivation. The normative foundation of Jaurès's welfare state is a concern with the inner life of the citizen and, above all, with the danger that each person's inner life might be cut off from the rest. Thus he writes: "Let there be not one single soul who feels ignored, lost, condemned by his isolation to a life of the deadened resignation or furious revolt that adds an overflow of anger and built-up hate to times of crisis. In all the complex life of modern society, let there be not one miserable and obscure corner where shines no ray of social justice, where penetrates none of the kindness of society's mutual obligations, no glimmer of new hope" (*AN*, 359).

Without rejecting the idea of the social ownership of property—the defining aim of nineteenth-century socialism—Jaurès relegates that goal to the margins of his agenda. He is not envisioning here a society in which class has been abolished or in which a premodern simplicity has been re-created. Instead, he calls for the amelioration of a particular aspect of injustice that he here calls "isolation" and that he has elsewhere referred to as being "lonely." This is a characteristically socialist argument in that it traces the roots of injustice to the class divide of a capitalist society and insists that inclusion in the human community requires some redistribution or socialization of material goods, although, making no pretense to a complete resolution of social injustice, it is socialist in a distinctly reformist way. The socialist element of the argument gives it its analytic weight, but what gives the argument its moral power is the republican idiom in which it is cast. Jaurès wants to place as one of the chief ends of political action what he at some points calls "common life" (*AN*, 449). The amelioration of loneliness, in Jaurès's argument, is not achieved in private life alone, but in the "mutual obligations" of society's members toward one another and in the visibility of society's members to one another. We are to picture society's members in a shared space filled with light: a promenade, perhaps, or a city square.

At the same time—and this is the second new element in his argument—Jaurès argues that this common life offers means of political action that do not themselves threaten common life. Common life, in other words, has the potential to reinforce itself: it generates a kind of moral community.

> Give the working class confidence in the power of progress through law. Design mechanisms by which it will have access, *as a class, as an organized and united collective*, to the vast wealth of modernity. Draw a broad, straight path before it. . . . And as the republican nation makes an effort to attain justice, it will be the duty of the working class, in return, to voluntarily organize and discipline itself. It will also be in its interest. It has nothing to gain by putting its protests into a brutal form. . . . Acts of destruction not only have the effect of betraying humanity . . . but by giving the illusion of immediate power, they also distract the workers from the pursuit of true power, which lies in forming ever larger groups and in taking ever more methodical action. (*AN*, 360)

As workers are included in the legal rights, material wealth, and common prospects of the nation, Jaurès proposes, their organizations acquire a duty to choose nonviolent methods. In other words, the entrance of previously excluded people into a nation's public life changes those people; it teaches or shapes them. Once they have a legal right to organize, once they experience a welfare state and other policies that promote egalitarian redistribution or socialization of wealth, once they share the public spaces of the nation on something like equal terms with members of other classes, workers have something more to lose than their chains, and they begin to think about the nation in a different way than they had before. When they had not experienced common life, they did not know its value; now that they have experienced it, they realize that they must refrain from disrupting it.

This is not a simply civic pedagogy. Notice that Jaurès introduces three forms of commonality in the passage quoted above, and that they come in a sequence from familiar to remote: the political experience of a *class* that is included in the *nation* leads to a realization of duty toward *humanity*. Class and nation appear here as forms of proximate commonality that point beyond themselves toward a commonality that is more encompassing than either, and more difficult to realize. When the labor movement declines to act in "brutal" ways, it is demonstrating its loyalty to humanity; it is also learning that human loyalty in a new way. This idea of loyalty to humanity as a whole and this pattern of loyalties that point toward higher loyalties are themes to which Jaurès will return.

Jaurès makes a negative argument here about the duty to refrain from violence. He also wants to make a positive argument about the alternative to violence that he is recommending to the labor movement. "True power," he writes, is based on "methodical action," the gradual and prosaic project of building mass-membership organizations such as trade unions and political parties. By itself, of course, this is not a claim that Jules Guesde, Karl Kautsky, or Rosa Luxemburg would have disputed. They also wanted methodical action; the question that divided them from Jaurès was whether the labor movement's organizational strength generated a kind of power that could plausibly be used to bring about social changes now, within a society still dominated by the power of capital. In defending the plausibility of political reform, Jaurès is also defending the efficacy of political power in the face of economic power. His argument rests on a certain conception of commonalities and common goods, building on what he has already said about the nature of public life in a modern society.

The modern republic, as Jaurès conceives it, presupposes a minimal common life, and goes on to produce other or richer commonalities. Political power is the power to preserve and extend those commonalities, and it is founded on those commonalities. Class conflict troubles those commonalities, but never eclipses them. Marx and Engels had insisted in their *Manifesto* that the modern state "is but a committee for managing the common affairs of the whole bourgeoisie."[32] This view denies the possibility of collective self-government by the two classes together, but Jaurès proposes that within "the democracy of today," the state "expresses the relationship between classes." Thus, even though the modern democratic state does tend to reinforce the primacy of whichever class is more powerful in economic life, and even though that state is affected by the conflict between the classes, it also has the function of "maintaining and protecting the guarantees of the common existence, order, and civilization of the two classes." The relationship between the classes includes not only their conflict, but also their members' shared environments, language, "organic habits," and so forth. The governing institutions of a republic based on popular sovereignty, Jaurès writes, are not "a homogeneous block" defined solely by the power of a dominant class, but a reflection of the complexity of social life, and thus complex and malleable (*AN*, 433–35). Thus collective self-government by a group of people is possible despite the conflicts among them. Because class conflict does not have the last word about political life, there is room—at least in a republic—for political power to bring about the reform of economic and social arrangements.

Conflicting classes in any era might be said to have some limited common life, of course. Jaurès argues that the two dominant classes of a modern society, the bourgeoisie and the proletariat, have something specific in common. The bourgeoisie may be guilty of all the "repugnant selfishness" and "insidious violence" of which Marx accused it, Jaurès writes, but Marx was also right to note "the grandeur of the bourgeoisie's work" in "breaking all the ancient forms, dissolving all the old powers and all the old beliefs, changing the habits of the world profoundly and reinventing its own techniques incessantly, unchaining the tragic beauty of unlimited productive forces, taking the dead property of church, nobles, and kings and making it into a living and energetic property, and throwing all the great sleeping forest of traditions into its ever-moving monstrous furnace blaze" (*AN*, 367–68). The bourgeoisie and the proletariat share this spirit of protest and progress.

From the Reformation's rediscovery of "the power of inner life" to the Enlightenment's critique of authority to the French Revolution's abolition of monarchy, the bourgeoisie had shown the proletariat how to rebel, and, in learning that lesson, the proletariat had begun to rebel in its turn against the bourgeoisie. But this new rebellion did not make the bourgeoisie's own rebellious legacy obsolete. The "reciprocal education" of the two classes would continue, not only despite their conflict but through their conflict (*AN*, 398–402). The bourgeoisie's work of breaking apart the premodern social order was not finished, and the proletariat's work was to make democratic the modern world the bourgeoisie had brought about: to apply the ideas of popular sovereignty, equal rights, and the constitutional limitation of power to economic and social life, as well as to the state—and perhaps also to expand the possibilities of "inner life" (*AN*, 402–3).

If a modern republic must be founded on the common life of all its citizens and also on the common modernist project of its two leading classes, then the presence of orderly representative and legal institutions like those of the Third Republic would seem to allow for, or even generate, a second set of commonalities, which could secure and deepen the first. Once class-based political parties compete in elections, and once unions are legally recognized and collective bargaining at least tacitly encouraged, Jaurès writes, the class struggle becomes "organized" and "systematized." Thus transformed, it is no longer a threat to the "patrie": conflict between workers and bosses can become "amplified" without becoming "so bitter that no common ground can remain, that the terrain is broken under the clash of the combatants" (*AN*, 411). Thus "the struggle between the two classes, despite its increasing intensity and scope, is not heading towards social dislocation, and it undermines neither the law of democratic evolution nor the fundamental unity of the *patrie*. This is because all the compromises, agreements, or reforms that interrupt the combat at various moments both represent the seriousness of the conflict and prepare solutions proportionate to the problem" (*AN*, 430). From larger, more encompassing strikes, Jaurès notes, come larger and more encompassing collective bargains (*AN*, 431). Dissenting from both revolutionary socialism and mainstream French republicanism, Jaurès thinks that the energy of class struggle can be conducted through institutional and legal forms, sustaining that energy and applying it to a constructive end: making the Republic more thoroughly republican. When socialists turn toward parliamentary politics and collective bargaining, Jaurès suggests, class struggle does not dissipate, but takes on a new character. Jaurès wants to pursue something he calls "class struggle" or "class politics," but that something is quite different from the class struggle that Marx had envisioned. Morally and institutionally bounded by an orientation toward bargaining and compromise, class struggle gains new structure and purpose. Instead of being expressed in sporadic outbursts that always end quickly and often produce misery for workers, class struggle shaped by and for republican political institutions becomes a continuous project of political and social reform aiming not only at the good of the working class, but also at some more inclusive good.

Socialist ends and socialist means, once again, turn out to be hard to distinguish. The welfare state appears to be both a condition for the inclusion of the working class within the nation and the outcome of the working class's turn toward reformist politics. Social inclusion and egalitarian public policy are mutually reinforcing, Jaurès suggests. The logic of reformist politics, in other words, is both cumulative and self-limiting. Each reformist achievement, however limited, makes more likely further reforms, even as the moderating effects of increased social inclusion preclude a movement that seeks a radically different form of society. Reforms lead away from revolution, and they are always incomplete because they only constrain the economic power of the bourgeoisie; they do not abolish it. Jaurès concedes that much to his revolutionary critics. But what the revolutionaries fail to see is that each reform establishes the ground for further reforms. To adopt the method of reform is to accept the longevity of capitalism and to work for a piecemeal socialization of property, rather than for a complete reordering of society. The revolutionary alternative promises perfect justice in the future, but Jaurès wants that alternative to be judged according to its immediate method rather than its ultimate end. The revolutionary method—were revolutionary parties to actually employ it—would fail the test of republican justice because it would rupture the tentative human bonds that survive in a capitalist society. The actual practice of revolutionary parties, meanwhile, fails the test because revolutionaries refuse to use the limited political power they already have, for fear of muddying their absolute opposition to the existing society, and thus they do less than they could to establish some measure of justice. At the same time, mainstream republicans make such inadequate gestures toward either equality or solidarity that their methods and policies also fail the test of republican justice. But a method of republican class struggle—that is, the daily activity of a labor movement oriented toward large-scale collective bargaining, majoritarian coalition building, and the gradual construction of a welfare state—can pass that test. Indeed, a regime that shapes, and is shaped by, such a movement might be able to approximate the impossible balance Jaurès wrote about in the *Histoire socialiste*: to be at the same time like an organism and like a lava flow.

Jaurès wants socialists, by pursuing that logic of reform, to make their homes within the republic, within political life. Does this diminish socialism? It seems that Jaurès is still haunted by the old charge against him: "You counsel the proletariat to settle on the capitalist earth." Again, he defends himself against this kind of criticism. This time the language of belief and grace is missing, but the echo of Jaurès's early writings is evident.[33]

> When I speak of democracy's sovereign arbitration over the struggling classes, of the settlements, the agreements, the compromises that necessarily mark each moment of the struggle, I am speaking of the series of ways that the socialist idea is made real, the ways it enters into the realm of facts; I am speaking of laws incomplete from the moment of their creation, of institutions shaky as soon as they are built. These laws and institutions are what will make ready, plan, and by degrees achieve, at last, the new order. I am not speaking of even the partial abdication of the ideal. The ideal is never compromised. (*AN*, 425)

Socialists find their incomplete victories frustrating. Jaurès wants his socialist readers to understand that frustration not as a sign that they are hemmed in by a boundary they have set for themselves unnecessarily, but as a sign that they are witnessing the "réalisation," the making real, of an ideal. These victories are incomplete not because socialists have erred in adopting the method of reform; their incompleteness is not reason to conclude either that socialists would have been better off pursuing revolution or that they should dispense with all talk of ideals. Their victories are incomplete because the realization of an ideal is necessarily incomplete. To experience every victory as incomplete, in other words, is to feel that one's political activity is guided by an ideal.

This frustration is exactly what Jaurès wants to cultivate. When the working class does manage to "establish a portion of social justice in laws and in institutions," Jaurès continues, it should "proclaim that its series of victories are for it nothing but degrees, moments, means. . . . In the thick of its struggle, the proletariat will only be able to adopt the superior method of democracy, of orderly and humane action, if it is conscious that each of its steady efforts *le rapproche d'un fin supérieure*, which the proletariat constantly affirms" (*AN*, 425–26). The phrase I leave untranslated here is both politic and suggestive. One possible meaning has to do with a change in proximity: the proletariat's political efforts bring it closer to a goal that it might at some point reach; its inferior achievements are steps towards a superior achievement. This is the sort of thing a leader of the SFIO might have been expected to say. But the phrase could also mean that these efforts give shape to the rapport between the proletariat and its most dearly held ideal. The ambiguity runs all the way back through the passage. The new order will be achieved, although only at the "last," a time that might be actual but could just as well be symbolic. The end or ideal of socialism—Jaurès switches back and forth in this passage between the words "fin" and "idéal"—is final, but in what sense? Jaurès yet again leaves room for his readers to think that the final goal of socialism might be final in a temporal sense, that the movement's ends might in the end be achieved. But Jaurès has already pointed out the continuity of socialist ends and socialist means and thus the impossibility of a socialist end radically different from its means. The only thing that Jaurès impresses on his readers with certainty here is that the ultimate end or ideal of socialist politics is to be "constantly affirmed" through proximate and imperfect means. The means are what we know of the end; the end, we might also say, is how we know what the means mean, the light that illuminates our present surroundings and activities.

The end toward which socialist reforms strive is, Jaurès writes, a "superior" end. Superior to what? Jaurès has already suggested that loyalties of class and nation point toward a commitment to humanity, but now he wants to suggest even more than this. As "human community" becomes a fact, Jaurès continues, its realization represents "*a new fact* in the universe, and the consciousness of this new fact, the consciousness of the highest possibilities of the world, will bring a profound renewal of the religious spirit" (*AN*, 427). It would be easy to forget that Jaurès is still writing about the work of democratic reform, what he at one point calls "propaganda and combat" (*AN*, 425), the effort to persuade and the recourse to the deployment of power that happens when persuasion fails (and that lurks in the background of all efforts to persuade). This is the stuff of political life, and it is rarely joyous or beautiful. Jaurès wants to turn his readers' attention to it, to ask them to live inside it. But he also wants to remind them that any end or ideal that deserves to be called "final" or "superior" stands somewhere, or points to something, outside the boundaries of the political.

Believers in such an ideal, Jaurès, insists, must not neglect inferior forms of community. Thus, when Marx and Engels proclaimed in their *Manifesto* that the workers of the world have no country, Jaurès writes, they were guilty of a disastrous exaggeration (*AN*, 436). The *Manifesto*'s authors should have known better: in other writings, they contradicted, or at least qualified, this "passionate outburst." Although, in its original context, their "famous sentence" served as a retort to "the polemics of bourgeois patriots who denounced communism as the destroyer of the *patrie*," Jaurès points out that, when read as a general claim, the *Manifesto*'s assertion that workers have no country amounted to a "sarcastic negation" of the dialectical insight that Marx himself at times displayed (*AN*, 436, 437). At his wiser moments, Marx (and, likewise, Engels) recognized that a revolution would play out through national political institutions: it would "democratize nations and socialize democracies" (AN, 439). Nevertheless, it was all too often the simplistic slogan and not the nuanced qualification that characterized Marx's thought—and Marxist parties' strategies. When taken seriously, the "sarcasms of the *Manifesto*" would render the labor movement nothing but "an odd sect of powerless and destructive visionaries" (*AN*, 440).

In his *Études socialistes*, Jaurès had suggested that Marx lacked an appreciation of how political bodies work. His point here is similar: that Marx lacked an appreciation of the spaces in which political life takes place. The labor movement should seek not to abolish the "patrie," Jaurès argues, but to turn the "patrie" into a forum for republican justice. Justice is necessarily a humanistic and thus international ideal. But just as there is no irreconcilable conflict between the "patrie" and the labor movement, Jaurès writes, so there is also no irreconcilable conflict between internationalism and patriotism—a tension, no doubt, but not a conflict that requires the defeat of one side by the other. Indeed, the pursuit of humanistic ideals can only take place within particular polities. To see the "patrie" as a stage that will be surpassed by the labor movement's new internationalism is to abandon the means by which justice can be brought into the world, to neglect the spaces in which justice can be made real. Internationalism, after all, has become possible because of political changes within particular countries. "As democracies are developed and nations constituted, the passion of the proletariat is naturally carried on toward other objects. New problems arise. Political democracy must be fulfilled by social democracy. The international spirit must enter each autonomous *patrie* and the evolution of social justice must be assured by the concerted effort of the workers of every country in a context of international peace. But democracy and the nation remain the essential and fundamental preconditions of all higher and superior creations" (*AN*, 442). It is not that patriotism as a principle or the nation as a collective body entails no dangers. Far from it: Jaurès warns that the "patrie" is all too often a "collective egoism," as expressed in "that detestable phrase, 'my country, right or wrong.'" Jaurès asserts that his kind of patriotism, rooted in public life and directed toward an ideal of universal justice, is quite different from the new nationalism that increasingly colored right-wing politics in his era. Patriotism need not pull us away from the "human *patrie*" if each country's citizens pull their "patrie" "away from classes and castes" to "truly make it the possession of all," Jaurès argues (*AN*, 452–53). A "patrie" inspired with the "international spirit" is still a "patrie," but a "patrie" of a different kind.

Conversely, if the international spirit has no place to come to earth, it is ineffectual and insubstantial. The "high ideal" of human reconciliation, Jaurès writes,

> can only be realized in the autonomous nation, according to the methods of action and struggle suggested or imposed by the history of each country, with the materials furnished by each nation's substance. . . . The hour is past when utopians could think of communism as an artificial plant that one could cultivate at will, under whatever climate was chosen by the leaders of a sect. Enough with Icarus! Socialism no longer separates itself from life; it no longer separates itself from the nation. It does not desert the *patrie*: it makes use of the *patrie* in order to transform it and make it greater. The abstract and anarchistic internationalism that scoffs at the conditions of struggle, of action, of evolution of each historic grouping will come to seem like nothing but an Icarus, only more artificial and antiquated than the original. (*AN*, 453–54)

At Amsterdam, Jaurès had argued against imposing the German Marxist model on all parties of the International. Here, he goes farther. It is not only that different political tactics are suited to the institutions and cultures of different countries. Jaurès wants to say now that the existence of many polities and the deep differences among them are permanent facts of political life. Like so many other things that the Marxists think will soon melt into air, the "patrie" is part of the earth on which citizens stand. To think otherwise, to wish otherwise, is to try to float above political life, and thus to have no real part in it.

There is no question for Jaurès that internationalism is "higher" than commitment to any particular polity. But that the higher depends continually on the lower is, he writes, not only a political fact but a fundamental feature of existence: "Throughout the hierarchy of life, as Aristotle and Auguste Comte have magnificently demonstrated, the superior presupposes the inferior. The higher overcomes the lower, but it does not abolish it. It transforms it. It appropriates it to itself." Just as spirit transforms nature within every living thing, Jaurès writes, just as within the properly ordered human psyche passion submits to the rule of reason without losing its worth, so "nations ascend to humanity without being dissolved" (*AN*, 456). Internationalism does not require the abandonment of patriotism any more than republican patriotism requires the abandonment of class struggle. What Jaurès does not say here, even though he has suggested it elsewhere, is that the lower limits the realization of the higher. Just as local bonds of affection moderate the higher loyalties that they nurture, so patriotism precludes a wholly disinterested internationalism. Again, Jaurès is content to leave implicit what he had warned in *De la realité du monde sensible*: that the gap between actuality and potentiality is a "hidden root of suffering."

The relationship—or, one might say, the dialectic—of lower and higher is in part a relationship between principles and in part a relationship between institutions. After praising the debates about antiwar tactics at the International's Copenhagen and Stuttgart congresses, Jaurès writes: "International and *patrie* are henceforth linked. It is in the International that the independence of nations finds its strongest safeguard; it is in the independent nations that the International finds its noblest and most powerful instruments. One might even say: a small internationalism removes us from the *patrie*; a great internationalism brings us back. A small patriotism removes us from the International; a great patriotism brings us back" (*AN*, 463–64). The International is an idea, a principle of human solidarity, but it is also a series of congresses, as Jaurès has reminded his readers a few sentences before. It seems strange to invoke those congresses here. Stuffy meeting halls hung with red banners, crowded with chairs and long tables, cacophonous with translations into multiple languages—this is where a great patriotism leads us? But this strangeness seems to be exactly the point. Jaurès's prose may at times sag with the weight of grand abstractions, but here, it seems, is the secret of those abstractions: he means them to invite a passionate engagement with quotidian acts and concrete relations. It is always in real spaces, Jaurès wants to say—in particular rooms, streets, cities, countries, along with the particular men and women there—that we can engage in the pursuit of such lofty ideals as internationalism or solidarity or "complete social justice" (*AN*, 1). He also wants to remind his readers, once again, that our activity in those spaces is most comprehensible, or at least most tolerable, to us when we understand it to be the coming-to-earth of those ideals, and when we recognize in advance that those ideals will necessarily be limited by the characteristics of the spaces where they touch ground, and that they will be limited in different ways by different spaces.

This relationship between patriotism and internationalism, Jaurès argues, should be understood not as a conflict but as a pedagogical dialogue. "Distinct *patries*, distinct groups, have been the precondition of the broader groups for which our evolution is preparing us," he writes, "and in each of these groups a common life has been developed that secures and deepens the life of all and of each. A shared consciousness is formed in which individual consciousnesses are united and exalted" (*AN*, 449). A political movement committed to a humanistic ideal of justice can teach a "patrie" what its purpose is; the experience of membership in a "patrie," to the extent that it is just—or, for that matter, the experience of membership in a political movement that opposes some form of injustice—can teach the citizens of the "patrie," or the members of the movement, what it is to aspire to humanistic ideals. Thus Jaurès writes: "It is not in the hazy old dream of humanity in the abstract, but within the solid and historic reality of a human group—a group sharing a life that is rich and ample, but still bounded, concrete, and graspable—that there can be an apprenticeship for life in common and for a deeply humane sensibility" (*AN*, 451). Any human group of "graspable" scope, it seems, holds some potential to provide this apprenticeship. But the quality of the civic and humanistic education offered by a group depends on how "rich and ample" a life it shares. With civic consciousness as with egalitarian public policy, Jaurès suggests, the logic of reform is cumulative. As common life becomes more ample, it prepares its members for still richer forms of common life.

The passage quoted above may call to mind the idea of civic education, dear to classical republicans and the founders of the Third French Republic alike. It is worth noting, however, that an apprenticeship is not just any kind of education, but, typically, an education in a craft. In that sense, the metaphor seems to be yet another way for Jaurès to get at what he had earlier called the "question of method." He is convinced that the defining choice is not so much a matter of political ends, but one of political method. Describing public life as an apprenticeship, Jaurès suggests that, in it, one learns a way of thinking and doing at the same time, a habit of pursuing any proximate end—like the crafting of a particular object—in part to achieve that end but also in part because of what one learns from doing so. In a craft, ends and means are both important and are not entirely distinct.

But, in another sense, the metaphor of apprenticeship returns Jaurès to a familiar ambiguity. An apprenticeship is an education for a limited time: apprentices aspire to become masters. Will human beings at some point become fully humane? Will we become master-practitioners of life in common? If so, how long will it take? Despite everything, Jaurès seems once again to wonder whether he might be able to calculate the date by which justice will have been fully realized.

When Jaurès was first elected to public office, he described his political views simply as "republican." Although other labels could now be added to it, the designation was still appropriate. Jaurès had come to think that in a modern society—a society marked by capitalism, by the centralized state, by new kinds of loneliness, by the threat of new kinds of war—older republican ideas could be usefully put to work. Like the advocates of the classical Greek "politeia" or the Roman "res publica," Jaurès wanted to think in terms of public space and what happens in it; he wanted to pursue a common good, but by balancing rather than by purifying. Thinking in a republican way, Jaurès now proposed, modern citizens could come to recognize the possibility of mixing class struggle and democracy; they might seek to give institutional form to the solidarity of citizens not only through representative legislatures and the rule of law but also through encompassing collective bargaining arrangements and an inclusive welfare state, through strikes as well as election campaigns. If socialists began to think in this way, they could turn their attention, and their affections, from imagined future times to real present spaces.

Up to a point, then, Jaurès's thought reflects his republican influences. But only up to a point: beneath its arguments about movement strategy and public policy, *L'armée nouvelle* retraces the theology of Jaurès's first doctoral thesis. Jaurès had not forgotten his old convictions about the dynamics of Being. In 1910, not long before he finished writing *L'armée nouvelle*, he responded to a conservative deputy who accused him of being antireligious, telling the Chamber: "Twenty years ago, I wrote a book about nature and God, and about the relationship between them, of which I do not disavow a single line, and which has remained the substance of my thought."[34] Jaurès is not concerned that every reader or listener notice how his public rhetoric echoes deeper beliefs, and he does not ask his readers and listeners to join him in his way of understanding Being itself. He does not propose that a person needs to ask questions about Being before asking questions about politics. But, for Jaurès himself, the dialectic of the ideal and the real that he had pursued in *De la realité du monde sensible* seems still to be the key to all questions, political as much as epistemological. The solidarity of union members, the moral force of the nation, peace among nations—in *L'armée nouvelle* Jaurès layers reconciliation on reconciliation into a grand system of political harmonies. The higher and the lower reflect one another: universal ethical principles are to be rooted in local bonds of affection, and local bonds of affection are to be informed by universal ethical principles. A modern republic mixes and balances and is defined by the spaces in which it operates, but in ways that disclose a deeper pattern of mixing and balancing and reveal an aspiration that no space can enclose. The moral story Jaurès tells in *L'armée nouvelle* is about potentiality bursting through into actuality—but always, he reminds us, incompletely. After all, if there were a guarantee of perpetual peace then no armies, old or new, would be necessary.

Attending only to the polemic within *L'armée nouvelle,* we would notice how Jaurès uses republican motifs to connect the pieces of reformist socialist politics. But the book's undercurrents lead elsewhere. Reading *L'armée nouvelle* in the light of *De la realité du monde sensible*, we are apt to see themes that have less to do with Athens than with Jerusalem. There is no need for a reader to take in Jaurès's theological system as a whole. It would be a mistake, however, not to notice that Jaurès is directing our attention toward social democracy's inner life. Jaurès wants to say that, even though political life can never be more than a dim reflection of the fullest justice, the deepest reconciliation, for which we are capable of hoping, still the inability of political life to fulfill those fundamental hopes does not mean that they cannot speak to us, or that we should not listen.

Jaurès brought a bill for a citizen militia before the Chamber of Deputies in 1911, but it was never debated or voted on.[35] Soon he found himself immersed in an increasingly urgent effort to forestall a European war. Traveling throughout France and across Europe, he spoke before crowds, met with leaders of the International, lobbied successive French governments, wrote steadily. Despite the enmity his relentless work for peace brought him from France's new right-wing nationalist organizations and journals, and despite the unmistakable imminence of war, he seemed never to lose heart.[36]

The story of Jaurès's last three years is a moving one, not least because we know how it will end: on the last day of July 1914, a young nationalist fanatic shot and killed him, and, by the time he was buried, the First World War had begun. I will not tell that story here; others have told it well.[37] I only want to suggest that, in thinking about the contours of inner life, we may find it worth considering the life, and not just the ideas, of someone like Jaurès. His tenacity in those final years is a testament to his way of thinking about politics. It is not unreasonable to imagine that we might find within Jaurès's political thought some notion of how people of good will might remain upright in the storm.

CONCLUSION
An Awkward Politics

In the decades after Jaurès's death, as social democrats went on to construct a new political model, they saw and did things that neither the liberal republicanism nor the Marxism of the nineteenth century had anticipated or could comprehend, but for which the political thought of Jaurès and other reformists in his generation should have prepared them. The end of the First World War did not restore liberal confidence in steady progress. Instead, the representative institutions and legal rights beloved of the old-style radicals seemed in danger of being overwhelmed by the rising power of industry and finance, and undermined by the loneliness of mass society and the furies to which modern moods gave rise. The revolutionary Left had expected that it could, someday, solve these problems once and for all. This expectation, however, proved a poor guide to the real political options, and, by the end of the twentieth century, parties of the democratic Left had abandoned the pretense that they aimed to transcend capitalism. Contradiction had not led to anything like the crisis predicted by Marx; private ownership of industry had proven resilient; the quest for a historical agent capable of revolutionary consciousness and revolutionary action had failed.

Instead of raising the world on new foundations, the democratic Left brought about a modern mixed regime, a peaceful if uneasy cohabitation of capitalism and democracy. The Left's great achievement, as it turns out, has been to bring the principles of freedom and solidarity down to earth, establishing the possibility that modern social life could be shaped by political decisions. The forms social democrats have given to their principles—welfare states, collective bargaining regimes, economic regulations, parties and unions and civic associations—have been imperfect and impermanent; they have needed vigilant defense and frequent adjustment. The method of democratic reform has never won such smashing victories as to make itself obsolete, but it has never proven incapable of generating something new. The battle to realize the Left's hopes has never been wholly won; it has also never been wholly lost.

Throughout the past century, the social democratic tradition has been defined by what Jaurès calls its "method" of reform. Although reformism has sometimes been taken to mean "programmatic minimalism" and at other times an alternate path to the old maximal revolutionary goals,[1] the reformism that Jaurès points to is something else—an ethos of democratic engagement, a procedure for political action that is democratic in both its means and its ends. This reformism is cumulative because reforms provide the ground on which further reforms are possible; it is political in character because no accumulation of reforms can make further reform unnecessary.

In his address to the 1903 Bordeaux congress of the Parti socialiste français, Jaurès tells the members of his party that "a day will come when we will see that the proletarian and socialist state has replaced the oligarchic and bourgeois state." But, he goes on to say, "I no longer believe that this will need to be like a sudden leap, a crossing of the abyss. Perhaps we will find that we have entered the zone of the socialist state as sailors notice that they have crossed the line of a hemisphere. No rope stretched over the ocean shows them that they have passed the line; instead, they know that their ship's course has carried them into a new hemisphere little by little."[2] The striking thing about this image is the continuity it portrays: picturing the scene, we know that on the day after their ship crosses a line of latitude or longitude, the sailors will do the same work as on the day before. They are sailors not because they have crossed or expect to cross a particular invisible line, but because they take soundings, scrub decks, mend rigging, watch the weather. Likewise, the defining question for social democratic politics as Jaurès explains it is not the degree to which social democrats expect to realize particular goals; differing expectations might distinguish optimists from pessimists, but this sort of speculation does not matter. What matters is that, regardless of whether their movements win dazzling victories or suffer smashing defeats, social democrats will need to organize, negotiate, and build coalitions, to find multiple ways of embodying freedom and solidarity, to balance conflict and commonality by bringing both to light in public spaces. To be a social democrat is to pursue social justice by doing the work of reform without expecting the necessity for that work to be eclipsed by either the failure or the success of that work.

Jaurès's political thought can help us develop an account of social democracy's history something like the one sketched out in the preceding paragraphs. Looking back on social democracy's achievements from a period in which they have come to seem fragile, we are likely to see a usable account of the Left's victories as no small thing. What I am most interested in, however, is the way that Jaurès's thought can help us reflect on what it would mean to revive the social democratic project in our time: to protect what social democrats have won, to extend that heritage in new ways—and perhaps to do it all better this time around. Writing when social democracy was new, Jaurès has something to say to those who would like to be part of social democracy's renewal. He offers an account not only of social democracy's successes, but also of the problems to which social democracy is prone—a social democratic critique of really existing social democracy.

A single theme runs through Jaurès's thought. When he writes about the presence of potentiality within actuality and about the gulf between them; when he describes a dialectic in which nothing is abolished; when he finds both "moral" and "material" interpretations of history insufficient; when he takes up the question of method; when he writes about the dependence of the "higher" and the "lower" on one another; and when he applies in new ways the old republican images of mixing and balancing, Jaurès is concerned with the incomplete reconciliation of the ideal and the real. Everything he has to tell us about the inward and outward aspects of social democracy, about both what the social democratic tradition has done well and what it might do better, stems from this notion of incomplete reconciliation.

In his speech at the PSF's Bordeaux congress, soon after talking about sailors crossing into a new hemisphere, Jaurès criticizes those members who would make the party's work "too easy" by distilling its politics to a single principle. This will not do, he argues: the politics he advocates will mix strikes and electoral coalitions, class struggle and common good, labor movement and parliament, partiality and unity, patriotism and internationalism. He says: "I recognize, yet again, that this complex politics which I am trying to present to the Party . . . is awkward [*malaisée*], that it will create for us grave difficulties at every moment."[3] These are surprising words for a party leader speaking to his members, but they are what we expect from Jaurès. His way of thinking is defined by its awkwardness, its gaps and remainders. When social democracy tries to evade its characteristic difficulties, he warns, it falters.

Following Jaurès, I propose that a renewed awkwardness will be essential to the renewal of social democracy in our time. Two kinds of awkwardness will be especially important for that renewal. Self-reflective social democrats and sympathetic critics of social democracy often remark that the movement's moral impulse has waned. One such writer reports that "social democrats today are defensive and apologetic"; another argues that social democracy has come to favor an "instrumental politics" at the expense of "speculative criteria for ethical judgment," leaving itself no course but a "politics of drift"; still another writes of the "loss of the idealism that has sustained the movement from the beginning"; yet another laments that "politics on the left . . . has been disenchanted."[4] There is obviously something to the idea that social democracy is starved for a sense of the ideal. There is something else, equally important, that is only implied by the common complaint about the social democratic movement's loss of ideals: namely, that social democracy today is a "movement" only in a loose and courteous sense of the term. The mainstream of social democracy is better described as a series of political parties directed, like other parties today, by a tier of professional politicians and operatives whose activities are opaque to the citizens on whose support they depend, citizens who are generally disengaged from political life except during the moment they spend in the voting booth.[5] Reviving social democracy will involve both recovering something of the movement quality of social democratic politics and restoring that movement's sense of the ideal. These tasks are related to each other, and both involve the sort of difficulties about which Jaurès fits us to think.

The differentiation of professional politics from the public lives of ordinary citizens is too much of a piece with other developments of the past century to be entirely reversed.[6] There is no way to eliminate the gap between political amateurs and the specialists who staff parties, unions, and the organs of the state. Nevertheless, any desirable future for the democratic Left requires a rich public life alongside the world of professional politics. A movement, in the sense I use the term, might at times encompass organizations that trade in policy ideas or operate election campaigns or administer benefits—activities that are often best carried out by experts or professionals who work inside the kinds of places that we refer to as "the halls of power," or who at least develop close relationships with those on the inside and work in a manner similar to theirs. But whether or not it includes such insiders, a movement necessarily incorporates political outsiders. A movement in this sense is an assortment of neighboring and overlapping campaigns and associations populated by ordinary citizens who plan and take action together.[7] Thus, even though it is too diverse and dispersed to be managed by a single set of leaders, a movement still has some sense of unity, some awareness of a common project, and some degree of mutual regard among its component parts and among their individual members.

Movements for reform are at their best when they encompass both insider and outsider politics: this is a lesson that the history of the Left makes unambiguously clear, and one that Jaurès can help us think about. The institutional position of insiders is a prerequisite for policy change, and governing institutions, at their best, can articulate more encompassing common goods than less authoritative associations can. At the same time, the tensions outsiders create are a necessary countervailing force against the tendency of even the best-intentioned insiders to accommodate themselves to the status quo. Moreover, the classical image of the active citizen is simply too valuable a legacy to abandon. Solidarity needs to take institutional form, Jaurès tells us; it needs to take form both through law and through civic experience, through public policy and through everyday practices of citizenship. All of these things are the business of political movements.

"Outsider" organizations will sometimes support and sometimes protest against the politicians and "insider" professionals closest to them. The relationship of outsider and insider politics is necessarily complicated, and it often requires a division of labor between those who are drawn, for whatever reasons of aptitude or temperament, to one or the other kind of politics. But the difference between the politics that happens within bureaucratic organizations, government institutions, or the election campaigns of those who seek to lead those institutions, on the one hand, and the politics of insurgent protest, on the other, should not be seen as a difference of principle. Frustrated by the stony face that professional politics so often turns toward the public, some activists on the Left (and, for that matter, on the Right) have claimed that it is such a difference, but they make things too simple. Furthering the divide between the two kinds of politics, political parties have too often encouraged the development only of citizen groups that will remain under their control or that will safely fade away when the next election has been won. These habits, too, make things simpler—and easier—than they should be. The difficulty lies in figuring out how a movement can make trouble for elected officials yet respect the logic of electoral politics and the nature of governance—and, conversely, how it can pursue legislative change and adopt bureaucratic forms of organization yet welcome disruptive or insurgent (or, simply, amateur) political engagements.

Suggesting that the logic of democracy is visible in both the "masses in motion" and the "play of parliament," Jaurès shows how we might hold outsider and insider politics together. Because the logic of democracy works itself out in more than one form, and because there is no one perfect embodiment of the principles of freedom or solidarity, Jaurès tells us, their various forms or embodiments stand in tension with one another. Although they do not achieve harmony, nevertheless, they aspire to it. Whether or not they know it, people who pursue the logic of democracy in any of its incarnations are moving together. For Jaurès, thinking in this way made it possible to appreciate the outsider and insider faces of his movement—and, most important, to understand these disparate concerns as contributions to a common project.

This is awkward work. A movement that makes room for both outsider and insider politics is necessarily ill at ease with itself. The relationships among its members are dissonant rather than harmonious. This is a dissonance that today's social democrats need to amplify.

Movements need members, and their greatest challenges are to find them and then to keep them together. Supporters of election campaigns return to private life after a few days or weeks of political activity, but movement members need to continue their work together. Why should they? Self-interest can certainly prompt a person's entry into political life. The pursuit of self-interest, however, can as easily lead to disengagement; my interests are most conveniently met, after all, if I leave the work of politics to someone else. Few political ends are so clear and so certain of achievement as to secure the commitment of large numbers of people for more than a short time. Ends aside, participation in a movement itself brings certain pleasures, above all, those of mutual endeavor and comradeship. But, as a source of sustained motivation, the pleasures of comradeship are no more reliable than the more obvious forms of self-interest. Comradeship, after all, has its aggravations as well as its pleasures, and the aggravations are as likely to drive us away from membership as the pleasures are to pull us in. Moreover, to the extent that we prize the virtues of private life—kindness, sincerity, intimacy—we will find, and should find, political life uncomfortable because it requires other virtues than these. Concrete ends and pleasing means are both important to movements, and much might be said about either. But, even together, they do not seem to be sufficient to sustain a movement. Movements, unlike less demanding forms of political participation, require some deeper or higher inspiration.

Nineteenth-century socialism drew and held its members in by claiming epic purposes. It sustained its members' political engagement with the promise that victory was certain—and not just any victory, but absolute victory in the "final conflict." In a surprisingly similar way, some versions of nineteenth-century liberalism promised a gradual progress toward perfection that differed from the revolutionaries' promise mainly in its sense of timing. Unaccustomed as we are to anything like that confidence, we may find it hard to grasp how radical a move it was for the early social democrats to deny the validity of these promises. Much of the time, Jaurès insists that the socialist ideal cannot be fully realized. To adopt the method of reform, he suggests, means accepting that no political path leads beyond the confines of politics— beyond the world of conflict and disagreement, partial and impermanent victories, and limited communities. Democratic reform leads to more democratic reform; it does not transcend political life. It is dishonest for a movement to promise its members that their efforts will, in the end, lead to the abolition of injustice. It is also ineffective: unrealistic hopes are easily converted into equally unrealistic hopelessness. The empty moral space left by the disappearance of revolutionary confidence may seem an alien concern to many today—

especially in America, where revolutionary movements have usually been marginal, and where their memory is in any case faint. The empty space where liberal confidence in progress used to be is—again, especially in America—a familiar concern indeed.

This is where the need for ideals and the need for movement politics intersect. The members of a movement need a plausible hope, a call to political participation and common purpose more compelling than self-interest or pleasure and more enduring than the old dream of revolution. They need, in other words, an ethical purpose, an ideal. Ideals are, by definition, unfulfilled, which is why they are able to furnish criteria for judgment and norms for evaluation of achievements. They are antidotes to complacency and instigations to hope. When carried out in the light of an ideal, political activity is inspiring in the way that movement politics needs to be if it is to sustain movement members in their common political commitments.

An ideal is different from a bold but potentially realizable policy. Creative policy proposals are good things, but to the extent they are achievable, they are not radical enough to serve as ideals. They are achieved or not achieved, and that is all there is to say about them. Policies are not my concern here. I am also not concerned here with the claim that certain ideals are universally valid in the sense that their pursuit is an imperative for everyone, everywhere, always. Some ethical imperatives may be universal—Jaurès, for one, thought that some are—but I am interested here in another property that certain ideas have.

By an "ideal," I mean a value or a moral commitment that has the power to call us where we did not expect to go, that compels us to look beyond the limited form in which we first come to know it. This is what I believe Jaurès meant when he wrote that our experience of quotidian things directs us toward an "ideal end." We do not get gradually closer to realizing an ideal, as we might get gradually closer to realizing a policy model: there is always an infinite distance between an ideal and the fragmentary forms in which we are able to realize it. Its very distance from us shows an ideal's power.

At the same time, what matters is not that we can demonstrate the rightness of an ideal, in the abstract, but that we recognize in it a power that is more than cognitive. We respond to an ideal intellectually, but also with a "feeling of duty" that is to us, as Jaurès told his students at Albi, as the core of the trunk is to the tree. When we see our actions in the light of an ideal—let us say, the ideal of justice—we come to understand our actions differently than we otherwise would have. We come to see that those actions have a limited capacity to realize justice, but we also come to see in them a depth and a significance that would not be apparent if we were not asking ourselves whether and how they contribute to the realization of that ideal. Perhaps the questions we are led to ask about our actions will then prompt us to see instances of injustice, and possibilities for joining with others in pursuit of justice, that we had previously ignored. An ideal, we might say, both judges and justifies our actions and our memberships. Or, more precisely: we can properly call a value or moral commitment an "ideal" when we find that it has these powers, that it surprises us in these ways. An ideal can be reflected in real actions, but an ideal is an ideal insofar as we cannot fully realize it. An ideal remains outside our experience. That is why it can inspire us in a way that self-interest or pleasure or false expectations or fully realizable goals cannot.

To reconcile ideals with politics, however, is trickier than it might seem. The problem is not that politics is tawdry; it can be, but ideals can touch earth in strange places. Rather, the problem is that, although ideals can inspire our political engagement, they can also distract us from political life—including, and perhaps especially, democratic political life. If we are guided by an ideal, then every pragmatic organization we might join, every strategic action we might take, every effective vote we might cast will be disappointing to us. Ideals can lead us away from an appreciation for the real and limited spaces in which politics takes place and the real and limited people with whom we take political action—and from our limits as individuals. A movement that admits the inspiration of an ideal will find that its shared ideal points to questions that political life cannot answer, problems that political action cannot resolve. Nevertheless, a movement that is political in character—that does not aim at absolute harmony or pure freedom or perfect justice—cannot escape the nonideal nature of political life. The possibility of politics, after all, arises as much from our frailties and divisions as it does from our capacities and commonalities. Thus one of the characteristic anxieties of the democratic Left is that it finds ideals both necessary and troubling.[8]

Jaurès has something to say about this feature of the democratic Left's inner life. At the heart of his political thought is the claim that devotion to an ideal of justice can lead us deeper into an appreciation for political life, but only if we attune ourselves to notice the ways that the ideal is already with us, reconciled incompletely with the world in which we live. A movement like social democracy, he wants to say, can inspire its members' political participation and moral commitment in a way that does not distract them from the humdrum work of democratic politics but rather leads them into a deeper affection for that work—if they can sense their ideal, if they can feel the presence of solidarity and see evidence of freedom in and around that work, and in and around its proximate results. All this can happen, Jaurès was convinced, without the ideal losing its power as a norm against which real achievements can be judged, as the ground against which political life stands out in clear relief and begins to make sense.[9]

Although Jaurès's political ideal is justice—the reconciliation of freedom and solidarity, individual and community—he is not interested in developing a systematic theory of the relationship between these. He wants instead to pose the ideal of justice as a problem to work at because to freeze the ideal into a fixed form would diminish its power. Justice is an ideal for him in that, once he decides to understand his political activity in its light, it asks more of him than he expected. This is the lesson he takes from the Dreyfus Affair: to his own surprise, he finds himself defending the rights of a bourgeois army officer because he sees in the case of Dreyfus an instance of injustice that he is compelled to take seriously. What Jaurès means is that, for modern citizens committed to a politics of democratic reform, commitment to an ideal of justice generates a plausible hope. When people who do the work of reformist politics think of that work as the imperfect realization of an ideal—that is, when the ideal to which they are committed both helps them make sense of what they have done and impels them to do more—they then have cause to keep doing the work of reform together, even though they do not expect their work to succeed in any full or final sense.

In his theology of Being, Jaurès gives an elaborate account of the relationship between the ideal and the real, and thus of the sources and characteristics of this plausible hope. Turning Kant inside out, he argues that the human being is a citizen of an ordered whole, that the human consciousness perceives order and yearns for harmony because all Being yearns for harmonious order and is forever both realizing and falling short of that ideal. For Jaurès, the yearning for socialism is justified by—and the hope of socialist victories, however fragmentary, is secured by—the nature of Being itself. This is too much. Jaurès's is a kind of natural theology, and like other members of that genre, it overreaches. *De la realité du monde sensible* asserts knowledge where expressions of desire would be more appropriate; it claims certainty where at most possibility is warranted; it depends too much on factual assumptions that may well be false—not least, the notion of an orderly, spatially infinite, and uniformly three-dimensional cosmos. But we learn most from Jaurès's theological thought if we judge it by its consequences instead of its literal content. Jaurès's all-embracing account of Being relieves him of the need to base his hope, implausibly, on claims about the march of mere human history. It has the surprising effect of freeing him to think about politics in ways that are contextual rather than abstracted, local rather than epic. In short, we need not accept Jaurès's argument about the *sources* of hope to learn something from what he says about the *characteristics* of a plausible hope. If nothing else, he shows us how to recognize, when we find it, the kind of hope that his kind of politics involves.

Here, as I understand them, are the criteria by which Jaurès thinks we can know the patterns of inner life appropriate to a social democratic movement. His socialism is a regulative ideal,[10] but of a certain kind: he is concerned as much with the "feeling of duty" as with the validity of that duty. He wants his political activities to be judged according to and justified by an ideal, a principle of justice, but he does not want that principle to be purely noumenal. The kind of ideal with which he is concerned is a moral claim that confronts the whole person, body and passions and mind, with a decision about whether and how to engage in political life. He wants to be moved by the ideal to which he is committed, and so he wants the ideal to be recognizable within the sensible world. He wants to experience the political organizations and institutions that he works in and works for as embodiments of that ideal. He wants the ideal to take shape within the world of visible and tangible things, and he wants to be able to claim that an ideal does not have to be fully realized to be found within the sensible world. At the same time, even though he generally declines to insist that the ideal *will be* realized, he wants to maintain an acute sense that the ideal *has not been* realized. Having displaced the ideal from the realm of political expectations, he wants to remember that it is absent from political life, even though he also wants to feel its presence within political life. Rejecting apocalyptic visions and implausible hopes, he wants to be able to cultivate a romance with the mundane, and thus he needs to be able to find the mundane worthy of romance. He wants, in short, a palpable ideal.

Jaurès's way of thinking about the relationship between ideals and reality is paradoxical—or dialectical, in his sense of that term. He wants to convince his readers that they do not need revolutionary dreams to inspire them because they can fall in love with the daily work of reformist politics—not merely because they find pleasure in it, as important as that pleasure might be, but because they find in that work the mediation of an ideal that political life can never fulfill. He wants to show them that they can put their hearts into the prosaic spaces and ungainly bodies of real politics—the unions, parties, legislatures, and bureaucracies where the work of organizing citizens and the work of making policy go on—because the principles they value have already taken surreptitious shape within those spaces and bodies. The moral sustenance that makes a movement for democratic reform possible, Jaurès thinks, comes from this way of looking at and thinking about the work of democratic reform. Social democracy is defined by both its commitment to an ideal and its engagement with the real, even though it has no way to seamlessly unite the two. But out of this awkwardness, somehow, a sustaining hope reveals itself: that is the crucial, and the most difficult, claim within Jaurès's awkward politics.

Jaurès tells us in the *Histoire socialiste* that hope can be, or perhaps must be, attached to a symbol. To be plausible, hope needs to be distinguished from optimism: it does not mean a literal expectation about the future. When he describes the ideal as if it has already taken a palpable form, he is trying to show how the hope that inspires a politics of democratic reform grows out of an experience in the present, understood in relation to an ideal. Recognizing the motif at the heart of his political thought as a paradox, we can also recognize its variations as a set of symbols, expressions that have the power to point beyond themselves, to indicate a quality of inner life that is impossible to express directly.[11]

In those passages where Jaurès departs from his usual way of thinking, where he seems to expect the ideal of justice to be fully realized at some point in the future, it is possible, even likely, that he is simply being inconsistent. But if we read his visions of a fulfilled ideal there symbolically—which, I would suggest, he has given us license to do—they offer us another way to talk about the palpability of the ideal. Understood symbolically, the experience of waiting is as close as we can get to an experience of simultaneous absence and presence. We may even say, when waiting for something, "It's so close I can taste it."[12] If there are occasions when we talk about the dream of a day of perfect justice and when our talking inspires us to engage in the political work at hand rather than leading us to disdain that work, it seems possible that talking about our dream of perfect justice has inspired our engagement because it makes our ideal feel present to us. We are hopeful not because we are convinced that a day of perfect justice is actually going to arrive, but because conversations like these allow us to feel the presence of the absent as we do when we wait for something we want.

Not despite its paradoxical quality but because of it, Jaurès's belief in the palpable ideal can help us give an account of what it is like to be committed both to an ideal of justice and to the steady work of democratic reform.[13] If we were to describe the dialectic of ideals and democratic reform in a nonparadoxical way, we would make it seem too easy. Jaurès wants to say all this as a philosopher, but, if he succeeds, it is because he is at least half a poet.

Perhaps his greatest legacy is that Jaurès described the outer and inner awkwardnesses without which the social democratic tradition would cease to be itself. He asked what consequences a commitment to the method of reform might have, and he traced those consequences into the inner lives of the members of a reformist movement, uncovering the difficulty of political ideals and political hope for those who have made their homes within the frustrating spaces of democratic politics. The political method he recommended is awkward in any number of ways, but its awkwardness is what we ought to appreciate most about it. He insisted that the gap between real politics and ideal ends cannot be reduced to nothing, but also that freedom and solidarity are real experiences. It is because they are, at the same time, both within our sensory experience and outside it that these ideals can be reconciled with democratic politics and can inspire a movement for democratic reform. That movement, in turn, will generate its own difficulties; the relationships among its components will involve their own incomplete reconciliations and impossible balances. But ideals come first. Without a palpable ideal, such a movement founders.

Jaurès was convinced that a movement like social democracy depends on the immediacy with which the movement's members sense the presence within political life of that which remains absent from political life. He was certain that once a group of "believers" accepts all this, something new happens: out of awkwardness emerges a moral poise and a persistent hope, a kind of grace. Those who want to combine a democratic politics and a politics of ideals will be sustained in their shared work if for them every proximate form of freedom and solidarity, every proximate instance of human reconciliation, is at once disconcerting, satisfying, and hopeful—disconcerting because it forces them to imagine an ultimate reconciliation of human with human, and of humanity with Being itself, that they know they cannot achieve; satisfying because it provides a taste of the ideal that directs them; and hopeful because the irrepressible possibility of further reconciliations, of deeper freedoms, of wider and more durable solidarities stretches out before them. I do not know whether he was right about all of this. It does seem possible that many people who have made lasting commitments to the democratic and political pursuit of justice, or who have come to terms with the frustrations of membership in a complex movement for democratic reform, have arrived at something like the inner awkwardness and the ensuing state of grace of which Jaurès gives an uncommonly vivid account. What I am certain of is that this is a proposition to be tested in practice, not one for which we ought to seek proofs in advance.

I am equally certain that, if social democracy is to be renewed, social democrats must not ignore the inner life of their movement. The core of what Jaurès's writings have to say to social democrats in our time is that we should not be dismayed when we are unable to resolve the disharmonies within our project, or when we find ourselves hungry for an experience of our ideal. Social democracy will be awkward because, rightly, it works to reconcile what it cannot reconcile. Thus social democrats should be suspicious of any strategy or theory that seeks to resolve the clashes between protest and governance, conflict and commonality, freedom and solidarity, or the particular and the universal, whether by rejecting either term within any of these tense pairings or by claiming to have put their tensions permanently to rest. Thus, too, whenever social democrats begin to think it easy to reconcile democratic politics and political ideals, it is most likely because they have begun to neglect either the shape of the real or the demands of the ideal.

Ideals expand, but politics is life within limits. It is impossible to embrace both the ideal of justice and the real world of politics; it is unnecessary to let go of either. Forgetting these contradictions would be all too easy. The alternative to forgetting, whatever else we might say about it, involves thoughtful observation, attentiveness, reflection—reflection not only on organizations and institutions, strategies and policies, but also on the currents of trouble, and perhaps hope, that run beneath the surface of political life.

NOTES

INTRODUCTION

1. The phrase "renewal of social democracy" comes from the seminal work in these debates: Giddens, *Third Way*, 1. For my own response to Giddens, see Kurtz, "Anthony Giddens's Third Way."

2. My understanding of social democracy is influenced in particular by Berman, *Primacy of Politics*. Other general works on social democracy's character and scope include Esping-Andersen, *Politics Against Markets*; Korpi, *Democratic Class Struggle*; Padgett and Paterson, *History of Social Democracy*; Przeworski, *Capitalism and Social Democracy*; Przeworski and Sprague, *Paper Stones*; and Sassoon, *One Hundred Years of Socialism*. For overviews of social democracy's development in recent decades, see Kitschelt, *Transformation of Social Democracy*; Moschonas, *In the Name of Social Democracy*; and Pierson, *Hard Choices*. For the most recent surveys of the state of social democratic politics, see Cramme and Diamond, eds., *After the Third Way* and Cronin, Ross, and Shoch, eds., *What's Left of the Left*. These studies are primarily (in most cases exclusively) focused on European social democracy. On the notion that trade unions and their allies have at times constituted an "invisible mass movement" for social democracy in the United States, see Harrington, *Socialism*, 305–29. For recent studies of this American version of social democracy, see Battista, *Revival of Labor Liberalism* and Rossinow, *Visions of Progress*.

3. On the concepts of political tradition and political project, see Bronner, *Ideas in Action*, 7–10; see also Smulewicz-Zucker, "Concepts, Traditions, and Actions." Sheri Berman posits something similar when she writes that "correctly understood, social democracy is far more than the defender of particular policies or values such as the welfare state, equality, or solidarity. Nor is it merely watered-down Marxism or bulked-up liberalism, but rather, at least as originally conceived, a distinctive ideology and political movement all its own" (*Primacy of Politics*, 200).

4. See Crick, *In Defense of Politics*. Berman labels this classical set of ideas "the primacy of politics and communitarianism," or "the conviction that political forces rather than economic ones should be the driving forces of history and that the 'needs' or 'goods' of society must be protected and nurtured" (*Primacy of Politics*, 6). In a more recent version of this argument, Berman drops the term "communitarianism" in favor of "cross-class cooperation" ("Social Democracy's Past and Future," 32). Although social democrats have pursued common goods in ways that the term "cross-class" does not adequately convey, Berman's new phrase does solve a problem in her earlier formulation. The term "communitarian" has a specific meaning in academic political theory. I would argue—and, given her shift in terminology, perhaps Berman would agree—that social democracy is as distinct from communitarianism, in the sense that academic political theorists use that term, as it is from liberalism or Marxism. For such a formulation, see Walzer, "Communitarian Critique of Liberalism," 96–97.

I use the term "talk" here (in preference to "speech") in a sense similar to that developed by political theorists such as Benjamin Barber (*Strong Democracy*, 173–98) and Michael Walzer ("Critique of Philosophical Conversation"), who have warned against the notion that political judgment must emerge from "perfectly rational forms of speech" (Barber, *Strong Democracy*, 176) and have argued, accordingly, that democratic political theory should be more concerned with the "real talk" of ordinary public life than with the "ideal speech" of philosophy (Walzer, "Critique of Philosophical Conversation," 35–36).

    5. See Schwartz, *Permanence of the Political*.

    6. On the emergence of social democracy, see Kloppenberg, *Uncertain Victory*. Classic studies of socialism and social democracy in this period include Braunthal, *History of the International*; Cole, *Second International*; and Joll, *Second International*. For an account that places early social democracy within the broader context of socialist political thought, see Bronner, *Socialism Unbound*. Note that early reformist socialists did not generally describe themselves as "social democrats"; they more often called themselves "socialists." I (and others) use the term "social democrat" to describe them because it is, in retrospect, the label most helpful in grouping like-minded thinkers.

    7. Whether because social democrats have prided themselves on their tradition's pragmatism, or because social democracy's coalition-building strategies have encouraged porous ideological boundaries, or because social democratic thought is often historicist rather than purely normative and social democratic writing is often oriented toward broad publics rather than being narrowly academic, there seems to be no commonly acknowledged canon of social democratic political theory. For an ambitious recent attempt to formulate a comprehensive statement of social democratic political theory, see Meyer with Hinchman, *Theory of Social Democracy*. For influential English-language works reflecting on social democracy, see Webb and Webb, *Industrial Democracy*; Rauschenbusch, *Christianity and the Social Crisis*; Niebuhr, *Moral Man and Immoral Society*; Polanyi, *Great Transformation*; Crosland, *Future of Socialism*; Marshall, *Citizenship and Social Class*; Walzer, *Spheres of Justice*; Harrington, *Socialism: Past and Future*.

    8. There has been no complete collection of Jaurès's writings. The most extensive compilation is the *Oeuvres de Jean Jaurès*, edited by Max Bonnafous. The French publishers Fayard and Vent Terral have begun two new series of Jaurès's works, launched in 2000 and 2005, respectively, of which only a few volumes have appeared so far. The principal biography of Jaurès in English is Goldberg, *Life of Jean Jaurès*; see also Pease, *Jean Jaurès*, and Jackson, *Jean Jaurès*. For studies of Jaurès's political thought in English, see Weinstein, *Jean Jaurès*; Kolakowski, "Jean Jaurès"; and Noland, "Individualism in Jean Jaurès' Socialist Thought." For a recent French biography of Jaurès, see Rioux, *Jean Jaurès*; one of the more useful older sources is Soulé, *Vie de Jaurès*. For an engaging and richly illustrated biographical sketch, see Rebérioux, *Jaurès*. Significant recent studies of Jaurès's political thought in French include Antonini, *État et socialisme*, and Peillon, *Jean Jaurès*. Goldberg includes a thorough bibliography of early and mid-twentieth-century editions of Jaurès's works (*The Life of Jean Jaurès*, 569–76). Antonini includes a more up-to-date bibliography of French editions of Jaurès' works (*État et socialisme*, 249–54) and works on and related to Jaurès written in French (254–74). See also the writings collected at http://fr.wikisource.org/wiki/Auteur:Jean Jaurès (accessed January 15, 2014).

    9. On Bernstein, see Steger, *Quest for Evolutionary Socialism*; and Gay, *Dilemma of Democratic Socialism*.

    10. For use of the term "Jaurèsism," see DeLeon, *Flashlights of the Amsterdam Congress*, 37, 49, 51, and passim. On Jaurès's place not only as the Second International's leading pro-

ponent of a reformist method but also as the spokesman within the International for a broader "way of looking at politics," see Joll, *Second International*, 3.

11. Howe, *Essential Works of Socialism*, 213. For an example of the dismissive view of Jaurès that Irving Howe describes, see Lichtheim, *Marxism*, 278–79.

12. I am influenced here by Walzer, "On the Role of Symbolism," and Walzer, *Interpretation and Social Criticism*.

13. On the notion of the "connected critic," see Walzer, *Interpretation and Social Criticism*, 39. For a recent social democratic apologia, see Judt, *Ill Fares the Land*.

14. I have argued elsewhere that Jaurès's account of social democracy is republican in a different way from that of ideas prominent in recent neorepublican political theory, such as the version expounded in Pettit, *Republicanism*. See Kurtz, "Apprenticeship for Life in Common."

15. Which writings and speeches? My intention has been show the scope of Jaurès's thought without covering the same ground too many times or following too many lines of thought tangential to my central purposes. This means that I have attended only briefly to his early works (other than his two dissertations) and have left out some speeches and writings that, though historically important or aesthetically notable, do not seem to me to be the best exhibitors of the substance of his thought: his much-loved "Discours à la jeunesse" (Address to the youth) is missing here, for instance, as is his moving invocation of Friedrich von Schiller's "Song of the Bells" at the Basel congress of the International. I have addressed only what I take to be the most telling portions of his *Histoire socialiste* and have scarcely touched on his voluminous topical writings and parliamentary speeches.

16. How much contextual information? As much as I have thought helpful, a standard that admittedly makes for idiosyncratic decisions. I attend more to some episodes—such as the gradual split between French reformists and revolutionaries in the first years of the twentieth century—than to others. I neglect some important historical events that do not seem to me to be essential to the reader's understanding of Jaurès's thought, like the Boulanger crisis and the Panama scandal, and I say little about the Dreyfus Affair or about the strikes of the 1890s and 1900s, and even less about the geopolitical events leading up to the First World War, although these would necessarily be major subjects in a full biography of Jaurès.

17. The principal exception is Jaurès, *Studies in Socialism*. See also Jaurès, *Democracy and Military Service*. The texts of these and other English translations of Jaurès's writings, including several previously unpublished translations, have been collected at http://www .marxists.org/archive/jaures/ (accessed January 15, 2014).

CHAPTER 1

1. Goldberg, *Life of Jean Jaurès*, 7–8; Pease, *Jean Jaurès*, 22–23.

2. Soulé, *Vie de Jaurès*, 9; Jackson, *Jean Jaurès*, 16; Goldberg, *Life of Jean Jaurès*, 4–9. Given his early experiences in Castres, it is interesting that Jaurès would later favor imagery drawn from the natural world: light, wind, water, trees, roots, soil. See the discussion of Jaurès's nature imagery in Grousselas, *Jaurès écrivain*, 45–77.

3. Pease, *Jean Jaurès*, 24; Goldberg, *Life of Jean Jaurès*, 11; Soulé, *Vie de Jaurès*, 12–17.

4. Goldberg, *Life of Jean Jaurès*, 12–13.

5. Ibid., 13–14.

6. Jaurès, as quoted in Soulé, *Vie de Jaurès*, 23–24. See also Goldberg, *Life of Jean Jaurès*, 13–14. Translations from French language works other than those by Jaurès are also mine, unless otherwise noted.

7. Goldberg, *Life of Jean Jaurès*, 16–17.

8. See Brooks, *Eclectic Legacy*, 248–56, for a description of the École's philosophy curriculum, and 31–34 for the relationship between the lycée and École courses of study. On Kant's place in Jaurès's schooling, see Goldberg, *Life of Jean Jaurès*, 17.

9. Goldberg, *Life of Jean Jaurès*, 18–19. On the friendship between Jaurès and Durkheim, see Lukes, *Émile Durkheim*, 44–48.

10. Jaurès, as quoted in Jackson, *Jean Jaurès*, 28. I have lowercased Jackson's "Socialist" to conform with the style I use elsewhere.

11. Jaurès, as quoted in Goldberg, *Life of Jean Jaurès*, 27–28.

12. On the founding of the Third Republic, see Derfler, *Third French Republic*, 11–25; Mayeur and Rebérioux, *Third Republic*, 25–41; Cobban, *History of Modern France*, 9–21; and Duclert, *République imaginée*, 102–25. On the French idea of a republic, see Nicolet, *Idée républicaine en France*, and Nora, "Republic." On French political thought in this period, see Judt, *Marxism and the French Left*; Mayer, *Political Thought in France*; Thomson, *Democracy in France*.

13. Adolph Thiers, as quoted in Derfler, *Third French Republic*, 109.

14. Jaurès's friend referred to here was Alexandre Zévaès, as quoted in Rimbert, "Jean Jaurès," part 1, 37.

15. Cobban, *History of Modern France*, 21–27; Derfler, *Third French Republic*, 29–33; Mayeur and Rebérioux, *Third Republic*, 79–100.

16. Rimbert, "Jean Jaurès," part 1, 47.

17. Goldberg, *Life of Jean Jaurès*, 22–23. The graduate Lesbazeilles, who would die four years later before making any name for himself, finished first. The philosopher Henri Bergson finished second (Rimbert, "Jean Jaurès," part 1, 35n2).

18. Jaurès, "Cours d'Albi," in *Philosopher à trente ans*, 52. Hereafter cited in text..

19. Goldberg, *Life of Jean Jaurès*, 24–27; Jean Jaurès to Charles Salomon, August 10, 1882, as quoted on 24.

20. Goldberg, *Life of Jean Jaurès*, 28–31, 34–35; Mayeur and Rebérioux, *Third Republic*, 123–25; Derfler, *Third French Republic*, 29; Cobban, *History of Modern France*, 32; Weinstein, *Jean Jaurès*, 35. On the Radicals of the Third Republic, see Stone, *Sons of the Revolution*. On Jaurès's evolving relationship with the Radicals, see Ducomte and Pech, *Jaurès et les radicaux*.

21. Bronner, *Socialism Unbound*, 2.

22. Marx and Engels, *Manifesto of the Communist Party*, 490.

23. My rendition of the (widely available) French text of "L'Internationale" draws freely on various English versions.

24. Derfler, *Third French Republic*, 44–47; Goldberg, *Life of Jean Jaurès*, 21; Joll, *Second International*, 14. On Proudhon and his influence, see Ehrenberg, *Proudhon and His Age* and Vincent, *Pierre-Joseph Proudhon*.

25. On Benoît Malon and reformist socialism, see Vincent, *Between Marxism and Anarchism*.

26. Gustave Rouanet, as quoted in Weinstein, *Jean Jaurès*, 27.

27. On the socialist groups in France in the 1880s, see Noland, *Founding of the French Socialist Party*, 6–25. See also Goldberg, *Life of Jean Jaurès*, 39–41; Mayeur and Rebérioux, *Third Republic*, 74–75; Joll, *Second International*, 13–16; and Mexandeau, *Histoire du Parti socialiste*, especially 22–55 (regarding the early years of the Third Republic) and 57–100 (regarding the period of Jaurès's career from the 1890s to the 1910s).

28. Goldberg, *Life of Jean Jaurès*, 38; Weinstein, *Jean Jaurès*, 44–47.

29. Thomson, *Democracy in France*, 103; Goldberg, *Life of Jean Jaurès*, 40–42. On the labor caucus (*groupe ouvrier*), see Derfler, *Third French Republic*, 44; Derfler, *Alexandre Millerand*, 29–30; Sagnes, *Jaurès*, 18.

30. On the legalizing of unions in 1884, see Rosanvallon, *Demands of Liberty*, 168–77; Mayeur and Rebérioux, *Third Republic*, 142; and Cobban, *History of Modern France*, 27.

31. Goldberg, *Life of Jean Jaurès*, 41–45; Rimbert, "Jean Jaurès," part 2, 6–9.

32. René Waldeck-Rousseau, as quoted in Rosanvallon, *Demands of Liberty*, 157.

33. Jaurès, "Fédération ouvrière," 171–74.

34. Jaurès, as quoted in Goldberg, *Life of Jean Jaurès*, 60.

35. France had by this time (1889) returned to the single-member district election system, which it would retain for the remainder of the Third Republic. Mayeur and Rebérioux, *Third Republic*, xv.

36. Goldberg, *Life of Jean Jaurès*, 61–63. Harvey Goldberg claims that Jaurès first described himself as a "socialist" in February 1890. I think his late-1889 writings express just as clear an identification with socialism, but the exact date is not important.

37. Jaurès, "Parti socialiste," 5, 7.

38. Jaurès, "Socialisme de la Revolution française," 205, 208.

39. Goldberg, *Life of Jean Jaurès*, 64.

40. On the relationship between Lucien Herr and Jaurès, see Goldberg, *Life of Jean Jaurès*, 62–63. On the lack of French translations of Marx's works at the time, see Mayeur and Rebérioux, *Third Republic*, 74.

41. On French higher education in the late nineteenth century, see Brooks, *Eclectic Legacy*, 33–34. On the writing of Jaurès's theses, see Goldberg, *Life of Jean Jaurès*, 26, 77–84. The theses are "De la realité du monde sensible," in *Philosopher à trente ans*, 113–374, and "De primis socialismi germanici lineamentis apud Lutherum, Kant, Fichte, et Hegel" in Adrien Veber's translation from the Latin, edited by Annick Taburet-Wajngart, "Des premiers linéaments du socialisme allemand chez Luther, Kant, Fichte, et Hegel," in *Philosopher à trente ans*, 383–436, both cited hereafter in text.

42. Kant's critical philosophy was experiencing a vogue in France, led by Jules Lachelier, and Lachelier is a key interlocutor in Jaurès's thesis (see especially *PTA*, 121–35). On the relationship between Jaurès's first thesis and neo-Kantianism, see Kolakowski, "Jean Jaurès," 120–25; Kloppenberg, *Uncertain Victory*, 225; and Goldberg, *Life of Jean Jaurès*, 77–81. Goldberg proposes that Jaurès was particularly influenced by Jules Lachelier and Émile Boutroux (*Life of Jean Jaurès*, 78); Kolakowski also cites Lachelier as a likely influence ("Jean Jaurès," 120). Unlike Kolakowski and Kloppenberg, I see Jaurès's argument less as a variant of neo-Kantianism than as a rejoinder to it.

43. Jaurès does not capitalize "l'être," but I will capitalize "being" when referring to the central concept of Jaurès's French thesis.

44. Note that Jaurès is writing his French thesis at the time when psychology was beginning to emerge as an observation-based discipline distinct from philosophy, and that psychology's early pioneers in France were, like Jaurès, philosophers trained at the École normale supérieure. See Brooks, *Eclectic Legacy*, 13.

45. On the influence of Neoplatonism on Jaurès's French thesis, see Taburet-Wajngart's introduction to *Philosopher à trente ans*, 29, and Antonini, *État et socialisme*, 28–33. Both Annick Taburet-Wajngart and Bruno Antonini identify Plotinus as the key source of Jaurès's Neoplatonic themes. Jaurès cites Plotinus once (*PTA*, 224).

46. Jaurès cites Aristotle's categories explicitly in his French thesis (*PTA*, 156); the key terms "acte" and "puissance" appear throughout the thesis.

47. On both occasions, Jaurès quotes the phrase "in God we live, and move, and have our being" (Acts 17:28) in Latin: "In Deo vivimus, movemur et sumus." This is a slight paraphrase of the Vulgate text, "In ipso enim vivimus, movemur et sumus" (In *him* we live, and move, and have our being). Given Jaurès's own rhetorical strategies, it is interesting that the phrase comes from a story in which Paul presents his "new doctrine" (Acts 17:19) to a group of Athenians in language that he thinks will sound familiar to them, telling his Greek audience that he is quoting from "your own poets." All English-language quotations of the Bible are from the King James Version here and throughout the notes to this volume.

48. See Goldberg, *Life of Jean Jaurès*, 14, regarding Jaurès's departure from the Church while in his late teens, and 68–69 regarding his attitude toward the Church around the time he was writing his theses.

49. Jaurès's French thesis has been aptly described as a "secular theology" (Blanc, "Patrie invisible," xcvii). On Jaurès's interest in religious matters, see the texts published posthumously in *Jaurès et la question religieuse*. On the relationship of those documents to "De la réalité du monde sensible" and to Jaurès's thought more broadly, see Peillon, *Jean Jaurès*, 201–13.

50. The concept of space and the related concepts of movement, form, and infinity (all of which Jaurès understands primarily in spatial terms) are each the subject of a chapter of his French thesis. See especially the chapter "De l'espace," in *Philosopher à trente ans*, 291–328.

51. Jaurès, "Au claire de lune." A translation titled "Moonlight" is included in Jaurès, *Studies in Socialism*, 184–92. See also Goldberg, *Life of Jean Jaurès*, 100.

52. Although the German Social Democratic Party would not reach the peak of its organizational strength until after its 1905 restructuring, even in the period I write about here, it seemed a model to many of Europe's left parties. By 1890, the Austrian, Swedish, Swiss, Norwegian, Danish, and Finnish socialist or labor parties—and of course Guesde's Parti ouvrier français—had adopted party structures and platforms based on that of the SPD, and its influence on eastern and southeastern European socialist movements was on the rise as well. Sassoon, *One Hundred Years of Socialism*, 9–12. See also Braunthal, *History of the International*, 200–201. On the SPD's internal organization in this period, see Gay, *Dilemma of Democratic Socialism*, 103–6, and Roth, *Social Democrats*, 266–67.

53. On the rise of Marxism within the German socialist movement, see Roth, *Social Democrats*, 171–92, and Sassoon, *One Hundred Years of Socialism*, 1–9.

54. In accordance with the conventions—or lack of conventions—of his day, Jaurès does not cite his sources in a consistent way. His discussion of Luther seems to be in response to three of Luther's texts: "On the Bondage of the Will," "The Commandment Against Usury," and "Commentaries on Genesis." See Dubief, "Jean Jaurès et Martin Luther," 347. Jaurès's chapter on Kant and Fichte seems to be a response to Kant's *Metaphysics of Morals* and Fichte's *Considerations on the French Revolution* (see editor's note, *PTA*, 400n1). In the titles of the last two chapters of his Latin thesis, he includes the names of the other works he has consulted: Fichte's *The Closed Commercial State* (*PTA*, 411), Hegel's *Philosophy of Right*, Marx's *Capital*, and Lassalle's *Capital and Labor* and *Program of the Workers* (*PTA*, 420). Jaurès does not seem to have made a comprehensive study of any of these thinkers' works; I do not know of evidence that he read, for instance, Kant's *Critique of Judgment* or Hegel's *Phenomenology of Spirit*.

55. Jaurès has in mind here the doctrine of the Declaration of the Rights of Man and of the Citizen, the great document of the Revolution of 1789, which begins: "Men are born, and always continue, free, and equal in respect of their rights," and which goes on to declare: "Political Liberty consists in the power of doing whatever does not injure another.

The exercise of the natural rights of every man has no other limits than those which are necessary to secure to every *other* man the free exercise of the same rights; and these limits are determinable only by the law." Quoted from the version in Paine, *Rights of Man*, 110.

56. By my count, Jaurès writes about fourteen pages on Luther, five on Kant, ten each on Fichte and Hegel, and six on Marx (with passing mentions of Lassalle), plus several pages of introductory, transitioning, and concluding remarks. Thus almost a third of the body of Jaurès's Latin thesis concerns Luther.

57. That Jaurès rarely wrote or spoke about Rousseau is interesting, given Rousseau's stature within the mainstream of French republican thought. Jaurès's reading of Rousseau is articulated most fully in his 1889 talk "Les idées politiques et sociales de J.-J. Rousseau," which he did not publish until 1912. By attacking the "oligarchy of money" and advocating a government based on the general will, Jaurès writes there, Rousseau called attention to the problem of property and the problem of sovereignty. The Third Republic had resolved the problem of sovereignty, Jaurès concludes, although through a representative parliament rather than through the direct democracy Rousseau had envisioned, but it had not yet confronted the problem of property ("Idées politiques et sociales de J.-J. Rousseau," 380–81).

58. Jaurès thought that Lassalle had to some extent preserved this theme of justice. Lassalle was more indebted to Fichte than was Marx, both with regard to Fichte's emphasis on the idea of justice and Fichte's program of the closed—and, in Jaurès's reading, collectivist—national state (see especially *PTA*, 418–19 and 433).

59. Benoît Malon, as quoted in Vincent, *Between Marxism and Anarchism*, 55. On Malon's influence on Jaurès, see Goldberg, *Life of Jean Jaurès*, 41 and Derfler, *Third French Republic*, 45–46. Jaurès had attempted to contact Malon's circle during his first term in the Chamber of Deputies but, feeling shy, he did no more than introduce himself and walk away (Goldberg, *Life of Jean Jaurès*, 41). Over time, however, Jaurès did develop ties to Malon and his associates. Malon published Jaurès's Latin thesis, in French translation, in his *Revue Socialiste* in 1892 (Jackson, *Jean Jaurès*, 33). In 1894, Jaurès wrote the introduction to a new edition of Malon's *La morale sociale* (*OJJ* 3:261–76) and in 1913 he spoke at Malon's funeral (Vincent, *Between Marxism and Anarchism*, 133–35).

CHAPTER 2

1. Editor's note, *Philosopher à trente ans*, 106n1.
2. Goldberg, *Life of Jean Jaurès*, 102–6; Scott, *Glassworkers of Carmaux*, 131–35.
3. Goldberg, *Life of Jean Jaurès*, 106–9.
4. Cobban, *History of Modern France*, 44–45.
5. Noland, *Founding of the French Socialist Party*, 11, 32; Mayeur and Rebérioux, *Third Republic*, 160.
6. Goldberg, *Life of Jean Jaurès*, 109–10; Mayeur and Rebérioux, *Third Republic*, 159–61; Derfler, *Third French Republic*, 41–46.
7. Noland, *Founding of the French Socialist Party*, 32; Mayeur and Rebérioux, *Third Republic*, 160.
8. Pease, *Jean Jaurès*, 33–34. The descriptions of Jaurès's voice are quotations from J. Ramsay MacDonald and Charles Rappoport, respectively; the description of Jaurès's oratorical energy is Margaret Pease's.
9. Goldberg, *Life of Jean Jaurès*, 111–36.
10. Jaurès, "Idéalisme et matérialisme dans la conception de l'histoire (controverse avec Paul Lafargue)" in *Oeuvres de Jean Jaurès* 6:3–35. Hereafter cited in text.

11. See, for instance, Lafargue's classic essay "The Right to Be Lazy." On Lafargue's political role in this period, see Derfler, *Paul Lafargue*; in particular, see 21 regarding Laura Marx's translation of the *Communist Manifesto* and 146–50 regarding Jaurès and Lafargue's debate.

12. Goldberg, *Life of Jean Jaurès*, 157–64. On Léon Bourgeois's political thought, see Thomson, *Democracy in France*, 130–31; Kloppenberg, *Uncertain Victory*, 301–5. On Bourgeois's 1895 government, see Kloppenberg, *Uncertain Victory*, 355–56.

13. Mayeur and Rebérioux, *Third Republic*, 143–46.

14. Braunthal, *History of the International*, 256; Mayeur and Rebérioux, *Third Republic*, 123, 159–60, 165; Noland, *Founding of the French Socialist Party*, 58–59.

15. Mayeur and Rebérioux, *Third Republic*, 165.

16. On Millerand, see Derfler, *Alexandre Millerand*.

17. Noland, *Founding of the French Socialist Party*, 48–57; Goldberg, *Life of Jean Jaurès*, 166–67.

18. Goldberg, *Life of Jean Jaurès*, 217. There are many works about the Dreyfus Affair. See, for example, Bredin, *Affair*, and Cahm, *Dreyfus Affair*. See also the summary of the affair in Mayeur and Rebérioux, *Third Republic*, 179–208. On Jaurès's activities during the Dreyfus Affair, see Goldberg, *Life of Jean Jaurès*, 131–32, 213–28, 238–42, 259–60.

19. Goldberg, *Life of Jean Jaurès*, 131–32. When Jaurès argued against this disparity in punishment, he was accused by right-wing politicians of being an antimilitary internationalist—curiously, the same charge he would face in even more vehement form once he took Dreyfus's side.

20. On Blum, who became France's first Socialist prime minister and who is often regarded as Jaurès's protegé, see Lacouture, *Léon Blum*, and Colton, *Léon Blum*.

21. Mayeur and Rebérioux, *Third Republic*, 191.

22. Jules Guesde, as quoted in Noland, *Founding of the French Socialist Party*, 63–64; see also Goldberg, *Life of Jean Jaurès*, 223–24.

23. Noland, *Founding of the French Socialist Party*, 69.

24. Goldberg, *Life of Jean Jaurès*, 229–30; Noland, *Founding of the French Socialist Party*, 68. The 1898 elections slightly increased the size of the socialist caucus in the Chamber and also shifted it a bit to the left: it gained Guesdist and Blanquist members, and lost several reformist deputies. Overall, the radical and socialist groups increased their representation slightly, but not enough to displace the conservative majority.

25. Goldberg, *Life of Jean Jaurès*, 236–41. See also Jaurès, *Les preuves*, hereafter cited in text in the most recent scholarly edition, as included in Jaurès, *Temps de l'affaire Dreyfus*.

26. The article and *Les preuves* chapter cited here are both entitled "L'interêt socialiste" (The socialist interest).

27. Note that, in addition to making room for cross-class alliances to be a normal part of socialist political life, Jaurès also made room here for intellectuals of bourgeois origin to be a normal part of the socialist movement. One of the most direct effects of Jaurès's writings and speeches during the Dreyfus Affair was to bring a number of young left-leaning intellectuals into the French socialist movement (Noland, *Founding of the French Socialist Party*, 84).

28. I will make reference to volumes 1 (1901) and 4 (1902) of *Histoire socialiste*, citing them hereafter in text as *HS* 1 and *HS* 4. On the writing of the *Histoire socialiste*, see Goldberg, *Life of Jean Jaurès*, 283–90, 571; Rioux, *Jean Jaurès*, 130. Jaurès's collaborators included a number of prominent reformist socialist politicians, such as Paul Brousse, Alexandre Millerand, Albert Thomas, and René Viviani. (Jules Guesde declined Jaurès's invitation to participate.) The volumes Jaurès did not write—those covering most of the nineteenth

century—emphasize the utopian socialists, especially Saint-Simon, and the development of the labor movement.

29. The frontispiece Jules Rouff added to the first volume of the *Histoire Socialiste* conveys something of this mood: along a pine branch, as on a family tree, appears a series of locket-shaped portraits, including images of François-Noël ("Gracchus") Babeuf, Claude Henri de Saint-Simon, Charles Fourier, Karl Marx, Louis Blanc, Pierre-Joseph Proudhon, and Auguste Blanqui. Aside from his picture's position in the middle of the lineage and his conspicuous place as the only non-Frenchman in this series of forefathers, Marx has no special prominence. Contrary to his reputation as a fiery curmudgeon, he is pictured here as a kindly, grandfatherly figure with a mild and tolerant smile. (The image is reproduced in Rebérioux, *Jaurès*, 41.)

30. Michelet, *The People*, 107.

31. Michelet, *History of the French Revolution*, 5.

32. Ibid., 8.

33. Declaration of the Rights of Man and the Citizen, as quoted in Paine, *Rights of Man*, 112.

34. Jaurès mentions Rousseau as such a protocommunist thinker; he also cites speeches and writings by several participants in the early stages of the Revolution: François Boissel, who receives extensive treatment in the fourth volume of the *Histoire socialiste,* as well as Jean-Baptiste Harmand, who called for legal protections for workers, and Jacques Nicolas Billaud-Varennes, who proposed an "individualist collectivism." See especially *Histoire socialiste* 4:1500–2.

35. This embrace of "the Revolution as a whole" put Jaurès close to the position of most Radicals; how he interpreted the Revolution, of course, was somewhat different. On the Radicals' enthusiasm for the Revolution, see Derfler, *Third French Republic*, 29.

36. Declaration of the Rights of Man, as quoted in Paine, *Rights of Man*, 110. Emphatic capitals are in the original.

37. See the discussion of the Le Chapelier law in Rosanvallon, *Demands of Liberty*, 157–60. Pierre Rosanvallon notes that Jaurès was "the first historian of the Revolution to attach such importance" to this law (310n43).

38. For a discussion of Jaurès's pluralist conception of socialist institutions, see Antonini, *État et socialisme*, 87–113. Here Jaurès shows the influence of Malon and Proudhon. On Proudhon's role in introducing pluralist themes to the French Left, see Vincent, *Pierre-Joseph Proudhon*, 127–65, 209–28, and 231–32. The appreciation of civil society evidenced here is among the reasons that Jaurès has been appropriately classified as a "liberal socialist." See Canto-Sperber with Urbinati, *Socialisme libéral*, especially 32–52, regarding the defining ideas of a liberal socialism and 67–78 for examples of Jaurès's most markedly liberal-socialist writings.

CHAPTER 3

1. Influenced by the anarchism of Pierre-Joseph Proudhon and of Mikhail Bakunin and eventually given its clearest expression in the writings of Georges Sorel—see especially his 1908 *Reflections on Violence*—syndicalism was the doctrine that the working class should eschew electoral campaigns and parliamentary action in favor of "direct action" by unions. Although in practice this meant scattered strikes and acts of small-scale sabotage, syndicalists held on to the dream of a general strike that would bring capitalism crashing down and allow a new society, based on unions themselves, to arise. Within the French

trade unions and *bourses du travail*, syndicalism was an increasingly influential force. Nevertheless, syndicalism was never universally accepted by French trade unionists, among whom could be found Marxists, reformist socialists, and adherents of various other ideologies. See the discussions of syndicalism in Joll, *Second International*, 56–76, and Noland, *Founding of the French Socialist Party*, 188–92.

2. Goldberg, *Life of Jean Jaurès*, 242; Noland, *Founding of the French Socialist Party*, 75.

3. Noland, *Founding of the French Socialist Party*, 86.

4. Ibid., 78–80; Goldberg, *Life of Jean Jaurès*, 243.

5. Goldberg, *Life of Jean Jaurès*, 243; Noland, *Founding of the French Socialist Party*, 80–82.

6. Jaurès, "L'unité socialiste," in *Temps de l'Affaire Dreyfus*, 511. Originally published in *Le Mouvement Socialiste* no. 1 (January 15, 1899).

7. Noland, *Founding of the French Socialist Party*, 86–87; Goldberg, *Life of Jean Jaurès*, 247–49.

8. Noland, *Founding of the French Socialist Party*, 88.

9. Ibid., 91–93; Goldberg, *Life of Jean Jaurès*, 250–53.

10. Alexandre Millerand, as quoted in Goldberg, *Life of Jean Jaurès*, 248.

11. Whether or not Millerand knew at the time of the Union socialiste meeting of June 21 that Waldeck-Rousseau would soon propose a new cabinet that included both himself and Gallifet is a point on which historians differ. Compare the account in Noland, *Founding of the French Socialist Party*, 90–91, with those in Derfler, *Alexandre Millerand*, 149–53, and Goldberg, *Life of Jean Jaurès*, 252–53.

12. Indeed, Dreyfus would be pardoned later in 1899 (Goldberg, *Life of Jean Jaurès*, 260).

13. Noland, *Founding of the French Socialist Party*, 92–93; Goldberg, *Life of Jean Jaurès*, 253–54. Note, however, that, when Waldeck-Rousseau presented his government to the Chamber for approval, the Guesdist and Blanquist deputies jeered but abstained from voting. Their abstention, coupled with the affirmative votes of the majority of the socialist deputies, secured the government's confirmation (see Noland, *Founding of the French Socialist Party*, 96; Goldberg, *Life of Jean Jaurès*, 255–56).

14. On the Allemanists' dual principles, see Duclert, *La république imaginée*, 244. The Allemanists' split was significant in part because it heralded a new conception of revolution on the French Left, no longer intertwined with the republican tradition and therefore open to new authoritarian versions of socialism. On the development of the French Left's idea of revolution, see Judt, *Marxism and the French Left*, especially 108.

15. July 1899 joint statement of the antiministerialist group, as quoted in Noland, *Founding of the French Socialist Party*, 97. I have lowercased Noland's "Socialist" before "political method" to conform with the style I use elsewhere in this volume. See also Noland, *Founding of the French Socialist Party*, 98–99, and Goldberg, *Life of Jean Jaurès*, 256–57. The Bloc des gauches would maintain a majority in the Chamber of Deputies for six years—a record for any parliamentary majority in the Third Republic.

16. On that new right-wing movement and its consequences, see Sternhall, *Neither Right nor Left*.

17. Noland, *Founding of the French Socialist Party*, 99.

18. Ibid., 102–14; Goldberg, *Life of Jean Jaurès*, 263–65.

19. Jaurès, as quoted in Goldberg, *Life of Jean Jaurès*, 262.

20. Paul Lafargue, as quoted in Noland, *Founding of the French Socialist Party*, 108.

21. Noland, *Founding of the French Socialist Party*, 110–15; Goldberg, *Life of Jean Jaurès*, 264–65.

22. Noland, *Founding of the French Socialist Party*, 115–17.

23. On the debates within Germany, see Braunthal, *History of the International*, 259–71; Joll, *Second International,* 89–95; and Tudor and Tudor, *Marxism and Social Democracy.*

24. Bronner, *Socialism Unbound*, 38.

25. Kautsky, *Road to Power*, 34.

26. Bernstein, "The Struggle of Social Democracy and the Social Revolution," in Tudor and Tudor, *Marxism and Social Democracy*, 149, 168–69.

27. Ibid., 168–69.

28. Bernstein, "A Statement," in Tudor and Tudor, *Marxism and Social Democracy*, 194. Originally published in *Vorwärts*, February 7, 1898.

29. Bernstein, *Preconditions of Socialism*. See also an earlier translation: Bernstein, *Evolutionary Socialism*. For discussions of this book's reception, see Braunthal, *History of the International*, 259–65; Joll, *Second International*, 89–93.

30. Bernstein, *Preconditions of Socialism*, 199.

31. Ibid., 209.

32. Most of the socialist parties existing in 1900 had been founded within the previous ten years. Sassoon, *One Hundred Years of Socialism*, 9.

33. Braunthal, *History of the International*, 197.

34. On developments within the socialist movements of the major European countries in the 1890s, see Braunthal, *History of the International*, 194–242; Sassoon, *One Hundred Years of Socialism*, 5–26. On the important case of Sweden, see Berman, *Primacy of Politics*, 38–65, and Tilton, *Political Theory of Swedish Social Democracy*, 15–38.

35. Jaurès, "Bernstein et l'évolution du methode socialiste" in *Oeuvres de Jean Jaurès* 6:119–40. Hereafter cited in text. See the account in Goldberg, *Life of Jean Jaurès*, 266–69.

36. Ignaz Auer to Eduard Bernstein, [no date given], as quoted in Joll, *Second International*, 94–95.

37. It is probably not an accident that this passage of Jaurès's Bernstein speech so closely follows the rhythm of Luke 17:20–21: "And when he was demanded of the Pharisees, when the kingdom of God should come, he answered them and said, The kingdom of God cometh not with observation: neither shall they say, Lo here: or lo there: for behold, the kingdom of God is within you."

38. Applause occurred after "as close to the believers as they believe," "a socialist state of grace," and "if it is not *ours*." According to the editor of the speech, the last of these three bursts of applause was "prolonged" (*OJJ* 6:135). Jaurès was interrupted by applause a total of fifteen times during the speech.

39. These two passages of Jaurès's Bernstein speech both received applause; this is the one part of the speech other than the "state of grace" passage in which Jaurès was interrupted by applause more than once within a few sentences.

CHAPTER 4

1. Noland, *Founding of the French Socialist Party*, 130n22.

2. The International is often referred to as the "Second International," to distinguish it from Marx's International Workingmen's Association (the "First International"), Lenin's Communist International (the "Third International"), and the present-day Socialist International, which was formed in 1951. The International's congresses—which had been held in Paris (1889), Brussels (1891), Zurich (1893), and London (1896)—drew delegates from many European countries, large and small, more and less industrialized. Delegates from

Canada, the United States, Argentina, South Africa, India, Australia, and Japan also attended in some years. On the Second International, see Joll, *Second International*, and Braunthal, *History of the International*.

3. Henry Hyndman, as quoted in Noland, *Founding of the French Socialist Party*, 124.

4. Noland, *Founding of the French Socialist Party*, 123–27; Joll, *Second International*, 95–99; Braunthal, *History of the International*, 272–74.

5. Noland, *Founding of the French Socialist Party*, 127–32.

6. Jaurès, "Les deux méthodes," in *Oeuvres de Jean Jaurès* 6:189–218. Hereafter cited in text.

7. Parti socialiste français, "A Program of 1902," in Ensor, *Modern Socialism*, 339–43.

8. See Noland, *Founding of the French Socialist Party*, 135–43. The difference between the names of the two French socialist parties may seem trivial at first glance, but it was in fact significant. "Parti socialiste de France" described the branch of an international movement located in France, suggesting a party that had no specifically *French* characteristics. In contrast, "Parti socialiste français" described a party that was "French" rather than merely "of France," suggesting that it was republican—that is, non-Marxist—in character and patriotic in principle. The two parties' governance structures also revealed significant differences: the PSF was a decentralized federation, whereas the PSdeF, though nominally federal, was in practice governed by a powerful Central Committee.

9. Jaurès, *Études socialistes*, in *Oeuvres de Jean Jaurès* 6:236–425. Hereafter cited in text. *Études socialistes* was also published in a slightly different form as Jaurès, *Studies in Socialism*, which I will cite in the notes at first mention of each "étude" in text.

10. For examples of Jaurès's appeals to the authority of orthodox Marxists, see Jaurès, "République et socialisme," in *Oeuvres de Jean Jaurès* 6:267–74, not included in *Studies in Socialism* and originally published October 17, 1901; and most of the selections grouped under the title "Évolution révolutionaire," in *Oeuvres de Jean Jaurès* 6:295–330; see also Jaurès, "Revolutionary Evolution," in *Studies in Socialism*, 43–105, originally published on various dates in August 1901. It should be noted that, among the writings by Wilhelm Liebknecht to which Jaurès refers, those from the period of Bismarck's Anti-Socialist Laws (1878–90), when Liebknecht and other SPD leaders were under severe legal and political constraints, may not be the most representative sample of Liebknecht's thoughts.

11. See also Jaurès, "Socialism and Life," in *Studies in Socialism*, 10–22; originally published September 7, 1901. Of course, that socialism stems from individual rights within a republic was much the same argument as the one those daring enough would find if they tackled the first two volumes of the *Histoire socialiste*, published three months later (for the publication dates, see Rioux, *Jean Jaurès*, 296).

12. See also Jaurès, "The General Strike and Revolution," in *Studies in Socialism*, 106–29, originally published August 29, 1901.

13. See also Jaurès, "Revolutionary Majorities," in *Studies in Socialism*, 51–59, originally published August 13, 1901.

14. See also Jaurès, "The Question of Method," in *Studies in Socialism*, 130–69.

15. For publication dates, see Rioux, *Jean Jaurès*, 296; on Jaurès's decision to publish his French thesis, see Goldberg, *Life of Jean Jaurès*, 571.

16. Note that, around the time of the *Études socialistes*, Jaurès's conspicuous lack of hostility toward religion led to a scandal within the Parti socialiste français. After Jaurès's daughter, Madeleine, took her first communion in July 1901, some of Jaurès's fellow socialists attacked him—with pompous indignity and considerable venom, first in print and then in a special hearing by the PSF's General Committee—for failing to expunge Roman Catholic practice from his own family. Defending himself, Jaurès argued that anticlerical public

policy was one thing and private faith another; although he opposed Church domination of education and although he himself had been without "formal religion" since adolescence, he held that he had no right to interfere with his wife's or daughter's decisions of conscience. (On the "cas Madeleine," see Goldberg, *Life of Jean Jaurès*, 281–83.)

17. The verbs that I translate with "embodied" are both forms of "incorporer." The phrase "the spirit floating over the waters" is a reference to Genesis 1:2: "And the earth was without form, and void; and darkness was upon the face of the deep. And the Spirit of God moved upon the face of the waters."

18. The passages from which this and the following two quotations are taken are not included in the *Studies in Socialism* version of "The Question of Method."

19. Noland, *Founding of the French Socialist Party*, 144–46; Mayeur and Rebérioux, *Third Republic*, 220–22, 225–26. Jaurès's vice presidency in the Chamber of Deputies made him the rough equivalent of a majority whip in the U.S. House of Representatives: in other words, he had more organizational responsibility than policy-making power.

20. Noland, *Founding of the French Socialist Party*, 146; Mayeur and Rebérioux, *Third Republic*, 226, 229–34; Goldberg, *Life of Jean Jaurès*, 296–99; Luebbert, *Liberalism, Fascism, or Social Democracy*, 27–28.

21. Mayeur and Rebérioux, *Third Republic*, 238.

22. Ibid., 235–36; Rosanvallon, *Demands of Liberty*, 181–82.

23. Noland, *Founding of the French Socialist Party*, 148–60.

24. Parti socialiste français, *Congrès socialiste de Bordeaux*, 76.

25. Secrétariat Socialiste Internationale, *Sixième Congrès*. There are accounts of the Amsterdam congress in Braunthal, *History of the International*, 274–83; Joll, *Second International*, 100–106; and Noland, *Founding of the French Socialist Party*, 163–74. See also the caustic and partisan account in DeLeon, *Flashlights of the Amsterdam Congress*. For Jaurès's main speech in the resolutions committee, see *Sixième Congrès*, 174–98; for his main speech on the floor of the congress, see 67–82.

26. On Bebel's and Kautsky's attitude toward confrontation between reformist and revolutionary socialists during this period, see Steger, *Quest for Evolutionary Socialism*, 178–82.

27. During the course of the Sixth Congress of the Socialist International, the Dresden resolution was amended to "reject" rather than "condemn" revisionism and to state that socialists would refuse to "seek" rather than refuse to "accept" ministerial positions; the latter was presented as an attempt to more accurately translate the original German, but both changes can reasonably be seen as small concessions to the reformists. The resolutions and the vote tallies for each are in Secrétariat Socialiste Internationale, *Sixième Congrès*, 113–16.

28. Ibid., 174. On Luxemburg, see Bronner, *Rosa Luxemburg*.

29. Secrétariat Socialiste Internationale, *Sixième Congrès*, 131, 186.

30. See J. Ramsay MacDonald's vivid description of the scene, as quoted in Pease, *Jean Jaurès*, 99–100.

31. Secrétariat Socialiste Internationale, *Sixième Congrès*, 174, 178. For a description of the interaction between Jaurès and Luxemburg, see DeLeon, *Flashlights of the Amsterdam Congress*, 3.

32. In addition to Jaurès, Adler, and Vandervelde, other speakers for the reformist side included Édouard Anseele from Belgium, J. Ramsay Macdonald from Britain, and Hjalmar Branting from Sweden. Bernstein, marginalized within his own party, was not a delegate to the Sixth Congress. Jaurès's speeches seem to have been the main events in the defense of the reformist position: they are generally longer, and inspire more reaction from the audience, than those of his allies.

33. Secrétariat Socialiste Internationale, *Sixième Congrès*, 179.
34. Jaurès, as quoted in ibid., 74–76.
35. Ibid., 76–77.
36. Braunthal, *History of the International*, 200, 274.
37. Secrétariat Socialiste Internationale, *Sixième Congrès*, 78–81.

CHAPTER 5

1. Secrétariat Socialiste Internationale, *Sixième Congrès*, 82.
2. Each delegation to the Amsterdam congress had two votes; some countries' delegations split their votes on one or both resolutions. The pattern of the votes is revealing, as Joll points out (*Second International*, 104). The group of delegations that supported the Adler-Vandervelde resolution—the first vote taken, and thus the better indication of each delegation's preference—included most of the delegations that would within a few decades go on to adopt reformist methods with at least some success—for instance, the delegations from Austria, Belgium, Britain, Denmark, Holland, Sweden, and Switzerland. (The Norwegian delegation split its vote between the two resolutions—as, of course, did the French.) The parties that voted against the Adler-Vandervelde resolution included those which would never become particularly strong, such as the American socialist party, along with several that would, by the 1930s, find themselves unable to resist the rise of authoritarian regimes within their countries, such as the Bulgarian, German, Hungarian, Italian, Japanese, and Spanish parties, as well as the Russian party, which would create its own brand of authoritarianism. For the complete vote results, see Secrétariat Socialiste Internationale, *Sixième Congrès*, 114–16. See also the accounts of the congress in Goldberg, *Life of Jean Jaurès*, 328; Joll, *Second International*, 105–6; Braunthal, *History of the International*, 283–84; and Noland, *Founding of the French Socialist Party*, 174.
3. Noland, *Founding of the French Socialist Party*, 174–87; Mayeur and Rebérioux, *Third Republic*, 258–61.
4. Noland, *Founding of the French Socialist Party*, 183–84; Derfler, *Alexandre Millerand*, 254–55, 262. Some other friends and close allies of Jaurès did join the SFIO, most notably, Léon Blum.
5. Goldberg, *Life of Jean Jaurès*, 364.
6. Margaret Minturn, in her introduction to Jaurès, *Studies in Socialism*, xlii. For a different interpretation, see Goldberg, *Life of Jean Jaurès*, especially 415–16 and 456–57. In Harvey Goldberg's view, Jaurès began to question reformism after 1904, and his thought acquired a "revolutionary urgency" (457) during his last years.
7. Noland, *Founding of the French Socialist Party*, 201–2; Weinstein, *Jean Jaurès*, 159–62. The policy of permitting second-round endorsement of nonsocialist candidates at the district level was reaffirmed in 1909, 1911, and 1914.
8. Weinstein, *Jean Jaurès*, 162; Derfler, *Alexandre Millerand*, 263–64.
9. Weinstein, *Jean Jaurès*, 160. When referring to members of the Parti socialiste, section française de l'Internationale ouvrière (SFIO), I will capitalize "socialists" since they are members of a single coherent party and not simply adherents of an idea.
10. Goldberg, *Life of Jean Jaurès*, 445–46.
11. The Radicals' rightward shift and the SFIO's growth were related: as the SFIO won over former Radical voters among the urban working class, the Radicals turned to rural and small-town propertied interests for support. See Derfler, *Third French Republic*, 55. On

strikes in this period, see Mayeur and Rebérioux, *Third Republic*, 245, 305. On the public employee unionization controversy and Jaurès's role in defending teachers' unions, see Goldberg, *Life of Jean Jaurès*, 365–69.

12. Derfler, *Third French Republic*, 56; Mayeur and Rebérioux, *Third Republic*, 300–9.

13. For a summary of social policy reforms in France during the Third Republic, see Luebbert, *Liberalism, Fascism, or Social Democracy*, 27–28. On the controversy within the SFIO regarding the 1910 pension law, see Goldberg, *Life of Jean Jaurès*, 404–7.

14. Jaurès, *Éloge de la réforme*, 15, 14, 19. Jaurès's speech at the Toulouse congress has been seen as the classic expression of a "Jaurèsian synthesis" in the SFIO. It should be clear by now that I am skeptical about the extent to which either Jaurès or the SFIO's revolutionary majority were ready to "synthesize" reform and revolution. On the idea that the SFIO's majority never absorbed much reformism, see Carlberg, "Cult of the Revolution." Carlberg points out that the proportion of the initial SFIO membership coming from the antiministerialist parties was similar to the proportion of the SFIO that voted fifteen years later to affiliate with Lenin's Communist International; moreover, the regions of France in which the Guesdists were particularly strong in 1905 were also the regions with the highest level of support for Leninism in 1920.

15. Jaurès, as quoted in Joll, *Second International*, 106–7.

16. On the Boer War and the expansion of European colonies in Africa and Asia and their significance for the International. see Joll, *Second International*, 108–9.

17. See Braunthal's chapter on the "colonial question" in *History of the International*, 305–19.

18. On French colonialism in Morocco, see Goldberg, *Life of Jean Jaurès*, 342–52, 369–75; Joll, *Second International*, 128; and Noland, *Founding of the French Socialist Party*, 385–88. On Jaurès's position regarding colonialism generally, see Weinstein, *Jean Jaurès*, 141–52. Weinstein points out that Jaurès was greatly concerned about the possibility of great-power wars stemming from colonial conflicts, yet, even though he consistently supported humane policies within France's colonies, he never called for their independence. Thus Jaurès's attitude toward colonialism was similar to that of those reformist socialists elsewhere who were his allies within the International. See, for example, MacDonald, *Awakening of India*. Jaurès's writings and speeches from 1903–1908 regarding the Morocco crisis and other issues of war and foreign policy are collected in *Oeuvres de Jean Jaurès* 2 and 5 (1931 and 1933).

19. On the new prominence of the war question in the International after 1907, see Joll, *Second International*, 128, and on Jaurès's role in these debates, 135–36. Braunthal (*History of the International*, 320–56) offers an extended discussion of the International's debates on the prevention of war. The fourth position in these debates—marginal at the time since it was held by only a few, but of substantial interest in retrospect—was the idea that socialists should use the occasion of war, when it inevitably arrived, to hasten the moment of revolutionary crisis. The chief proponents of this position were Rosa Luxemburg in Germany and, curiously, both Vladimir Lenin and Julius Martov, the leaders of opposing factions within the Russian Social Democratic Labor Party (see Braunthal, *History of the International*, 337). On the parallel debates within the SFIO, see Goldberg, *Life of Jean Jaurès*, 378–80; and Weinstein, *Jean Jaurès*, 162–67.

20. See the union membership statistics in Braunthal, *History of the International*, 301n1; regarding the Italian strike, see 341. That Jaurès himself came to doubt the feasibility of his general strike proposal is suggested by the fact that at the extraordinary session of the International Socialist Bureau held on July 29, 1914, the day after Austria declared war on Serbia, Jaurès declined to press the idea of a general strike and instead held out hope that

diplomatic measures might avert war (Braunthal, *History of the International*, 351; Goldberg, *Life of Jean Jaurès*, 464–67).

21. As noted above, however, many socialists did accept the colonization of peoples not yet organized into nation-states.

22. On the ubiquity of socialist support for citizen militias, see Braunthal, *History of the International*, 325. On the 1880 platform of the Parti ouvrier français and the 1902 platform of the Parti socialiste français, see Noland, *Founding of the French Socialist Party*, 7 and 140, respectively.

23. On the writing of *L'armée nouvelle*, see Goldberg, *Life of Jean Jaurès*, 385–89. On the concept of the "nation armée," which Jaurès invokes often in *L'armée nouvelle*, see Challener, *Nation in Arms*.

24. Editor's introduction to *L'armée nouvelle*, vii.

25. Goldberg, *Life of Jean Jaurès*, 388; Joll, *Second International*, 113.

26. Émile Vandervelde wrote that *L'armée nouvelle* contains "the most complete and mature exposition of his Socialist doctrine that Jaurès ever made" (as quoted in Jackson, *Jean Jaurès*, 142–43). It is interesting that, even when Jaurès writes something close to a grand statement of political theory, his writing remains topical, contextual, and engaged.

27. That French military leaders had not dealt with France's inability to defend itself against Germany is one of the chief themes of chapter 3, "Défense mutilée et défense complète," in *L'armée nouvelle*, 40–59. Note that, although an alliance with a larger country would have been one way to supplement France's small army, Jaurès was consistently opposed to France's alliance with tsarist Russia, Europe's most reactionary regime (see Goldberg, *Life of Jean Jaurès*, 206–8, 430–31, 460–63).

28. The terms "military force" and "moral force" occur a number of times in *L'armée nouvelle*, beginning with the title of chapter 1, "Force militaire et force morale" (*AN*, 1).

29. Condemnation of offensive war was a staple of socialist party platforms in Jaurès's era (see Joll, *Second International*, 112).

30. I use the French "patrie" in this chapter because none of the obvious English equivalents—country, homeland, fatherland—both retains the ease of the French and leaves intact the connection with the concept of patriotism, a connection crucial to understanding *L'armée nouvelle*.

31. Jaurès is referring to Homer's *Odyssey*, 17.322–23. The Greek word he translates as "âme" (soul) is actually a form of "aretē," a key term in classical political thought usually translated into English as "virtue" or "excellence."

32. Marx and Engels, *Manifesto of the Communist Party*, 475.

33. Jordi Blanc ("Patrie invisible," cxiii) remarks that, in *L'armée nouvelle*, Jaurès "renews the faith" expressed twenty years earlier in his theology of Being.

34. Jaurès, as quoted in Jordi Blanc's foreword to Jaurès, *De la réalité du monde sensible* (vol. 2 of *Oeuvres philosophiques*), v.

35. Goldberg, *Life of Jean Jaurès*, 388; Joll, *Second International*, 113.

36. On French antiwar politics in this period, see Miller, *From Revolutionaries to Citizens*, 145–200.

37. On Jaurès's antiwar activities between 1911 and 1914, see Goldberg, *Life of Jean Jaurès*, 417–57; and Joll, *Second International*, 126–57; on the final years of Jaurès's life, see Goldberg, *Life of Jean Jaurès*, 458–74; Joll, *Second International*, 158–69; and Jackson, *Jean Jaurès*, 174–85.

CONCLUSION

1. Moschonas, *In the Name of Social Democracy*, 5; consider the subtitle of one important work on social democratic thought: Tilton, *Political Theory of Swedish Social Democracy: Through the Welfare State to Socialism*.

2. Jaurès, as quoted in Parti socialiste français, *Congrès socialiste de Bordeaux*, 67.

3. Ibid., 76. "Awkward" may not be the most obvious translation of "malaisée," but it suits the occasion; I borrow that choice of word from R. C. K. Ensor. See Ensor's translation of Jaurès's speech "The Revolutionary and Reformist Controversy, as Illustrated at the Bordeaux Congress of the French Socialist Party," in Ensor, *Modern Socialism*, 175–77.

4. Judt, *Ill Fares the Land*, 6; Bronner, *Socialism Unbound*, iv; Berman, *Primacy of Politics*, 217; Jacobs, "Reason to Believe."

5. Kitschelt, *Transformation of Social Democracy*; Moschonas, *In the Name of Social Democracy*, 120–44. On the notion of political "tiers," see McWilliams, "Two-Tier Politics."

6. On these other developments and their consequences, see Crouch, *Post-Democracy* and Rosanvallon, *Counter-Democracy*.

7. My use of the terms "movement," "associations," and "campaigns" is informed by Walzer, "What Is the 'Good Society'?"

8. That the democratic Left finds ideals both necessary and troubling is the dilemma referenced in the title of Gay, *Dilemma of Democratic Socialism*.

9. Something of this experience of an ideal is captured in the call-and-response rally chant "Tell me what democracy looks like! / This is what democracy looks like."

10. On the idea of socialism as a regulative "class ideal," see Bronner, *Socialism Unbound*, 147, 164–67. In Kurtz, "Socialist State of Grace," I argued that Jaurès understood socialism as a regulative ideal, plain and simple. I now think that Jaurès shows us how the relationship between the ideal and the real is not asymptotic but paradoxical.

11. See Paul Tillich's definition of "symbol" (with its broader implications for a "theology of culture") in Tillich, "Nature of Religious Language."

12. Paul Tillich writes that "waiting means *not* having and having at the same time" (Tillich, "Waiting," 149).

13. I borrow the phrase "steady work" from Howe, *Steady Work*.

BIBLIOGRAPHY

WORKS BY JAURÈS

Jaurès, Jean. "Au claire de lune." *La Dépêche de Toulouse*, October 15, 1890.

———. *De la realité du monde sensible.* Vol. 2 *of Oeuvres philosophiques.* Edited by Jordi Blanc. Valence d'Albigeois: Vent Terral, 2009.

———. *Democracy and Military Service: An Abbreviated Translation of "L'armée nouvelle" by Jean Jaurès.* Translated by George G. Coulton. Edited by Dennis Sherman. 1916. Reprint, New York: Garland, 1972.

———. *Études socialistes.* Paris: Éditions de Cahiers, 1902.

———. *Éloge de la réforme: Discours de Jean Jaurès au Congrès de Toulouse, 1908.* Paris: Fondation Jean Jaurès, 1998.

———. "Fédération ouvriére." *La Dépêche de Toulouse*, August 20, 1887. Reprinted in Louis Soulé, *La vie de Jaurès*, 170–75. Paris: L'Émancipatrice, 1921.

———, ed. *Histoire socialiste, 1789–1900.* 13 vols. Paris: Jules Rouff, 1901–8.

———. "Les idées politiques et sociales de J.-J. Rousseau." *Revue de Métaphysique et de Morale* (1912): 371–81.

———. *Jaurès et la question religieuse.* Edited by Michel Launay. Paris: Éditions de Minuit, 1958.

———. *Oeuvres de Jean Jaurès.* 9 vols. Edited by Max Bonnafous. Paris: Rieder, 1931–39.

———. *L'organisation socialiste de la France: L'armée nouvelle.* 2nd ed. Paris: L'Humanité, 1915.

———. "Le Parti socialiste." *La Dépêche de Toulouse*, October 27, 1889.

———. *Philosopher à trente ans.* Vol. 3 of *Oeuvres de Jean Jaurès.* Edited by Annick Taburet-Wajngart. Paris: Fayard, 2000.

———. *Les preuves.* Paris: La Petite République, 1898.

———. "Le socialisme de la Revolution française." *La Dépêche de Toulouse*, October 22, 1890. Reprinted in Louis Soulé, *La vie de Jaurès*, 204–8. Paris: L'Émancipatrice, 1921.

———. *Studies in Socialism.* Edited and translated by Margaret Minturn. London: Putnam's, 1906.

———. *Les Temps de l'affaire Dreyfus, novembre 1897–septembre 1898.* Vol. 6 of *Oeuvres de Jean Jaurès.* Edited by Éric Cahm and Madeleine Rebérioux. Paris: Fayard, 2000.

WORKS BY OTHERS

Antonini, Bruno. *État et socialisme chez Jean Jaurès.* Paris: L'Harmattan, 2004.

Barber, Benjamin R. *Strong Democracy: Participatory Politics for a New Age.* Berkeley: University of California Press, 1984.

Battista, Andrew. *The Revival of Labor Liberalism*. Champaign: University of Illinois Press, 2008.

Berman, Sheri. *The Primacy of Politics: Social Democracy and the Making of Europe's Twentieth Century*. Cambridge: Cambridge University Press, 2006.

———. "Social Democracy's Past and Potential Future." In *What's Left of the Left: Democrats and Social Democrats in Challenging Times*, edited by James Cronin, George Ross, and James Shoch, 29–49. Durham: Duke University Press, 2011.

Bernstein, Eduard. *Evolutionary Socialism: A Criticism and Affirmation*. Translated by Edith C. Harvey. New York: Schocken Books, 1961.

———. *The Preconditions of Socialism*. Edited and translated by Henry Tudor. Cambridge: Cambridge University Press, 1993.

Blanc, Jordi. "La patrie invisible." Introduction to Jean Jaurès, *De la réalité du monde sensible*, vol. 2 of *Oeuvres philosophiques*, edited by Jordi Blanc, xi–clxxi. Valence d'Albigeois: Vent Terral, 2009.

Braunthal, Julius. *History of the International*, vol. 1, *1864–1914*. Translated by Henry Collins and Kenneth Mitchell. New York: Frederick A. Praeger, 1967.

Bredin, Jean-Denis. *The Affair: The Case of Alfred Dreyfus*. Translated by Jeffrey Mehlman. New York: George Braziller, 1986.

Bronner, Stephen Eric. *Ideas in Action: Political Tradition in the Twentieth Century*. Lanham, Md.: Rowman and Littlefield, 1999.

———. *Rosa Luxemburg: A Revolutionary for Our Times*. University Park: Pennsylvania State University Press, 1997.

———. *Socialism Unbound*, 2nd ed. Boulder, Co.: Westview Press, 2001.

Brooks, John I., III, *The Eclectic Legacy: Academic Philosophy and the Human Sciences in Nineteenth-Century France*. Newark: University of Delaware Press, 1998.

Cahm, Éric. *The Dreyfus Affair in French Society and Politics*. New York: Longman, 1994.

Canto-Sperber, Monique, with Nadia Urbinati, eds. *Le socialisme libéral: Une anthologie: Europe–États-Unis*. Paris: Éditions Esprit, 2003.

Carlberg, Russell L. "The Cult of the Revolution: French Socialism and the Creation of Communism in France, 1871–1920." Ph.D. diss., Indiana University, 2000.

Challener, Richard D. *The French Theory of the Nation in Arms, 1866–1939*. New York: Columbia University Press, 1955.

Cobban, Alfred. *A History of Modern France*, vol. 3, *1871–1962*. New York: Penguin, 1965.

Cole, G. D. H. *The Second International, 1889–1914*. 2 vols. New York: St. Martin's Press, 1956.

Colton, Joel G. *Léon Blum: Humanist in Politics*. Durham: Duke University Press, 1987.

Cramme, Olaf, and Patrick Diamond, eds. *After the Third Way: The Future of Social Democracy in Europe*. London: I. B. Tauris, 2012.

Crick, Bernard. *In Defense of Politics*, 2nd ed. Chicago: University of Chicago Press, 1972.

Cronin, James, George Ross, and James Shoch, eds. *What's Left of the Left: Democrats and Social Democrats in Challenging Times*. Durham: Duke University Press, 2011.

Crosland, Anthony. *The Future of Socialism*, rev. ed. New York: Schocken Books, 1957.

Crouch, Colin. *Post-Democracy*. Cambridge: Polity Press, 2004.

DeLeon, Daniel. *Flashlights of the Amsterdam Congress*. New York: New York Labor News, 1904.

Derfler, Leslie. *Alexandre Millerand: The Socialist Years*. The Hague: Mouton, 1977.

———. *Paul Lafargue and the Flowering of French Socialism, 1882–1911*. Cambridge: Harvard University Press, 1998.

———. *The Third French Republic, 1870–1940*. Princeton: Van Nostrand, 1966.

Dubief, Henri. "Jean Jaurès et Martin Luther." *Bulletin de la société de l'histoire de protestantisme français*, July–September 1983: 345–56.

Duclert, Vincent. *La république imaginée, 1870–1914*. Paris: Belin, 2010.

Ducomte, Jean-Michel, and Rémy Pech. *Jaurès et les radicaux: Une dispute sans rupture.* Toulouse: Éditions Privat, 2011.

Ehrenberg, John. *Proudhon and His Age*. Atlantic Highlands, N.J.: Humanities Press, 1996.

Engels, Frederick [Friedrich]. *The Condition of the Working-Class in England in 1844.* Translated by Florence Kelley Wischnewtzky. London: Allen and Unwin, 1952.

Ensor, R. C. K., ed. and trans. *Modern Socialism, as Set Forth by Socialists in Their Speeches, Writings, and Programmes*. 3rd ed. London: Harper, 1910.

Esping-Andersen, Gøsta. *Politics Against Markets: The Social Democratic Road to Power.* Princeton: Princeton University Press, 1985.

Gay, Peter. *The Dilemma of Democratic Socialism: Eduard Bernstein's Challenge to Marx.* New York: Collier Books, 1962.

Giddens, Anthony. *The Third Way: The Renewal of Social Democracy*. Cambridge: Polity Press, 1998.

Goldberg, Harvey. *The Life of Jean Jaurès*. Madison: University of Wisconsin Press, 1968.

Grousselas, Camille. *Jaurès écrivain*. Paris: Éditions Européennes ERASME, 1990.

Harrington, Michael. *Socialism*. New York: Bantam Books, 1972.

———. *Socialism: Past and Future*. New York: Arcade, 1989.

Howe, Irving, ed. *Essential Works of Socialism*, 2nd ed. New Haven: Yale University Press, 1976.

———. *Steady Work: Essays in the Politics of Democratic Radicalism*. New York: Harvest Books, 1966.

Jackson, J. Hampden. *Jean Jaurès: His Life and Work*. London: George Allen and Unwin, 1943.

Jacobs, Michael. "Reason to Believe." *Prospect*, October 20, 2002.

Joll, James. *The Second International, 1889–1914*. London: Routledge and Kegan Paul, 1974.

Judt, Tony. *Ill Fares the Land*. New York: Penguin Books, 2010.

———. *Marxism and the French Left: Studies in Labor and Politics in France, 1830–1931.* Oxford: Clarendon Press, 1986.

Kautsky, Karl. *The Road to Power*. Translated by Raymond Meyer. Atlantic Highlands, N.J.: Humanities Press, 1992.

Kitschelt, Herbert. *The Transformation of European Social Democracy*. Cambridge: Cambridge University Press, 1994.

Kloppenberg, James T. *Uncertain Victory: Social Democracy and Progressivism in European and American Thought, 1870–1920*. Oxford: Oxford University Press, 1986.

Kolakowski, Leszek. "Jean Jaurès: Marxism as a Soteriology." In *Main Currents of Marxism*, vol. 2., translated by P. S. Falla, 115–40. Oxford: Oxford University Press, 1978.

Korpi, Walter. *The Democratic Class Struggle*. London: Routledge and Kegan Paul, 1983.

Kurtz, Geoffrey. "Anthony Giddens's Third Way: A Critique." In *The Logos Reader: Rational Radicalism and the Future of Politics*, edited by Stephen Eric Bronner and Michael J. Thompson, 81–97. Lexington: University Press of Kentucky, 2005.

———. "An Apprenticeship for Life in Common: Jean Jaurès on Social Democracy and the Modern Republic." *New Political Science* 35, no. 1 (2013): 65–83.

———. "Jean Jaurès: A Portrait." *Logos: A Journal of Modern Society and Culture* 5, no. 2 (2006). http://www.logosjournal.com/issue_5.2/kurtz.htm.

———. "A Socialist State of Grace: The Radical Reformism of Jean Jaurès." *New Political Science* 28, no. 3 (2006): 401–18.

Lacouture, Jean. *Léon Blum*. Translated by George Holoch. New York: Holmes & Meier, 1982.

Lafargue, Paul. "The Right to Be Lazy." In Irving Howe, ed., *Essential Works of Socialism*, 2nd ed., 219–24. New Haven: Yale University Press, 1976.

Lichtheim, George. *Marxism: A Historical and Critical Study*, 2nd ed. New York: Praeger, 1964.

Luebbert, Gregory M. *Liberalism, Fascism, or Social Democracy: Social Classes and the Political Origins of Regimes in Interwar Europe*. Oxford: Oxford University Press, 1991.

Lukes, Steven. *Émile Durkheim, His Life and Work: A Historical and Critical Study*. Stanford: Stanford University Press, 1985.

MacDonald, J. Ramsay. *The Awakening of India*. London: Hodder and Stoughton, 1910.

Marshall, T. H. *Citizenship and Social Class*. Cambridge: Cambridge University Press, 1950.

Marx, Karl. *Capital: A Critique of Political Economy*. Edited by Frederick Engels. Revised and amplified by Ernest Untermann. Translated by Samuel Moore and Edward Aveling. New York: Modern Library, 1936.

———. *Critique of Hegel's "Philosophy of Right."* Edited by Joseph O'Malley. Translated by Annette Jolin and Joseph O'Malley. Cambridge: Cambridge University Press, 1970.

Marx, Karl, and Friedrich Engels. *The Manifesto of the Communist Party*. In *The Marx-Engels Reader*, edited by Robert C. Tucker, 2nd ed., 469–500. New York: W. W. Norton, 1978.

Mayer, J. P. *Political Thought in France from the Revolution to the Fifth Republic*, 3rd ed. London: Routledge and Kegan Paul, 1961.

Mayeur, Jean-Marie, and Madeleine Rebérioux. *The Third Republic from its Origins to the Great War, 1871–1914*. Translated by J. R. Foster. Cambridge: Cambridge University Press, 1984.

McWilliams, Wilson Carey. "Two-Tier Politics and the Problem of Public Policy." In *The New Politics of Public Policy*, edited by Marc K. Landy and Martin A. Levin, 268–76. Baltimore: Johns Hopkins University Press, 1995.

Mexandeau, Louis. *Histoire du Parti socialiste, 1905–2005*. Paris: Tallandier, 2005.

Meyer, Thomas, with Lewis Hinchman. *The Theory of Social Democracy*. Cambridge: Polity Press, 2007.

Michelet, Jules. *History of the French Revolution*. Translated by Charles Cocks. Edited by Gordon Wright. Chicago: University of Chicago Press, 1967.

———. *The People*. Translated by John P. McKay. Urbana: University of Illinois Press.

Miller, Paul B. *From Revolutionaries to Citizens: Antimilitarism in France, 1870–1914*. Durham: Duke University Press, 2002.

Moschonas, Gerassimos. *In the Name of Social Democracy: The Great Transformation: 1945 to the Present*. Translated by Gregory Elliott. New York: Verso, 2002.

Nicolet, Claude. *L'idée républicaine en France (1789–1924)*. Paris: Gallimard, 1982.

Niebuhr, Reinhold. *Moral Man and Immoral Society*. New York: Scribner's, 1932.

Noland, Aaron. *The Founding of the French Socialist Party (1893–1905)*. Cambridge: Harvard University Press, 1956.

———. "Individualism in Jean Jaurès' Socialist Thought." *Journal of the History of Ideas* 22, no. 1 (1961): 63–80.

Nora, Pierre. "Republic." In *Critical Dictionary of the French Revolution*, edited by François Furet and Mona Ozouf, translated by Arthur Goldhammer, 792–805. Cambridge: Harvard University Press, 1989.

Padgett, Stephen, and William E. Paterson. *A History of Social Democracy in Postwar Europe*. New York: Longman, 1991.

Paine, Thomas. *The Rights of Man*. New York: Penguin Books, 1985.

Parti socialiste français. *Congrès socialiste de Bordeaux, tenu les 12, 13, et 14 avril 1903*. Paris: L'Émancipatrice: Imprimerie Communiste, 1903.

Pease, Margaret. *Jean Jaurès, Socialist and Humanitarian*. London: Swarthmore Press, 1916.

Peillon, Vincent. *Jean Jaurès et la religion du socialisme*. Paris: Bernard Grasset, 2000.

Pettit, Philip. *Republicanism: A Theory of Freedom and Government*. Oxford: Oxford University Press, 1997.

Pierson, Christopher. *Hard Choices: Social Democracy in the Twenty-First Century*. Cambridge: Polity Press, 2001.

Polanyi, Karl. *The Great Transformation: The Political and Economic Origins of Our Time*, 2nd ed. Boston: Beacon Press, 2001.

Przeworski, Adam. *Capitalism and Social Democracy*. Cambridge: Cambridge University Press, 1985.

Przeworski, Adam, and John Sprague. *Paper Stones: A History of Electoral Socialism*. Chicago: University of Chicago Press, 1986.

Rauschenbusch, Walter. *Christianity and the Social Crisis*. New York: Macmillan, 1907.

Rebérioux, Madeleine. *Jaurès: La parole et l'acte*. Paris: Gallimard, 1994.

Rimbert, Pierre. "Jean Jaurès: L'évolution vers le socialisme," part 1. *L'OURS* 14 (1970).

———. "Jean Jaurès: L'évolution vers le socialisme," part 2. *L'OURS* 15 (1970).

———. "Jean Jaurès: L'évolution vers le socialisme," part 3. *L'OURS* 16 (1971).

Rioux, Jean-Pierre. *Jean Jaurès*. Paris: Perrin, 2005.

Rosanvallon, Pierre. *Counter-Democracy: Politics in an Age of Distrust*. Translated by Arthur Goldhammer. Cambridge: Cambridge University Press, 2008.

———. *The Demands of Liberty: Civil Society in France Since the Revolution*. Translated by Arthur Goldhammer. Cambridge: Harvard University Press, 2007.

Rossinow, Doug. *Visions of Progress: The Left-Liberal Tradition in America*. Philadelphia: University of Pennsylvania Press, 2008.

Roth, Guenther. *The Social Democrats in Imperial Germany: A Study in Working-Class Isolation and National Integration*. Totawa, N.J.: Bedminster Press, 1963.

Sagnes, Jean. *Jaurès*. Béziers: Aldacom, 2009.

Sassoon, Donald. *One Hundred Years of Socialism: The West European Left in the Twentieth Century*. New York: New Press, 1996.

Schwartz, Joseph M. *The Permanence of the Political: A Democratic Critique of the Radical Impulse to Transcend Politics*. Princeton: Princeton University Press, 1995.

Scott, Joan Wallach. *The Glassworkers of Carmaux: French Craftsmen and Political Action in a Nineteenth-Century City*. Cambridge: Harvard University Press, 1974.

Secrétariat Socialiste Internationale [Second International]. *Sixième Congrès socialiste internationale, tenu à Amsterdam du 14 au 20 août 1904*. Brussels, 1904.

Smulewicz-Zucker, Gregory R. "Concepts, Traditions, and Actions: Rescuing Political Theory from the History of Political Thought." In *Rational Radicalism and Political Theory: Essays in Honor of Stephen Eric Bronner*, edited by Michael J. Thompson, 209–27. Lanham, Md.: Lexington Books, 2011.

Sorel, Georges. *Reflections on Violence*. Edited by Jeremy Jennings. Cambridge: Cambridge University Press, 1999.

Soulé, Louis. *La vie de Jaurès*. Paris: L'Émancipatrice, 1921.

Steger, Manfred B. *The Quest for Evolutionary Socialism: Eduard Bernstein and Social Democracy*. Cambridge: Cambridge University Press, 1997.

Sternhall, Zeev. *Neither Right nor Left: Fascist Ideology in France*. Translated by David Maisel. Princeton: Princeton University Press, 1986.

Stone, Judith F. *Sons of the Revolution: Radical Democrats in France, 1862–1914*. Baton Rouge: Louisiana State University Press, 1996.

Thomson, David. *Democracy in France: The Third and Fourth Republics*, 3rd ed. London: Oxford University Press, 1958.

Tillich, Paul. "The Nature of Religious Language." In *Theology of Culture*, edited by Robert C. Kimball, 53–67. Oxford: Oxford University Press, 1959.

———. "Waiting." In *The Shaking of the Foundations*, 149–52. New York: Scribner's, 1948.

Tilton, Timothy. *The Political Theory of Swedish Social Democracy: Through the Welfare State to Socialism*. Oxford: Clarendon Press, 1990.

Tudor, Henry, and J. M. Tudor, eds. and trans. *Marxism and Social Democracy: The Revisionist Debate 1896–1898*. Cambridge: Cambridge University Press, 1988.

Vincent, K. Steven. *Between Marxism and Anarchism: Benoît Malon and French Reformist Socialism*. Berkeley: University of California Press, 1992.

———. *Pierre-Joseph Proudhon and the Rise of French Republican Socialism*. New York: Oxford University Press, 1984.

Walzer, Michael. "The Communitarian Critique of Liberalism." In *Thinking Politically: Essays in Political Theory*, edited by David Miller, 96–114. New Haven: Yale University Press, 2007. Originally published in *Political Theory* 18, no. 1 (1990): 6–23.

———. "A Critique of Philosophical Conversation." In *Thinking Politically: Essays in Political Theory*, edited by David Miller, 22–37. New Haven: Yale University Press, 2007. Originally published in *Philosophical Forum* 21 (1989–1990): 182–96.

———. *Interpretation and Social Criticism*. Cambridge: Harvard University Press, 1987.

———. "On the Role of Symbolism in Political Thought." *Political Science Quarterly* 82, no. 2 (1967): 191–204.

———. *Spheres of Justice: A Defense of Pluralism and Equality*. New York: Basic Books, 1983.

———. "What Is 'The Good Society'?" *Dissent* (Winter 2009): 74–78.

Webb, Sidney, and Beatrice Webb. *Industrial Democracy*. 2nd ed. London: Longmans, Green, 1920.

Weinstein, Harold R. *Jean Jaurès: A Study of Patriotism in the French Socialist Movement*. New York: Columbia University Press, 1936.

as antiministerialist, 78–79, 100–102, 178 n. 13
in coalition with non-socialists, 49, 53, 59, 76
as orthodox Marxist, 16, 42, 183 n. 14

Hague conferences (1899 and 1907), 127–28
Hardie, Keir, 83
Harmand, Jean-Baptiste, 177 n. 34
Hébertists, 68
Hegel, Georg Wilhelm Friedrich, 31, 37–45
Henry, Joseph, 56
Herr, Lucien, 20, 54, 55
Hervé, Gustave, 128, 129, 130
history, 25. *See also* change, political and social; Marx, Karl, ideas of, history, materialist theory of
determinist accounts of, 10, 36
idealist accounts of, 42–43, 49–50, 62–63, 156
materialist accounts of, 42–43, 49–50, 60, 62, 86
Homer, 10, 184 n. 31
hope, 28, 64
ideals and, 117, 160–67
problem of, 3–4, 7, 21, 91–94, 152–53
symbols and, 66, 165
Howe, Irving, 5–6
Hyndman, Henry, 100

ideals and the ideal
as absent or unreal, 23, 93–94, 161–64, 166–67
definition of, 161
and movements, 45, 59, 104–5, 117, 152, 157–67
as present in a mediated form, 26–30, 62, 145, 151–52, 155–59, 162–67; as "grace," 33–34, 93–94, 96–97, 166–67; with symbols of embodiment or incarnation, 40, 44, 105–6, 115, 122; with symbols of light or illumination, 50, 117, 161–63
as realized fully, 35, 40, 114, 151, 160, 164–65
as regulative or normative, 50, 73, 93, 161–64, 166, 185 n. 10
incarnation. *See also* Christ; institutions, as political bodies or organisms
as Christian doctrine, 34, 40
as symbol, 113–15
Independent Labor Party, 83
independent socialists, 16, 53, 59, 79, 117
inner life, 1, 94, 139, 142–43, 152–53
of social democracy, 3, 4, 7, 162–67
institutions, 62, 65, 116
and political consciousness 77, 105, 110–11, 150

as political bodies or organisms, 73, 114–16, 122, 147, 159, 164–65; Hegel's understanding of, 39–40
pluralism in, 71, 74, 115, 177 n. 38
International (groupings of socialists)
Amsterdam congress of (1904), 119–22, 124–25, 148, 181 n. 27, 181 n. 32, 182 n. 2
First (International Workingmen's Association), 16, 179 n. 2
Second (Socialist International), 100, 179–80 n. 2, 183–84 n. 20; anti-war politics and, 128–129, 149, 152, 183 n. 19
Third (Communist International), 179 n. 2, 183 n. 14
Internationale (song), 15
internationalism, 53, 147–50, 157
isolation. *See* loneliness

Jacobins, 14, 16, 17, 62, 68–70
Jaurès, Jean, 5–8, 9
career in public office of: Chamber of Deputies, activities in, 17–18, 48–49, 117–19, 126–27, 151, 152; Chamber of Deputies, candidacies for, 14, 48, 55, 117; Toulouse city council, 20, 21
death of, 5, 152, 154
and Dreyfus Affair, 54–59, 163, 176 n. 19, 176 n. 27
efforts to forestall war, 152–153, 183–84 n. 20
foreign policy views of, 183 n. 18, 184 n. 27
journalism of, 126–27, 152; in *La Dépêche de Toulouse*, 14, 18–21; with *L'Humanité*, 125; in *Le Mouvement Socialiste*, 76–77; in *La Petite République*, 55–56, 102
labor movement, relations with, 17–18, 21
major speeches and writings of: *L'Armée nouvelle*, 129–52, 184 n. 26, 184 n. 33; "Bernstein et l'évolution du methode socialiste," 84–98, 105, 112, 115, 116, 144–45, 179 n. 37, 179 n. 38, 179 n. 39; debate with debate at the Amsterdam Congress, 119–22, 181 n. 32; Jules Guesde, 101; debate with Paul Lafargue, 49–52; "De la réalité du monde sensible," 9, 21–30, 33, 47, 50, 113–14, 136, 149, 151–52, 163–64, 175 n. 56, 184 n. 33; "De primis socialismi germanici lineamentis," 30–46, 47, 50; *Études socialistes*, 102–17; *Histoire socialiste*, 59–74, 75, 103, 144, 176–77 n. 28, 177 n. 29, 180 n. 11; *Les preuves*, 55–59
as orator, 49, 126–27, 152, 171 n. 15, 175 n. 8